Fraud Examinations in White-Collar Crime Investigations

This book reviews a range of reports written by fraud examiners after completing internal investigations. These reports are normally kept secret and are the property of client organizations, which do not wish to disclose potential wrongdoing that can harm the reputation of the businesses.

Fraud Examinations in White-Collar Crime Investigations was able to retrieve several recent reports, including foreign aid kickbacks, Russian favors to the Biathlon president, and Leon Black's deals with Jeffrey Epstein. While not claiming that the obtained reports are representative for the outcome of the private investigation industry, the reports do provide insights into the variety of issues that fraud examiners address in their internal investigations and the quality of their work. This book identifies convenience themes and assesses investigation maturity across the reports analyzed. It considers the motives of and opportunities for white-collar criminals, as well as their willingness to engage in unlawful activity, and assesses to what extent fraud examiners are either efficient or deficient in their work.

A compelling read, this book will appeal to students and scholars of criminology, sociology, law, and politics, and all those interested in fraud examinations in relation to white-collar crime.

Petter Gottschalk is Professor Emeritus at the Department of Leadership and Organizational Behavior at BI Norwegian Business School, Norway.

Routledge Studies in Crime and Society

For more information about this series, please visit: www.routledge.com/Routledge-Studies-in-Crime-and-Society/book-series/RSCS

Fraud Examinations in White-Collar Crime Investigations

Convenience Themes and Review Maturity

Petter Gottschalk

LONDON AND NEW YORK

First published 2023
by Routledge
4 Park Square, Milton Park, Abingdon, Oxon OX14 4RN

and by Routledge
605 Third Avenue, New York, NY 10158

Routledge is an imprint of the Taylor & Francis Group, an informa business

British Library Cataloguing-in-Publication Data
A catalogue record for this book is available from the British Library

ISBN: 978-1-032-42717-1 (hbk)
ISBN: 978-1-032-42718-8 (pbk)
ISBN: 978-1-003-36393-4 (ebk)

DOI: 10.4324/9781003363934

Typeset in Times New Roman
by Apex CoVantage, LLC

Contents

Figures

Tables

Introduction

This book reviews a number of reports written by fraud examiners after completing internal investigations. The purpose of the reviews is to identify convenience themes for offenders and assess investigation maturity of examinations. Identifying convenience themes in suspected white-collar crime cases is important in the study of white-collar offenders' motives, opportunities, and willingness for deviant behaviors. Assessing investigation maturity is important to learn from both deficient and efficient work by fraud examiners. A fraud examiner is a financial detective in the private policing business undertaking internal investigations in client organizations by collecting evidence. The fraud examiner conducts commercial inquiries by undertaking factual reviews of documents, interviews with whistleblowers and suspects, and other investigative steps. The client expectation is that fraud examiners will uncover and verify the facts of the case, reconstruct past events and sequences of events, and thereby help the client to make informed decisions to either litigate or resolve matters on a commercial basis (King, 2021; Meerts, 2020).

Very often, the first signs of misconduct and crime are reported anonymously to investigative journalists at major media houses. An example from Norway might illustrate the evolution of a white-collar crime case involving fraud examiners. The major Norwegian business newspaper received an anonymous tip and investigated the matter of alleged corruption in the municipality of Oslo. The newspaper published its first report in 2017. Then the municipality hired corporate investigators at the audit firm BDO to review the matter. More information was revealed by the newspaper, and then the municipality hired corporate investigators at audit firm Deloitte to review the matter in 2018 and 2019. The Norwegian national authority for investigation and prosecution of economic and environmental crime started a police investigation and eventually charged a consultant for having bribed municipal officials. The trial took place in Oslo district court in 2022 where the prosecutor asked for imprisonment of the defendant for three years and six months (Feratovic et al., 2022).

A corporate investigation serves the purpose of finding answers to questions such as: What happened? When did it happen? How did it happen? Who did what to make it happen or not happen? Why did it happen? When whistleblowers, the media, or other sources claim misconduct in organizations, accused organizations

DOI: 10.4324/9781003363934-1

in both the private and public sectors tend to hire corporate investigators to conduct an independent examination of allegations and accusations (Button, 2020; Wood, 2020).

White-collar crime is typically financially motivated crime committed by persons of respectability and high social status in the course of the offender's occupation. White-collar offenders are privileged individuals who abuse their organizational positions for personal or corporate gain (Sutherland, 1939, 1983; Wingerde and Lord, 2020).

White-collar crime might be explained by convenience theory (Asting and Gottschalk, 2022; Braaten and Vaughn, 2019). Convenience is savings in time and effort, reduction in pain and strain, and other factors that make a certain path or choice attractive. Convenience is the state of being able to proceed with something with little effort or difficulty, avoiding barriers. Convenience addresses the time and effort exerted before, during, and after an action or avoidance of action (Collier and Kimes, 2012; Mai and Olsen, 2016; Sundström and Radon, 2015).

Reports by fraud examiners after internal investigations are normally kept secret. Reports are the property of client organizations, which do not wish to disclose potential wrongdoing that can harm the reputation of the businesses. Only in exceptional circumstances do investigation reports become publicly available and thus accessible for research. This research was able to retrieve several recent reports. While not claiming that the obtained reports are representative for the outcome of the private investigation industry, the reports do provide insights into the variety of issues that fraud examiners address in their internal investigations and the quality of their work.

- Chapter 1: Leon Black deals with Jeffrey Epstein that were investigated by law firm Dechert (2021) in New York City. Apollo Global Management was an enterprise established by Leon Black that made deals with Jeffrey Epstein.
- Chapter 2: University president in solo projects without involvement of others at the institution. Bergen University in Norway was investigated by PwC (2021), who examined potential financial misconduct by the university president.
- Chapter 3: University coach causing donations. The University of California at Berkley in the United States was investigated by State Auditor (2020), who examined corrupt practices at admission in the athlete departments.
- Chapter 4: Cruise management showed reluctance to report at virus outbreak. Hurtigruten Cruises in Norway was investigated by law firm Wiersholm (2020), who examined executive reluctance to report a Covid-19 outbreak in order to continue the voyage.
- Chapter 5: Russian favors were provided to the president of the International Biathlon Union in Austria. The alleged wrongdoing was investigated by ERC (2021), who examined the union president's potentially corrupt visits to Russia.
- Chapter 6: Foreign aid was linked to local kickback schemes. Mercy Corp foreign aid in Congo was investigated by Henze et al. (2020), who examined the extent of corrupt practices among local aid workers.

- Chapter 7: Camaraderie seemed present in peninsula business. Rumors of financial misconduct and business activities that did not promote but rather hindered recreational activities caused the investigation by Aust-Agder (2019) in Norway.
- Chapter 8: Mayor reprisals against an employee caused a non-traditional investigation that was not related to fraud. Rather, law firm Simonsen (2020) was hired to examine gender-related allegations from a female employee regarding the male mayor in Norway.
- Chapter 9: Municipal benefits seemed provided to relatives. There was suspicion of corruption in the municipality in Norway. Audit firm Nordhordland (2019) was hired to investigate the matter of private costs covered by the municipality.
- Chapter 10: State victimization of social security clients occurred. Social security recipients in Norway were illegally sentenced to prison if they had stayed in other European countries while receiving social support (NOU, 2020).
- Chapter 11: Donald Trump was investigated by both James (2020) in a petition by the Attorney General of the State of New York to the Supreme Court of the State of New York and by Eisen et al. (2021) in the series of Brookings Governance Studies.
- Chapter 12: Strange financial flows in South Sudan were researched by Schoultz and Flyghed (2020) and by the Commission (2021) in examination of human rights violations and related economic crime in the country.
- Chapter 13: Danish clothing store chain Bestseller produced their garments in Myanmar that was in contravention of sanctions by the European Union. Corporate investigators Christoffersen and Mikkelsen (2021) reviewed the matter of Bestseller production in Myanmar.
- Chapter 14: Embezzlement of client funds. This chapter does not present another case study of fraud examiners in corporate investigations. Instead, the chapter reviews the case of attorney fraud in a law firm.
- Chapter 15: Similar to the previous and following chapters, this chapter does not present another case study. Instead, the chapter compares a number of case studies where crime convenience as dependent and corruption rank as independent are applied to predict the extent of convenience. This is exploratory research that needs more empirical study.
- Chapter 16: Again, a sample of investigation reports is applied in an analysis of a white-collar phenomenon. The question is whether competitors lose or gain when an industry peer is hit by a scandal. It is indeed an interesting issue in white-collar crime cases what the outcome is for competitors in the same industry: whether they suffer from the stigma effect or enjoy the competition effect as discussed in the chapter.

In the 13 fraud examination case studies in Chapters 1 to 13, two theoretical frameworks are applied. The structural model of convenience theory is the first framework to identify convenience themes for alleged wrongdoing. The structural model is illustrated in Figure 0.1. The extent of white-collar crime convenience manifests itself by motive, opportunity, and willingness. The motive is either occupational crime to benefit the individual or corporate crime to benefit the organization because of possibilities or threats (Dodge, 2020; Huisman, 2020; Shichor and Heeren, 2021). The ability of white-collar offenders to commit and conceal crime links to their privileged position status, legitimate access to resources, institutional deterioration by decay, lack of oversight and guardianship as chaos, and criminal market forces as collapse (Barak, 2012, 2017; Kawasaki, 2020; Wingerde and Lord, 2020).

The personal willingness for deviant behavior manifests itself by offender choice and perceived innocence. The choice of crime can be caused by deviant identity, rational consideration, or learning from others. Social identity is an individual's self-concept as an organizational member (Piening et al., 2020). The perceived innocence at crime manifests itself by justification and neutralization (Schoultz and Flyghed, 2021).

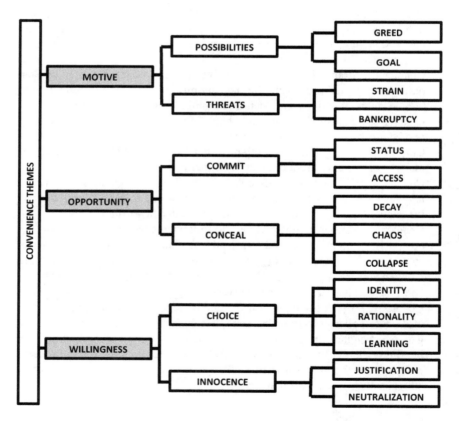

Figure 0.1 Theoretical model of white-collar crime convenience

As argued by Ghazi-Tehrani and Pontell (2022: 38), "using fraud examiner reports of financial crime cases in Norway and the United States, Gottschalk showed the utility of convenience theory in explaining these violations". In the case studies in this book, the theoretical model of white-collar crime convenience in Figure 0.1 is repeated and applied to each specific case by identifying some of the 14 issues on the right-hand side as relevant to that specific case.

The other theoretical framework is the stage model for investigation maturity level. Stages of growth models for maturity levels help to assess and evaluate a variety of phenomena (e.g., Masood, 2020; Röglinger et al., 2012). Stage models predict the development or evolution of investigative maturity from basic performance to superior results (Iannacci et al., 2019: 310):

> They also suggest that this development is progressive (i.e., each successive stage is better than the previous one), stepwise (i.e., each step is a necessary prerequisite for the following step in the sequence), and prescriptive (i.e., each step must occur in a prescribed order in accordance with a pre-existing plan or vision), thus emphasizing the chain of successful events rather than the mechanisms by which subsequent stages come about.

Here we apply the concept of stages in terms of maturity levels (Chen et al., 2021) to evaluate private internal investigations. The purpose is to develop characteristics of investigations at different maturity levels. The four maturity levels in the stage model in Figure 0.2 for fraud examinations have the following descriptions:

1 *Activity-oriented investigation: The examination is a chaos.* The investigation focuses on activities that may have been carried out in a reprehensible manner. The examiners look for activities and prepare descriptions of these. Then examiners make up their minds as to whether the activities were reprehensible or not. Here it is often auditors and others with financial knowledge. They are to assess financial transactions and management of assets. The investigation at level 1 is often passive, fruitless, and characterized by unnecessary use of resources. At this lowest maturity level, investigators typically attempt to find an answer to the question: What happened?

2 *Problem-oriented investigation: The examination is a mess.* The investigation focuses on an issue that needs clarification. Examiners are looking for answers. Once examiners believe they have found answers, the investigation is terminated. It is important to spend as little resources as possible on the investigation, which should take the shortest possible time. Management is important for success. The client had an unresolved problem, and the client regulates premises for the investigation. There is no room for investigators to pursue other paths than those that address the predefined problem. Here it is often lawyers and others with legal knowledge. They are to map the facts. At this second maturity level, investigators typically attempt to find an answer to the question: How did it happen?

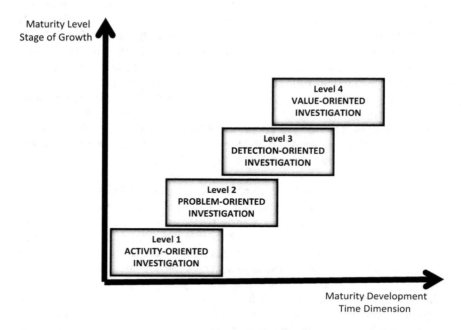

Maturity Level
Stage of Growth

Level 4
VALUE-ORIENTED
INVESTIGATION

Level 3
DETECTION-ORIENTED
INVESTIGATION

Level 2
PROBLEM-ORIENTED
INVESTIGATION

Level 1
ACTIVITY-ORIENTED
INVESTIGATION

Maturity Development
Time Dimension

Figure 0.2 Maturity model for internal private investigations with four stages

3   *Detection-oriented investigation: The examination is a disclosure.* The investigation focuses on something being hidden, which should be revealed. Investigators choose their tactics to succeed in exposing possible misconduct and perhaps even financial crime. Investigative steps are adapted to the terrain, where different sources of information and methods are used to get as many facts on the table as possible. Here it is often police-trained investigators and other private detectives. They are to uncover possible crime. While level 1 and level 2 are focused on suspicions of financial crime, level 3 is focused on suspicions against potential financial criminals. There are always criminals who commit crime. Level 3 has a focus on individuals, while level 3 has a focus on activities. Level 3 is characterized by the search for responsible persons who may have abused their positions for personal or corporate gain. This is a more demanding examination, because suspicions and suspects must be handled in a responsible manner in relation to the rule of law and human rights. Level 3 investigations are active with significant breakthroughs in the examinations. Investigation projects are carried out in a professional and efficient manner. At this third maturity level, investigators typically attempt to find an answer to the question: Why did it happen?

4   *Value-oriented investigation: The examination is a clarification.* The investigation focuses on value created by the examination, where the

investigation is an investment by the client with an expectation of benefits exceeding costs. The ambition of the investigation is that the result will be valuable to the client. The value can lie in clean-up, change, simplification, renewal, and other measures for the future. The investigation also focuses on being justifiable. A number of explicit considerations are identified and practiced throughout the inquiry. The investigation has in addition a focus on explicit decisions regarding information strategy, method strategy, configuration strategy, and system strategy. By explicit strategic choices, the investigation becomes transparent and understandable to the parties involved and affected. It is often examiners in interdisciplinary teams who are to contribute to value creation for the client. Level 4 investigations are characterized by the active use of strategies, with significant and decisive breakthroughs in the inquiries, which lay the foundation for learning and value creation in the client's organization. The value may, for example, be that detected deviations and wrongdoings become sanctioned and corrected in a satisfactory manner. At level 4, detection, disclosure, clarification, and solution are seen in context. There will be less to detect in the future if prevention is strengthened. It will be better in the future if the case is completely resolved. The examiners create value by proper investigation. Value is created before, during, and after the investigation. Before the investigation, risk understanding, and prioritization are developed. During the investigation, method understanding is developed. After the investigation, barriers are built against fraud, holes are closed, routines are developed and practiced, and evaluation is established on a continuous basis. At this top maturity level, investigators try to find the answer to the questions: What went wrong, what can the client learn, and how can wrongdoing be prevented from happening again in the future?

It is important to emphasize that the maturity model is applied in a static rather than a dynamic way in each case study. Usually, the concept of maturity equates to growth, that is, from underdeveloped to highly developed. In each of the investigations presented in this book they are considered static events that may have started at level 1 and stayed there throughout their entire life-course, or indeed at level 2, 3, or 4. The life-course of an investigation is typically a few months. There is no growth for each individual investigation. The growth perspective is implicit not for each individual investigation but for a series of investigations by the same corporate investigator at different points in time and for a series of investigations by different corporate investigators at the same point in time. The first dynamics is not spelled out in this book, as there is no empirical material available to study the performance of specific corporate investigators over time. The life-course of an investigator is typically several years and even decades. The second kind of dynamics is illustrated by various corporate investigators that perform fraud examinations at different levels of maturity within a time span of collected investigation reports.

Fraud examination strategies influence the level of maturity, where distinctions can be made between five strategies. First, knowledge strategy defines the areas of expertise that fraud examiners must apply to the task of reconstructing past events and sequences of events, where knowledge sharing from different professionals is required. Very often, knowledge of the law is the dominating expertise applied, while there is a lack of organizational and accounting knowledge in the investigation.

Next, information strategy defines sources of information that contribute to reconstructing past events and sequences of events. Very often, formal documents such as minutes of meetings are the dominating source applied, while there is a lack of investigative interviewing and visits to potential crime scenes.

Third, value configuration strategy defines the primary activities in the investigation. Very often, the value chain is the dominating configuration, where tasks follow in a sequential manner, while the alternative of the value shop is a more relevant configuration, where tasks follow each other iteratively in a spiral by returning to earlier tasks. Conducting effective investigations requires an investigative mindset that refers to "the use of a disciplined approach that ensures the decisions made are appropriate to the case, are reasonable and can be explained to others" (McLean et al., 2022).

Fourth, systems strategy defines the application of information technology and digitalization in the investigation. Very often, simple search words are used in digital queries that provide few and inconclusive instances of suspicious activities. Finally, methods strategy defines the overall approach and perspectives in the investigation. Very often, fraud examiners conduct interviews in a confrontational rather than cooperation manner. Very often, examiners have a thinking style of systematic analysis rather than the challenge style or the risk style of investigative thinking.

References

Asting, C. and Gottschalk, P. (2022). Attorney fraud in the law firm: A case study of crime convenience theory and crime signal detection theory, *Deviant Behavior*, doi: 10.1080/01639625.2022.2071657.

Aust-Agder. (2019). *Avtaler og beslutningsprosesser knyttet til Hove-saken (Agreements and decision-making processes related to the Hove case)*, audit firm Aust-Agder Revisjon, Arendal, Norway, September, p. 61.

Barak, G. (2012). *Theft of a Nation: Wall Street Looting and Federal Regulatory Colluding*, Rowman & Littlefield Publishers, New York.

Barak, G. (2017). *Unchecked Corporate Power: Why the Crimes of Multinational Corporations Are Routinized Away and What We Can Do about It*, Routledge, New York.

Braaten, C.N. and Vaughn, M.S. (2019). Convenience theory of cryptocurrency crime: A content analysis of U.S. federal court decisions, *Deviant Behavior*, doi: 10.1080/01639625.2019.1706706.

Button, M. (2020). The "new" private security industry, the private policing of cyberspace and the regulatory questions, *Journal of Contemporary Criminal Justice*, 36 (1), 39–55.

Chen, W., Liu, C., Xing, F., Peng, G. and Yang, X. (2021). Establishment of a maturity model to assess the development of industrial AI in smart manufacturing, *Journal of Enterprise Information Management*, doi: 10.1108/JEIM-10–2020–0387.

Christoffersen, J. and Mikkelsen, M.S. (2021). *Redegjørelse: Bestseller A/S' samfundsansvar i Myanmar (Statement: Bestseller Ltd.'s Social Responsibility in Myanmar)*, law firm Offersen Christoffersen, Copenhagen, Denmark, May 10, p. 122.

Collier, J.E. and Kimes, S.E. (2012). Only if it is convenient: Understanding how convenience influences self-service technology evaluation, *Journal of Service Research*, 16 (1), 39–51.

Commission. (2021). *Human Rights Violations and Related Economic Crimes in the Republic of South Sudan* (Human Rights Council, Forty-eighth session: Agenda item 4 Human rights situations that require the Council's attention), 13 September–08 October 2021. Conference room paper of the Commission on Human Rights in South Sudan.

Dechert. (2021). *Investigation of Epstein/Black Relationship and Any Relationship between Epstein and Apollo Global Management*, law firm Dechert, report of investigation, New York, p. 21.

Dodge, M. (2020). Chapter 8: Who commits corporate crime? in: Rorie, M. (editor), *The Handbook of White-Collar Crime*, John Wiley & Sons, Hoboken, pp. 113–126.

Eisen, N., Perry, E.D., Ayer, D. and Cuti, J.R. (2021). *New York State's Trump Investigation: An Analysis of the Reported Facts and Applicable Law*, Brookings Governance Studies, Washington, DC, www.brookings.edu.

ERC. (2021). *Final Report of the IBU External Review Commission, ERC (External Review Commission)*, International Biathlon Union, Austria, 28 January, p. 220.

Feratovic, L., Sæter, K., Solem, L.K. and og Gjernes, K. (2022). Ber om 3,5 år i fengsel for tiltalt Boligbygg-konsulent (Asks for 3.5 years in prison for accused housing construction consultant), *Daily Norwegian Business Newspaper Dagens Næringsliv*, 26 January, p. 13.

Ghazi-Tehrani, A.K. and Pontell, H.N. (2022). *Wayward Dragon: White-Collar and Corporate Crime in China*, Springer Nature, Berlin.

Henze, N., Grünewald, F. and Parmar, S. (2020). *Operational Review of Exposure to Corrupt Practices in Humanitarian Aid Implementation Mechanisms in the DRC*, Adam Smith International, London, p. 88.

Huisman, W. (2020). Chapter 10: Blurred lines: Collusions between legitimate and illegitimate organizations, in: Rorie, M.L. (editor), *The Handbook of White-Collar Crime*, Wiley & Sons, Hoboken, pp. 139–158.

Iannacci, F., Seepma, A.P., Blok, C. and Resca, A. (2019). Reappraising maturity models in e-government research: The trajectory-turning point theory, *Journal of Strategic Information Systems*, 28, 310–329.

James, L. (2020). *The Trump Organization, Inc.; DJT Holdings LLC; DJT Holdings Managing Member LLC; Seven Springs LLC; Eric Trump; Charles Martabano; Morgan, Lewis & Bockius, LLP; Sheri Dillon; Mazars USA LLC; Donald J. Trump; Donald Trump, Jr.; and Ivanka Trump*, Petition by the Attorney General of the State of New York to the Supreme Court of the State of New York, January 18.

Kawasaki, T. (2020). Chapter 27: Review of comparative studies on white-collar and corporate crime, in: Rorie, M.L. (editor), *The Handbook of White-Collar Crime*, Wiley & Sons, Hoboken, pp. 437–447.

King, M. (2021). Profiting from a tainted trade: Private investigators' views on the popular culture glamorization of their trade, *Journal of Criminological Research Policy and Practice*, 7 (2), 112–125.

Mai, H.T.X. and Olsen, S.O. (2016). Consumer participation in self-production: The role of control mechanisms, convenience orientation, and moral obligation, *Journal of Marketing Theory and Practice*, 24 (2), 209–223.

Masood, T. (2020). A machine learning approach for performance-oriented decision support in service-oriented architecture, *Journal of Intelligent Information Systems*, doi: 10.1007/s10844-020-00617-6.

McLean, F., Meakins, A. and White, E. (2022). Conducting effective investigations: Rapid evidence assessment, *College of Policing*, 73 pages, July, www.college.police.uk.

Meerts, C. (2020). Corporate investigations: Beyond notions of public-private relations, *Journal of Contemporary Criminal Justice*, 36 (1), 86–100.

Nordhordland. (2019). *Forenkla forvaltningskontroll (Simplified management control)*, audit firm Nordhordland Revisjon, December 20, Alver, Norway, p. 32.

NOU. (2020). Blindsonen: Gransking av feilpraktiseringen av folketrygdlovens oppholdskrav ved reiser i EØS-området (The blind spot: Investigation of the incorrect practice of the National Insurance Act's residence requirements when traveling in the EEA area), *Norges offentlige utredninger* (Norway's public inquiries), 2020 (9), 328.

Piening, E.P., Salge, T.O., Antons, D. and Kreiner, G.E. (2020). Standing together or falling apart? Understanding employees' responses to organizational identity threats, *Academy of Management Review*, 45 (2), 325–351.

PWC. (2021). *Universitet i Bergen: Gjennomgang av "konseptet" (The University of Bergen: Review of "the concept")*, investigation report, PricewaterhouseCoopers, Oslo, 11 March, p. 68.

Röglinger, M., Pöppelbuss, J. and Becker, J. (2012). Maturity model in business process management, *Business Process Management Journal*, 18 (2), 328–346.

Schoultz, I. and Flyghed, J. (2020). Denials and confessions: An analysis of the temporalization of neutralizations of corporate crime, *International Journal of Law, Crime and Justice*, doi: 10.1016/j.ijlcj.2020.100389.

Schoultz, I. and Flyghed, J. (2021). "We have been thrown under the bus": Corporate versus individual defense mechanisms against transnational corporate bribery charges, *Journal of White Collar and Corporate Crime*, 2 (1), 24–35.

Shichor, D. and Heeren, J.W. (2021). Reflecting on corporate crime and control: The Wells Fargo banking saga, *Journal of White Collar and Corporate Crime*, 2 (2), 97–108.

Simonsen. (2020). *Rapport om mottatt varsel vedrørende forhold ved jordmortjenesten i Ørland kommune (Report on notification received regarding conditions at the midwifery service in Ørland municipality)*, law firm Simonsen Vogt Wiig, report of investigation, May 20, Oslo, p. 36.

State Auditor. (2020). *University of California, California State Auditor, 621 Capitol Mall*, report of investigation, Sacramento, CA, p. 82.

Sundström, M. and Radon, A. (2015). Utilizing the concept of convenience as a business opportunity in emerging markets, *Organizations and Markets in Emerging Economies*, 6 (2), 7–21.

Sutherland, E.H. (1939). White-collar criminality, *American Sociological Review*, 5 (1), 1–12.

Sutherland, E.H. (1983). *White Collar Crime – The Uncut Version*, Yale University Press, New Haven.

Wiersholm. (2020). *Granskingsrapport: Utbrudd av covid-19 på Hurtigruten-skipet MS Roald Amundsen 17–31 Juli 2020 (Investigation report: Outbreak of covid-19 on Hurtigruten ship MS Roald Amundsen July 17–31, 2020)*, law firm Wiersholm, Oslo, p. 51.

Wingerde, K. and Lord, N. (2020). Chapter 29: The elusiveness of white-collar and corporate crime in a globalized economy, in: Rorie, M.L. (editor), *The Handbook of White-Collar Crime*, Wiley & Sons, Hoboken, pp. 469–483.

Wood, J.D. (2020). Private policing and public health: A neglected relationship, *Journal of Contemporary Criminal Justice*, 36 (1), 19–38.

1 Leon Black Deals with Jeffrey Epstein

Leon Black was one of the founders and chief executive at Apollo Global Management when the criminal acts he was accused of were carried out. He was ambitious and powerful with substantial influence in the company. Assuming that the accusations against him were correct, his motive in convenience theory terms can be described by the perspective of rational self-interest, where one does what is best for oneself. His membership in the financial elite in the economical metropole of New York City gave him an extremely high status in the inner circles of power. Personal willingness for deviant behavior means a positive attitude toward individual actions that violate social norms, including formally enacted rules and informal nonconformity. The investigation report by Dechert is assigned maturity level 3 for a detection-oriented investigation. After release of the report by Deckert, Leon Black stepped down from his role as CEO of Apollo Global.

The media reported in 2020 that "the billionaire who stood by Jeffrey Epstein", "Dechert's Leon Black investigation: things you may have missed", "what a sad tale of sycophants: Wall Street is not buying Leon Black's Epstein story", "Jeffrey Epstein's deep ties to top Wall Street figures", "billionaire Leon Black is leaving Apollo following scrutiny over ties to Jeffrey Epstein", and "billionaire Leon Black, revealed to pay Jeffrey Epstein $158, is stepping down" (Gara and Voytko, 2021). These headlines emerged as law firm Dechert (2021) concluded an investigation on behalf of Apollo Global Management board. Jeffrey Epstein committed suicide in jail in August 2019 after being convicted as a sex offender abusing underage female prostitutes (Sampson, 2020). The suspected fraud was concerned with Black's involvement with Epstein.

Offender Convenience Themes

Leon Black was one of the founders and chief executive at Apollo Global Management when the criminal acts he was accused of were carried out. He was ambitious and powerful with substantial influence in the company. Assuming that the accusations against him were correct, his motive in convenience theory terms can be described by the perspective of rational self-interest, where one does what is best for oneself (Pillay and Kluvers, 2014). The economic model of rational self-interest is all about weighing up the pros and cons of alternative courses of

DOI: 10.4324/9781003363934-2

actions. The model considers incentives and probability of detection (Welsh et al., 2014). This applies to both private and professional life. Human behavior finds motivation in the self-centered quest for satisfaction and avoidance of suffering (Hirschi and Gottfredson, 1987).

The economic model of rational self-interest does not imply that every individual in the same situation will conclude and act in the same way. There will be different choices in the same situation because rationality is a subjective matter. For example, the objective detection risk will be the same in the same situation for everyone, while the subjective detection risk will vary with individual variation in risk perceptions, risk willingness and risk aversion (Berghoff and Spiekermann, 2018: 293):

> Risk-averse people seldom, if ever, violate criminal laws. On the other hand, those who are risk-tolerant or even risk-seeking, i.e., who display fundamental characteristics of entrepreneurial personalities, are much more likely to become criminals.

The gain in this case was access to the pedophile community, and Black must have thought that the advantages outweighed the disadvantages. Due to his position in the company, there would be little likelihood of detection. The sex adventures that Epstein offered Black are not easily accessible to people, and therefore his involvement might be seen as a status symbol that can enhance the prestige he already enjoyed among like-minded people. Black did it for his own pleasure and not for the business. Media reports have documented that Epstein's pedophile network consisted of people in high positions with much power where Black could extend his business network. Black's need to achieve personal gain might be connected to Maslow's (1943) hierarchy of needs where self-realization and recognition are important elements toward the top of the pyramid. He realized the American dream of prosperity (Schoepfer and Piquero, 2006), and he probably satisfied his need for acclaim as a narcissist (Chatterjee and Pollock, 2017). From the perspective of philanthropy, he may also have satisfied his desire to help others out of social concern (Agnew, 2014).

In the organizational opportunity dimension of convenience theory, Black had a convenient opportunity because of his position and access to funds. He could easily embezzle and pay Epstein what was required to become a member of the pedophile community. As a CEO, the person has many degrees of freedom, and even more so as one of the founders of the company. There is little or no control by others. The opportunity can be explained by the principal–agent perspective, where the board at Apollo Global Management is the principal and CEO Black is the agent. The board has given Black authority, responsibility, duty, and trust, and he has taken advantage of the board's inability to control him, using company assets to gain access to Epstein's services. He enjoyed the trust of board members as part of the elite. Black's misconduct was because he wanted to, and not because of pressure or threats. Both his status and his access to resources that come with such a position have enabled him to get involved in the Epstein network.

His membership in the financial elite in the economical metropole of New York City gave him an extremely high status in the inner circles of power as indicated in Figure 1.1. Status is an individual's social rank within a formal or informal hierarchy or the person's relative standing along a valued social dimension. Status is the extent to which an individual is respected and admired by others, and status is the outcome of a subjective assessment process (McClean et al., 2018). High-status individuals enjoy greater respect and deference from, as well as power and influence over, those who are positioned lower in the social hierarchy (Kakkar et al., 2020: 532):

> Status is a property that rests in the eyes of others and is conferred to individuals who are deemed to have a higher rank or social standing in a pecking order based on a mutually valued set of social attributes. Higher social status or rank grants its holder a host of tangible benefits in both professional and personal domains. For instance, high-status actors are sought by groups for advice, are paid higher, receive unsolicited help, and are credited disproportionately in joint tasks. In innumerable ways, our social ecosystem consistently rewards those with high status.

In the willingness dimension for deviant behavior in convenience theory, Leon Black found it convenient to commit financial crime by embezzlement potentially to enjoy underage female prostitutes, which in itself is a criminal act from pedophilia. To understand the behavioral willingness, one must focus both on the proceeds and what the proceeds enable in the situation. As illustrated in Figure 1.1, the embezzlement to gain access to sexual services seems based on both choice and innocence. The perspective of deviant affiliation explains Black's behavior by choosing to associate with like-minded people, in this case Epstein, and avoiding people who are skeptical of their attitudes. When you are with people who have the same opinions and thoughts as yourself, a kind of neutralization of potential guilt feelings can easily occur.

The idea of neutralization techniques (Sykes and Matza, 1957) resulted from work on Sutherland's (1983) differential association perspective. According to this perspective, people are always aware of their moral obligation to abide by the law, and they are aware that they have the same moral obligation within themselves to avoid illegitimate acts. The perspective postulates that criminal behavior learning occurs in association with those who find such criminal behavior favorable and in isolation from those who find it unfavorable (Benson and Simpson, 2018). Crime is relatively convenient when there is no guilt feeling for doing something learned from others. The differential association perspective suggests that whether individuals engage in white-collar crime is largely based on their socialization within certain peer groups. In an elite setting, interactions with deviant others promote criminal activity (Sutherland, 1983).

Personal willingness for deviant behavior means a positive attitude toward individual actions that violate social norms, including formally enacted rules and informal nonconformity (Aguilera et al., 2018). "Deviance" is a term to describe

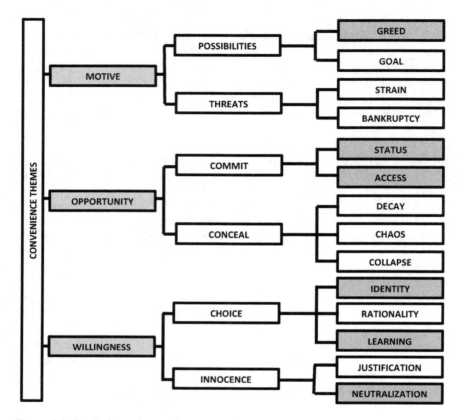

Figure 1.1 Convenience themes for Leon Black

behavior that contravenes accepted norms, values, and ethical standards (Smith and Raymen, 2018). The offender may explain the act of wrongdoing as morally justifiable (Schnatterly et al., 2018).

The convenient choice theme of identity is relevant in the case of Black because he has characteristics of a business elite member and a founder of his own successful global asset management. Identity of an individual is the person's self-concept in terms of the knowledge structure that contains all information relevant to self. Piening et al. (2020: 327) define three self-concept levels:

> First, people define themselves in terms of their personal attributes (e.g., personality, abilities, and interests). At this individual level, one's sense of uniqueness and self-esteem is based on favorable comparisons with other people in a given social context. Second, the relational level involves self-definition based on connections and role relationships with others, with one's self-worth being influenced by the quality of these relationships. Third, the collective level refers to defining oneself in terms of the social groups one belongs to.

The identity makes deviant behavior acceptable for the elite (Petrocelli et al., 2003), often combined with narcissistic identification with own business enterprise (Galvin et al., 2015). Narcissists expect preferential treatment (Zvi and Elaad, 2018), they tend to exaggerate self-enhancement after receiving positive feedback, and they tend to discount failure (Howes et al., 2020).

Narcissistic identification is a special type of narcissism, where the offender sees little or no difference between self and the corporation. The company money is personal money that can be spent in whatever way the narcissist prefers (Galvin et al., 2015). Identification with the organization is the process through which an individual's identity becomes entangled with, and imprinted by, the corporation. The person's unique sense of self comes to be understood in reference to that organization, where the organization defines individual self (Toubiana, 2020).

Lack of self-control is a convenience theme among many seemingly successful individuals. As argued by Gottfredson and Hirschi (1990), human behavior finds innocence in the self-centered quest for satisfaction and avoidance of suffering. Self-control is the blockade that stands between the individual and criminal activity. Lack of self-control is lack of such a blockade, making the short-term pleasure seeking dominate the mind. Lack of self-control implies that the offender lacks the ability and tendency to consider potential implications of a deviant action (Kroneberg and Schultz, 2018), as they are impulsive and unstable (Craig and Piquero, 2016; Jones et al., 2015). Those lacking self-control will typically have a short-term focus and be adventuresome, risk-willing, and indifferent.

Fraud Investigation Outcome

The mandate for the investigation by Dechert (2021: 1) had the following formulation:

> In October, 2020, the Conflicts Committee of Apollo Global Management, Inc. ("Apollo") retained Dechert In October 2020, the Conflicts Committee of Apollo Global Management, Inc. ("Apollo") retained Dechert LLP ("Dechert") as independent counsel to conduct a thorough investigation into (1) the relationship between Leon Black ("Black") and Jeffrey Epstein ("Epstein"), including any financial, business or personal dealings between Black and any Black affiliate, on the one hand, and Epstein and any Epstein affiliate on the other; (2) any work performed for, or services rendered to, Black or any Black affiliate by Epstein or any Epstein affiliate; (3) the financial or other relationship, if any, between Apollo or any Apollo affiliate, and Epstein and any Epstein affiliate, including without limitation, any financial or other dealings between them; and (4) any statements made by or on behalf of Black or Apollo referring, relating to or characterizing either Black's or Apollo's relationship with Epstein.

According to the Dechert (2021) report, which was dated January 22, 2021, and then filed with the Securities and Exchange Commission in the United States,

Black and Epstein had a social relationship from the mid-1990s to 2018. They were introduced by an unnamed mutual friend. Black viewed Epstein as someone who was very intelligent and knowledgeable regarding issues relating to estate planning and taxation. In 1997, Black appointed Epstein to be one of the initial directors of the Black Family Foundation, established to facilitate his charitable giving. Black was apparently impressed that David Rockefeller had appointed Epstein to the board of Rockefeller University, a scientific research university on the East Side of Manhattan (Cohan, 2021).

According to Dechert (2021), it was Black's understanding that Epstein was extremely knowledgeable about science and technology, as well as a strong proponent of scientific research and development. According to Cohan (2021), Epstein had somehow convinced Black, one of the most gifted financial engineers, that he was the ultimate autodidact, exceptionally skilled in both the arcane rules of tax structuring and estate planning and also of scientific research. Epstein introduced Black to well-regarded researchers at the Massachusetts Institute of Technology and Harvard University. Epstein stayed on the Black Family Foundation board for ten years, until he resigned in mid-2007, the year before his 2008 conviction for pedophilia.

According to Cohan (2021), Black's reputation was as a ruthless dealmaker:

> He learned his craft at Drexel Burnham Lambert, the defunct investment bank, and from its superstar banker Michael Milken, a recently pardoned convicted criminal who helped create the junk bond market. Black was head of mergers and acquisitions at Drexel before it blew up. In one of Apollo's earliest deals, it negotiated to buy, at a significant discount, the bond portfolio of Executive Life Insurance Company, which had failed after, among other things, buying too many Drexel-underwritten junk bonds. Black was highly adept at fighting for the last penny in deals and was one of Wall Street's most feared vulture investors, the people who buy bonds of distressed companies at a discount and then get control of companies by converting the debt they own to equity. As Apollo grew, Black and his growing team engineered bigger and bigger deals. Among its biggest successes are LyondellBasell, a chemical company, ADT, the security company, and among its biggest flops are Caesars Entertainment and Linens'n Things.

For reasons that Dechert (2021) does not completely make clear, Black had a soft spot for Epstein, even after his 2008 guilty plea for soliciting prostitution and procuring a person under the age of 18 for prostitution. Examiners found that Black believed in rehabilitation and in giving people second chances. That was also why Black stayed friendly with Martha Stewart, who had spent time in prison. Black viewed Epstein as a friend worthy of his trust. They attended social events together, Black confided in Epstein on personal matters, and Black introduced Epstein to his family. Black regularly visited Epstein's townhouse in New York either to discuss business or to meet other prominent guests who were visiting Epstein, including well-known businessmen, political figures, diplomats, scientists, and celebrities. One-on-one breakfast meetings between Black and Epstein would be more common for business meetings, whereas afternoon meetings with other guests would be more common for social visits.

Dechert (2021: 3) draw the following conclusions after their investigation:

1   Dechert has seen no evidence that Black, or any employee of the Family Office or Apollo was involved in any way with Epstein's criminal activities at any time. There is no evidence that Epstein ever introduced Black, or offered to introduce Black, to any underage woman.

2   Black and others at Apollo and the Family Office were aware that Epstein had been convicted in 2008 for the charges of solicitation of prostitution and procuring a person under 18 for prostitution. There is no evidence suggesting knowledge of any other of Epstein's criminal activity or the scope and details of such activity, at any time prior to such activities being publicly reported in late 2018 and culminating with Epstein's arrest in July 2019. When Black first retained Epstein, he believed that Epstein had served his time for the originally charged offenses and believed that it was not inappropriate to give Epstein a second chance, as many other prominent figures in business, science, politics and academia had done.

3   From approximately the mid-1990s to 2018, Black had a social relationship with Epstein, and from 2012 to 2017, Epstein provided professional services to Black as well. There is no evidence that Black paid Epstein for any services after April 2017, although the two men did continue to communicate until October 2018. Professionally, Black retained Epstein to advise Black and the Family Office on a variety of topics related to trust and estate planning, tax issues, philanthropic endeavors, and the operation of the Family Office. Socially, Black was friendly with Epstein and confided in Epstein regarding personal matters. Epstein would, at times, allude to their personal relationship when attempting to negotiate aspects of their business relationship, but Dechert has seen no evidence suggesting that either their professional or personal relationships ever touched upon Epstein's criminal activities or any other illegal activity.

4   Epstein regularly advised Black on a variety of issues related to trust and estate planning, tax, philanthropy, and the operation of the Family Office. Although witnesses agreed that: (a) not all of Epstein's advice was useful and (b) Epstein was generally a disruptive and caustic force within the Family Office, many witnesses believed that Epstein had creative ideas that no other advisor had proposed and would push Family Office employees to achieve greater performance than they might have achieved on their own. As a result of Epstein's work, Black believed, and witnesses generally agreed, that Epstein provided advice that conferred more than $1 billion and as much as $2 billion or more in value to Black.

5   Black compensated Epstein for his work in amounts that were intended to be proportional to the value provided by Epstein. Those payments for work performed over the period 2012 through 2017 totaled $158 million. In 2013,

payments were memorialized in signed and unsigned agreements. After that point, payments were made on an *ad hoc* basis based on Black's perceived value of Epstein's work. Dechert has seen no evidence suggesting that Black ever compensated Epstein for any service other than Epstein's legitimate advice on trust and estate planning, tax issues, issues relating to artwork, Black's airplane, Black's yacht, and other similar matters, philanthropic issues, and the operation of the Family Office. Moreover, such advice was vetted consistently by Black's other advisors, including Family Office employees, Paul Weiss, and other outside legal, accounting and tax professionals.

6   Beginning in 2016, Black and Epstein's professional and personal relationship deteriorated over a payment dispute that had long been brewing, with Black refusing to pay Epstein tens of millions of dollars that Epstein believed he had earned. Black's last payment to Epstein was made in April 2017; in 2018, Epstein repaid a portion of two loans that were outstanding to Black but never repaid the balance. Black and Epstein ceased communications in or around the fall of 2018, prior to the renewed public revelations of Epstein's conduct and Epstein's arrest and suicide.

7   Epstein and his entities did not invest in any Apollo-managed funds. However, in 2011, one of Epstein's entities, Financial Trust Company, purchased 263,257 shares of Apollo's stock in its initial public offering. Those shares appear to have later been transferred to a second Epstein entity, Southern Financial LLC, and appear to have been held through at least September 2019. Aside from this stock purchase, and the tangential matters described below, Dechert has seen no evidence of Epstein or any Epstein entity having any relationship with Apollo or any Apollo-managed fund.

8   Epstein made repeated efforts to ingratiate himself with other senior executives at Apollo and appears to have relied on Black to help him make those introductions. Despite these efforts, Dechert has seen no evidence of any other Apollo executive ever retaining Epstein for his services.

Review Information Sources

The documentary *Jeffrey Epstein: Filthy Rich* presents insights into Epstein's power, influence, network, wealth, and activity. His behavior might be explained by the perspective of sensation seeking to experience adventure. Craig and Piquero (2017) suggest that the willingness to commit financial crime by some white-collar offenders has to do with their inclination for adventure and excitement. Offenders are not only seeking new, intense, and complicated experiences and sensations, as well as exciting adventures, they are also accepting the legal, physical, financial, and social risks associated with these adventures. They attempt to avoid boredom by replacing repetitive activities such as regular meetings with thrill and adventures. Individuals like both Epstein and Black with low self-control tend to be impulsive, self-centered, out for adventure, and out for immediate pleasure. Immediate pleasure may be achieved more conveniently by white-collar crime than by legal activities.

When the Dechert (2021) report was published, some questioned the conclusions, arguing that Wall Street would not buy Leon Black's Epstein story (Cohan, 2021):

> Dechert's report on the Apollo cofounder's decades long dealings with the late convicted sex offender, including payments of $158 million, is raising eyebrows – and more questions – on Wall Street. One lawyer dismissed it as a "whitewash". "Nice try, Leon. You must think we are pretty stupid, gullible, or insane to believe the tale you spun to Dechert, the Wall Street law firm, about your decades-long involvement with Jeffrey Epstein, the late convicted pedophile. Well, I, for one, am not buying it, not any of it, and neither are many other smart Wall Streeters". "What a sad tale of sycophants", was the way one longtime Wall Street banker explained it to me. Added a Wall Street lawyer; "It's preposterous".
>
> Leon is, of course, Leon Black, one of the billionaire cofounders of Apollo Global Management, the publicly traded private-equity and investment firm with around $350 billion under management. Of course, he has a private jet and a luxury yacht and lots of fancy homes.

Cohan (2021) argued that Black could hire what appeared to be a reputable law firm to put their stamp of approval on a version of the truth that is not likely to be independently verified by anyone not getting paid by Black or Apollo. One of the ignored allegations against Black on the Wall Street is that Black used Epstein for laundering money from criminal activities. Black was using Epstein's services to pass money to people who he did not want to be associated with by name.

According to Cohan (2021), it was an article in the *New York Times* that caused Apollo to hire Dechert for the investigation of Black. The article about "the billionaire who stood by Jeffrey Epstein" was written by Matthew Goldstein, Steve Eder, and David Enrich. The three journalists had interviewed four people who were knowledgeable about Black and Epstein (Goldstein et al., 2020):

> The billionaire financier Leon Black, one of Wall Street's most powerful executives, was facing questions from clients after Jeffrey Epstein was arrested last year on federal sex trafficking charges. The two men had known each other for decades, and investors of Mr. Black's investment company, Apollo Global Management, wanted to know how close they had been. Such questions were valid, Mr. Black said, according to a transcript of a call with analysts in July 2019. He said in a letter that same day to investors that he had had a "limited relationship" with Mr. Epstein, a convicted sex offender, and had consulted him "from time to time" on personal financial matters.

Fraud Investigation Evaluation

In October 2020, the conflicts committee at Apollo Global Management decided to engage the law firm Dechert LLP to conduct an investigation on behalf of the company. The reason for the engagement was that there had been a lot of speculation in the media regarding Apollo's CEO, Leon Black's, relationship to the pedophile convict Jeffrey Epstein. The *New York Times* published an article in which Black was said to have paid millions to Epstein. The newspaper article was the trigger for Apollo's perception that there was a need for an investigation. Often the best starting point for an investigation is that the company itself recognizes that an examination is required, rather than having external pressures force the company to conduct an investigation. Without the media attention, Apollo would most likely not have initiated an investigation. The situational factor was the suspicion of financial crime and illegal relations between Black and Epstein. The Dechert (2021) report indicated that Apollo had willingness for change and was motivated to take on the possible consequences that could come from the investigation.

Dechert is a global law firm with 24 active locations. They advise on domestic and cross-border matters. They work on transactions and disputes. The firm claimed that it had conducted an independent investigation into the allegations against Black. While Cohan (2021) expressed surprise that Apollo did not ask the company's regular outside counsel Paul, Weiss, Rifkind, Wharton & Garrison, it is indeed a positive attribute of an investigation if it is conducted by a firm that is not the regular outside counsel. In fact, there is no indication of Dechert having done other business with Apollo, which strengthens the impression of independence. There is no sign or evidence to suggest that Apollo and Dechert had any relationship before they were hired to carry out the investigation. On the other hand, it might be questioned whether Dechert is independent when they are paid large sums of money for the assignment, where the client and the person to be investigated are more or less the same.

The mandate for the investigation seems relevant and appropriate. The mandate is clearly formulated and is controllable so that it is possible to achieve the examination objectives. The mandate is formulated so that Dechert will report the facts and provide an assessment of whether there had been a relationship between Apollo, Black, and Epstein, and any description of that relationship.

The investigation process by Dechert (2021) is not described in their report, which makes one wonder how examiners approached their assignment. In terms of knowledge categories, the investigation conducted by the law firm applied mainly legal knowledge, where psychology knowledge and investigative interviewing skills would be more appropriate to gain insights into personal relationships in this group of deviant elite members. In terms of information sources, examiners reviewed many documents and interviewed 20 people. One potential interviewee refused cooperation. Frequently in investigations, those who refuse to participate tend to be the most important information sources. While Dechert (2021) argued that the person did not have high value for the investigation, it is nevertheless an interesting issue why the person denied being interviewed. The reason might be information that the person did not want to disclose, or the reason might be lack of trust in the examiners in terms of how information is obtained and used.

The reviewed documents were preselected by Apollo. There is no indication of examiners having requested more documents. A suspicion of biased selection thus emerges. Frequently, investigated organizations leave out documents that might guide examiners in different directions because they – in their struggle for confidentiality and secrecy – want to avoid attention to certain aspects of their business (Gottschalk and Tcherni-Buzzeo, 2017). A sign of professional inquiry is when examiners can search documents themselves in the client organization rather than being handed a selection of documents from the client.

When it comes to the result in the investigation report, it is important to evaluate the extent to which the mandate has been answered, and whether conclusions are based on a clear and objective analysis. Dechert (2021) goes thoroughly through each of the points they have examined and explain their findings. Dechert explains the relationship between Epstein and Blacik and emphasizes that it was only professional and that there is nothing to indicate that Black has been introduced to underage girls, or that he knew about Epstein's criminal activities. Dechert has managed to find factual evidence that there is no proof of a criminal relationship between Epstein and Apollo. This means that the objective and mandate are fulfilled.

Investigation Maturity Assessment

Despite the criticism and skepticism by Cohan (2021) and others, the report by Dechert (2021) is trustworthy. Over a period of three months, Dechert reviewed more than 60,000 documents obtained from Black, Apollo, Elysium Management LLC (Black's "Family Office"), and Paul, Weiss, Rifkind, Wharton & Garrison LLP, outside legal counsel to Black and the Family Office. Such documents included emails, text messages, banking statements, and other forms of communication. Potentially relevant documents were collected from Apollo for current and former employees of Apollo dating back to 1998 as well as for all current and former employees of the Family Office, including from the inception of the Family Office and prior to implementation of the separate Family Office (Elysium) email address. Text messages were also collected from Black's cell phone.

Dechert was assisted in its document collection efforts by Paul, as well as by Apollo's legal counsel for the purpose of this investigation, Milbank LLP. Paul and Milbank also assisted Dechert in providing access to not only materials but also various witnesses thought to be relevant to the investigation. Dechert interviewed more than 20 witnesses (some more than once), including Black, current and former Apollo employees, the cofounders of Apollo, current and former Family Office employees, and current and former legal counsel to obtain their recollection of events that may have been relevant to Dechert's investigation. With only one exception, Dechert interviewed every witness that it had requested; that witness, a former employee of the Family Office, declined to participate in the investigation but is not believed to have any additional information likely to be material to the investigation.

The report concludes that there was no wrongdoing on the part of Black related to the crime by Epstein. This is an interesting and valuable conclusion, as it seemed in 2020 that everyone who had been dealing with Epstein must have done something wrong. The media were hunting individuals who at some point in time had communicated with Epstein. An anecdotal piece of evidence is the Norwegian crown princess who attended an event with Epstein in New York, where Norwegian press later tried to link potential wrongdoing to participation at the event. The crown princess then had to announce publicly that she condemned Epstein's abuse of minors and that she regretted ever having accepted an invitation from him.

The issue here, however, is whether some people doing business with Epstein ever was involved in Epstein's criminal activities. The answer from Dechert (2021) is no in the case of Leon Black. This detection-oriented conclusion has substantial value for him and his Apollo firm, as suspicion is removed from one of the founders of the firm. Figure 1.2 thus indicates that it was a detection-oriented investigation. The examination was a disclosure. A detection-oriented investigation focuses on something being hidden, which should be revealed. Investigators choose their tactics to succeed in exposing possible misconduct and perhaps even financial crime. Investigative steps are adapted to the terrain, where different sources of information and methods are used to get as many facts on the table as possible. Examiners are successful in identifying and documenting some new facts. The investigation has a clear perspective.

After release of the report by Dechert (2021), Leon Black stepped down from his role as CEO of Apollo Global. However, he would remain as chairman at the assets firm. He was replaced by cofounder Marc Rowan. The reason Black stepped down was his payment of $158 million in fees for services from Epstein as well as a loan to Epstein of $30 million and a donation of $10 million to Epstein's charity.

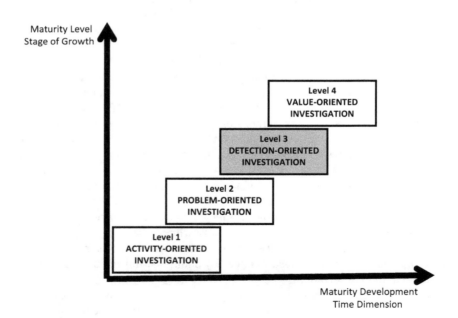

Figure 1.2 Maturity assessments for the Dechert (2021) report

All these figures were multiples of what was previously reported. Another reason was that Black was turning 70 years old and had been one of Wall Street's most prominent dealmakers for decades (Gara and Voytko, 2021).

References

Agnew, R. (2014). Social concern and crime: Moving beyond the assumption of simple self-interest, *Criminology*, 52 (1), 1–32.

Aguilera, R.V., Judge, W.Q. and Terjesen, S.A. (2018). Corporate governance deviance, *Academy of Management Review*, 43 (1), 87–109.

Benson, M.L. and Simpson, S.S. (2018). *White-Collar Crime: An Opportunity Perspective*, (3rd Edition), Routledge, New York.

Berghoff, H. and Spiekermann, U. (2018). Shady business: On the history of white-collar crime, *Business History*, 60 (3), 289–304.

Chatterjee, A. and Pollock, T.G. (2017). Master of puppets: How narcissistic CEOs construct their professional worlds, *Academy of Management Review*, 42 (4), 703–725.

Cohan, W.D. (2021). "What a sad tale of sycophants": Wall Street isn't buying Leon Black's Epstein story, *Vanity Fair*, January 29, www.vanityfair.com.

Craig, J.M. and Piquero, N.L. (2016). The effects of low self-control and desire-for-control on white-collar offending: A replication, *Deviant Behavior*, 37 (11), 1308–1324.

Craig, J.M. and Piquero, N.L. (2017). Sensational offending: An application of sensation seeking to white-collar and conventional crimes, *Crime & Delinquency*, 63 (11), 1363–1382.

Dechert. (2021). *Investigation of Epstein/Black Relationship and Any Relationship between Epstein and Apollo Global Management*, law firm Dechert, report of investigation, New York, p. 21.

Galvin, B.M., Lange, D. and Ashforth, B.E. (2015). Narcissistic organizational identification: Seeing oneself as central to the organization's identity, *Academy of Management Review*, 40 (2), 163–181.

Gara, A. and Voytko, L. (2021). Billionaire Leon Black, revealed to pay Jeffrey Epstein $158 million, is stepping down, *Forbes*, January 25, www.forbes.com.

Goldstein, M., Eder, S. and Enrich, D. (2020). The billionaire who stood by Jeffrey Epstein, *The New York Times*, October 13, www.nytimes.com.

Gottfredson, M.R. and Hirschi, T. (1990). *A General Theory of Crime*, Stanford University Press, Stanford.

Gottschalk, P. and Tcherni-Buzzeo, M. (2017). Reasons for gaps in crime reporting: The case of white-collar criminals investigated by private fraud examiners in Norway, *Deviant Behavior*, 38 (3), 267–281.

Hirschi, T. and Gottfredson, M. (1987). Causes of white-collar crime, *Criminology*, 25 (4), 949–974.

Howes, S.S., Kausel, E.E., Jackson, A.T. and Reb, J. (2020). When and why narcissists exhibit greater hindsight bias and less perceived learning, *Journal of Management*, 46 (8), 1498–1528.

Jones, S., Lyman, D.R. and Piquero, A.R. (2015). Substance use, personality, and inhibitors: Testing Hirschi's predictions about the reconceptualization of self-control, *Crime & Delinquency*, 61 (4), 538–558.

Kakkar, H., Sivanathan, N. and Globel, M.S. (2020). Fall from grace: The role of dominance and prestige in punishment of high-status actors, *Academy of Management Journal*, 63 (2), 530–553.

Kroneberg, C. and Schultz, S. (2018). Revisiting the role of self-control in situational action theory, *European Journal of Criminology*, 15 (1), 56–76.

Maslow, A.H. (1943). A theory of human motivation, *Psychological Review*, 50 (4), 370–396.

McClean, E.J., Martin, S.R., Emich, K.J. and Woodruff, T. (2018). The social consequences of voice: An examination of voice type and gender on status and subsequent leader emergence, *Academy of Management Journal*, 61 (5), 1869–1891.

Petrocelli, M., Piquero, A.R. and Smith, M.R. (2003). Conflict theory and racial profiling: An empirical analysis of police traffic stop data, *Journal of Criminal Justice*, 31 (1), 1–11.

Piening, E.P., Salge, T.O., Antons, D. and Kreiner, G.E. (2020). Standing together or falling apart? Understanding employees' responses to organizational identity threats, *Academy of Management Review*, 45 (2), 325–351.

Pillay, S. and Kluvers, R. (2014). An institutional theory perspective on corruption: The case of a developing democracy, *Financial Accountability & Management*, 30 (1), 95–119.

Sampson, A. (2020). Art billionaire and collector Leon Black investigated over financial dealings with Epstein, *Tatler*, August 25, www.tatler.com.

Schnatterly, K., Gangloff, K.A. and Tuschke, A. (2018). CEO wrongdoing: A review of pressure, opportunity, and rationalization, *Journal of Management*, 44 (6), 2405–2432.

Schoepfer, A. and Piquero, N.L. (2006). Exploring white-collar crime and the American dream: A partial test of institutional anomie theory, *Journal of Criminal Justice*, 34 (3), 227–235.

Smith, O. and Raymen, T. (2018). Deviant leisure: A criminological perspective, *Theoretical Criminology*, 22 (1), 63–82.

Sutherland, E.H. (1983). *White Collar Crime – The Uncut Version*, Yale University Press, New Haven.

Sykes, G. and Matza, D. (1957). Techniques of neutralization: A theory of delinquency, *American Sociological Review*, 22 (6), 664–670.

Toubiana, M. (2020). Once in orange always in orange? Identity paralysis and the enduring influence of institutional logics on identity, *Academy of Management Journal*, 63 (6), 1739–1774.

Welsh, D.T., Ordonez, L.D., Snyder, D.G. and Christian, M.S. (2014). The slippery slope: How small ethical transgressions pave the way for larger future transgressions, *Journal of Applied Psychology*, 100 (1), 114–127.

Zvi, L. and Elaad, E. (2018). Correlates of narcissism, self-reported lies, and self-assessed abilities to tell and detect lies, tell truths, and believe others, *Journal of Investigative Psychology and Offender Profiling*, 15, 271–286.

2 University President Solo Project

The president at the University of Bergen in Norway, Dag Rune Olsen, was accused of financial misconduct causing economic loss for the university. He spent university money on a project developed by his friend Tom Knudsen, who had been a business executive before developing the project with the university. The project was a concept of a working life portal that would link discipline students at the university to potential employers. The project was a collaboration between Olsen and Knudsen paid for by the University of Bergen (UiB). The university was to pay NOK 20 million (USD 2 million) for Knudsen's idea and buy annual services for NOK 5 million in five years. However, the project was discontinued, and Knudsen was temporarily employed at the university at a salary level out of the ordinary. The university also paid a sum of NOK 540,000 to Knudsen's company for costs related to the preparation of the concept (Eikefjord, 2021; Haga et al., 2020). The suspected fraud was concerned with the president's abuse of university funds.

When investigative journalists at the local newspaper detected the potential scam (Lindberg, 2021), fraud examiners from PricewaterhouseCoopers (PwC, 2021) were hired by the university board to review the matter. Fraud examiners concluded that Knudsen's concept was worthless and that the university should pay nothing for it. Furthermore, they concluded that the hiring of Knudsen as well as the refund of costs should not have taken place.

In the report, PwC (2021) concludes that it is contrary to the laws and regulations governing the university for the president to buy Knudsen's company and that it is also contrary to laws and regulations to hire Knudsen temporarily as the University of Bergen is a public institution and there must have advertised the position. Knudsen had for several years worked at the top of the Confederation of Norwegian Business and Industry's main organization (NHO), and it is therefore less believable that he did not know that his employment was contrary to the law. While our focus here is on Olsen at the university, the behavior of Knudsen could also deserve a study.

DOI: 10.4324/9781003363934-3

Motive Convenience Themes

Assuming that the allegations against Olsen are justified, we can apply convenience theory to study his motive, opportunity, as well as willingness. A relevant motive was the convenience theme of concern for others as defined by Agnew (2014), since the external partner to the university had a relevant project that suffered from a serious funding shortage. The motive of concern for others is reflected in climbing the hierarchy of needs (Maslow, 1943). This is illustrated in Figure 2.1 by motive-possibility-individual. He might claim that his motive was to strengthen the university's position in the labor market and thus emphasize motive-possibility-corporate (Schoultz and Flyghed, 2020a, 2020b, 2021; Walburg, 2020; Zysman-Quirós, 2020).

The motive for the agreement between Olsen and Knudsen was a possibility at the organizational level, which both of them thought could be beneficial for the university, but also in Knudsen's favor. It can be argued that Knudsen's motive was a possibility at the individual level as he was to receive some benefits when establishing the company (Hystad et al., 2020). The agreement between the two might thus be considered profit-driven misconduct carried out on the basis of

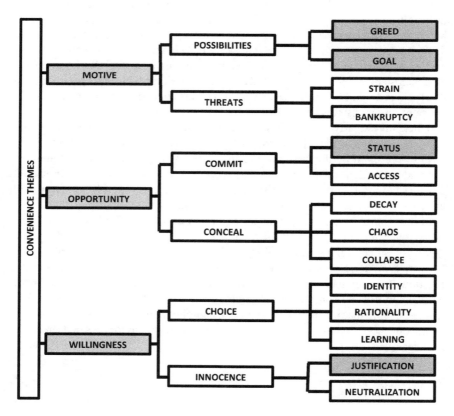

Figure 2.1 Structural model of convenience themes for the university dean

rational self-interest where one does what is best for oneself (Pillay and Kluvers, 2014). The economic model of rational self-interest is all about weighing up the pros and cons of alternative courses of actions. The model considers incentives and probability of detection (Welsh et al., 2014). This applies to both private and professional life. Human behavior finds motivation in the self-centered quest for satisfaction and avoidance of suffering (Hirschi and Gottfredson, 1987).

One of Olsen's motives was to compensate Knudsen (PwC, 2021: 60):

> According to PwC's assessment, UiB was not legally obliged to pay for costs invoiced from Bodoni, TK's lawyer and the company Best Practices AS totaling NOK 540,000. Furthermore, UiB has not fulfilled the requirement in the state's financial regulations related to the specification of the services with a sufficient indication of the nature, scope and time and place of delivery of services. It appears from the investigation that TK spent some time getting more players to invest in his idea and that he thus carried out marketing work with a desire to succeed commercially. In PwC's assessment, however, there is no indication that any form of technology development or other development has taken place that made it possible to present a concept of commercial value.
>
> In interviews with PwC, it appears that the president and UiB's lawyer have different views on what the payment to TK's companies where justified in. While UiB's lawyer was aware that the value of the concept could not be assessed and that the payments therefore, partly for hours TK had worked and partly for specific expenses/costs, the president believed that the payment secured UiB the rights to "the concept" of TK.

In this case, it was undoubtedly the possibilities that governed the actions that were committed. There were no threats to persons or the university by not implementing the agreement. The president had hoped that the prospect would give UiB great innovative competitive advantages in the future. Therefore, he chose to work for an agreement that would cost significant amounts as a basic investment in a company, which was to be followed up by the purchase of services for NOK 5 million per year up to and including 2025, where UiB would subsequently take over the business.

We must look at whether these actions were committed for UiB's gain or individual gain, or possibly both. Through the report, it never becomes clear why the president continues to carry out this project when he was repeatedly made aware that the actions were outside of his authority.

The possibilities for the individual include climbing the hierarchy in need of status and success (Maslow, 1943). Here, the question must be asked whether the reason why the president continued the project was to give himself a higher status, if the project for which he had high hopes was to be a success. Olsen's last term as president at the University of Bergen was to expire in 2021, and he had no intention of returning to his regular position as professor of biomedical physics as a cancer researcher. He was interested in a new position in society, where he could have power and influence. He applied for the position of president at another university in Norway, and he was then appointed president at the University of Tromsø. Before starting in the new position, the Bergen scandal became public. Grinde (2021) indicated that because of his professional network, he did not lose his new job. This happened despite the fact that he had to leave the position of president at the University of Bergen early before his term ended.

President Olsen saw the concept as a great possibility and believed that the idea was worth thousands of millions, despite the fact that the idea did not have much business value and would only serve Tom Knudsen in the long run. The president envisioned that the concept would benefit academia, and this was, according to the investigators, a major misjudgment. The concept that UiB was close to buying could cost them large sums, and it would probably take a long time before the concept would generate value, if at all. In other words, this was a risky project for UiB that was to secure Knudsen's company capital.

Securing capital for Knudsen might be analyzed in the perspective of concern for others. Agnew (2014) introduced the motive of social concern and crime, where there is a desire to help others, thus moving beyond the assumption of simple self-interest. However, as argued by Paternoster et al. (2018), helping others can be a self-interested, rational action that claims social concern. Olsen's social concern could also include university students who might enter into practice through the concept. By doing more for the students, the president might climb higher in the hierarchy for admiration.

Opportunity Convenience Themes

The opportunity to hire his friend Knudsen was possible based on the status of Olsen as the university president and the rule that short-term contracts can be signed with employees without announcement of vacant positions, even though Knudsen was obviously not qualified (PwC, 2021: 58):

> By employing Knudsen in a position of up to six months' duration, these rules were avoided. In PwC's assessment, this seems to be a deliberate circumvention, precisely in order to get past the requirements. In this connection, reference is made to the president, who in an interview with PwC said that he initially wanted to buy the company from Knudsen, as it was not relevant to hire him due to the qualification principle: "Hiring him was not relevant either, because then the position had to be advertised in the usual way – and then it is the qualification principle in the state that applies. Whether he had an idea and a concept that we wanted to further develop is irrelevant in such an appointment case. We could have done that too, but it might have been a bit complicated. It might have to be done as a six-month commitment in the first place. Salary in a position at UiB would also not include a financial compensation for the idea."

The incident can in many ways be considered a cover-up, at least initially when Olsen detected that he had no support for his actions. The principal–agent perspective is thus relevant here. "Principal" is the term for a body or person that entrusts work tasks to an agent. The principal in this case is the board where the agent is the president. The chance of misconduct from an organizational aspect increases when the agent is set to solve the tasks more independently and alone. President Olsen had a very free playing field, which is evident from both the investigation report and the media, and he did not talk to others than Knudsen when he experienced resistance. The perspective of principal and agent suggests that when a principal delegates tasks to an agent, the principal is often unable to control what the agent is doing. Agency problems occur when principal and agent have different risk willingness and different preferences, and knowledge asymmetry regarding tasks exists (Bosse and Phillips, 2016).

While president Olsen did not have formal authority to enter into business transactions with outside vendors, his position enabled him nevertheless to do so. The investigation report states that the president did not have his own business powers. It was the university director as head of the university administration who had overall responsibility for all financial matters. However, in his second and final term as president, no one stood in the way of him being allowed to conduct negotiations for a long time. PwC (2021) concludes that the administration at UiB was reluctant to intervene and avoided questioning the president regarding transactions with Knudsen. In that the president utilized the university director's powers, there must have been poor collaboration and poor communication between the top leaders of the university, which directs attention toward the convenience theme of lacking transparency. Lack of transparency makes concealment in accounting convenient (Davidson et al., 2019; Goncharov and Peter, 2019). Trusted offenders can withhold bad news by not telling and not reporting what expenses represent (Bao et al., 2019), since financial statements are a substantive component of an organization's communications with its stakeholders (Gupta et al., 2020).

Olsen was able to ignore skepticism in the university administration against the deal with Knudsen because of his status, where "status is a property that rests in the eyes of others and is conferred to individuals who are deemed to have a higher rank or social standing in a pecking order on a mutually valued set of social attributes" (Kakkar et al., 2020: 532).

Olsen felt innocent when he was interviewed by examiners from PwC (2021: 59):

> That said, my experience is that these are two things: One is the work the University of Bergen does as preparation to put students out into practice, and the other is my research project that relates to matching. But, of course, there is an interaction between these two parts because the experience and inputs he collects influences what the matching algorithm should contain.

As illustrated in this quote, strange language is applied in most of Olsen's statements in interviews with examiners. Executives and others in the elite may use language that followers do not necessarily understand. Followers nevertheless trust executive messages. Language shapes what people notice and ignore (Ferraro et al., 2005), and language is a window into organizational culture (Holt and

Cornelissen, 2014; Srivastava and Goldberg, 2017; Weick, 1995). Offender language can cause obedience among followers (Mawritz et al., 2017).

Willingness Convenience Themes

Within the willingness dimension of convenience theory, university president Olsen probably made choices based on identity and rationality. In terms of identity, Olsen has acted on his own by ignoring both the university board and the ministry for higher education. In many ways, he made his own rules. He chose not to listen to warnings from either the internal administration or external stakeholders. In terms of rationality, it was a matter of individual perception of potential benefits exceeding potential costs.

In the investigation report, several neutralization techniques can be highlighted in the president's statements. An example of claiming that the action is within his blunder quota is the president's response when he agreed to give Knudsen a salary at a higher level than was agreed with the management at the university. His response was that he "takes it in stride" and that "agreement is agreement" without any further explanation. He claimed a blunder quota.

Claiming blunder quota is often happening when the offender finds it was a necessary shortcut to get things done. The offender argues that what he or she did is acceptable given the situation and given his or her position. The person feels that after having done so much good for so many for so long time, others should excuse him or her for more wrongdoings than other people deserve forgiveness for. Others should understand that the alleged crime was an acceptable mistake. This is in line with the metaphor of the ledger, which uses the idea of compensating bad acts by good acts. That is, the individual believes that he or she has previously performed a number of good acts and has accrued a surplus of goodwill, and, because of this, he or she can afford to commit some bad actions. Executives in corporate environments neutralize their actions through the metaphor of the ledger by rationalizing that their overall past good behavior justifies occasional rule breaking.

Some white-collar offenders take on a professional deviant identity (Obodaru, 2017). The identity perspective suggests that individuals develop professional identities where they commit to a chosen identity. It is a process of generating possible selves, selecting one, and discarding others. Professional identity is how an individual sees himself or herself in relation to work. The self-concept is a complex cognitive structure containing all of a person's self-representations. According to the identity perspective, roles, and identities are interdependent concepts. Identity enactment refers to acting out an identity or claiming the identity by engaging in behaviors that conform to role expectations and that allow the identity to become manifest. Deviant behavior finds an anchor in a person's professional identity, where the deviant leader must claim and assume a leader identity by their followers.

Investigators attempted to identify president Olsen's justification (PwC, 2021: 62):

> Despite our assessment that the idea of TK did not constitute any value, it was
> the president's opinion that TK was the rightful owner of the idea and that

it would be wrong for UiB to take the idea without TK receiving any form of compensation. The president further believed that he himself was not the right person to determine the value of the idea and he therefore asked for help with such a calculation. The president reacted to the administration's focus on what was wrong with the draft agreement instead of correcting it so that it could be accepted. The president believed that it must be possible to find a solution where the idea could be further developed in a limited company. Not even the comments from the ministry did the president think were impossible to dissolve.

The slippery slope is a relevant perspective here. Arjoon (2008: 78) explained slippery slope in the following way: "As commonsense experience tells us; it is the small infractions that can lead to the larger ones". A series of small infractions gradually increase over time. Committing small indiscretions over time gradually will lead people to complete larger unethical acts that they otherwise would have judged impermissible (Murphy and Dacin, 2011; Pettigrew, 2018). The slippery slope perspective is relevant since people whom he initially talked to were neutral and reluctant to express their opinions when he presented his idea of cooperating with the developer and the software firm. When skepticism emerged, he escalated his efforts with Knudsen and ignored warnings from others. Lack of self-control, a desire to control others, and sliding on a slippery slope are all factors that make the willingness for deviant behavior grow. The slippery slope perspective suggests that a person can slide over time from legal to illegal activities without really noticing.

Lack of self-control is a frequent explanation for executive deviance and crime in general (Gottfredson and Hirschi, 1990). While many might be tempted, only those lacking self-control will actually do it. Self-regulation monitors self-control, where self-regulation represents a process of using self-regulatory resources to control undesirable impulses and override subsequent behavioral responses. As argued by Mawritz et al. (2017), individuals possess varying and limited self-regulatory resources that inhibit responses that may arise from physiological processes, habit, learning, or the strain of the situation. When resources that regulate self-control are depleted, individuals struggle to constrain their urges and engage in behavior almost unwittingly, using quick, thoughtless responses. They move down the slippery slope from the right side of the law to the wrong side of the law (Arjoon, 2008). Self-control processes deplete self-regulatory resources and impair one's ability to control subsequent inappropriate responses.

Olsen felt that the act of wrongdoing was morally justifiable (Schnatterly et al., 2018) based on upper-echelon information selection (Gamache and McNamara, 2019). Justification and also neutralization can cause perceived innocence of wrongdoing.

Identity, rationality, learning, justification, and neutralization all contribute to making white-collar wrongdoing a convenient behavior for offenders, where justification seems to be the most prominent convenience item in the case of Dean Olsen.

Investigation Report Outcome

The president at the University of Bergen, Dag Rune Olsen, hired his friend Tom Knudsen and promised to pay millions for Knudsen's innovative company, according to a news report (PwC, 2021: 5):

> But when the agreement was sent to the Ministry of Education, they came up with a number of objections.

Fraud examiners from PwC (2021) were hired to investigate the matter. They concluded that dean Olsen had violated the law when hiring Knudsen and promising millions (Strand, 2021):

> – This is not how you hire in a temporary position; certain conditions must be met in order to be able to use such positions. When we have looked at why they chose to hire Tom Knudsen, hiring him was a temporary decision that could be made at the administrative level, without having to involve an appointing body.
>
> This is what Stig Rune Johnsen from PwC said when the board at the University of Bergen (UiB) on Thursday was presented with the investigation report on the practice portal case and the contact between former rector Dag Rune Olsen and former NHO leader Tom Knudsen. The two collaborated on a working life portal – a concept PwC concludes has no business value.

The alleged law violation by Olsen is concerned with financial infidelity. Anyone who acts against another's interests that he controls or supervises, with the intention of obtaining an unjustified gain for himself or others is punishable according to Norwegian law. While it is not obvious that Olsen enriched himself, it is more likely to assume that he could have the intention of obtaining an unjustified gain for Tom Knudsen, with whom he had collaborated in various settings before (Svarstad, 2021). Olsen was accused of paying Knudsen an unjustified salary at the university, for refunding Knudsen's expenses that did not relate to university activities, for expensive entertainment paid by the university, and for offering a large sum of university money for procurement of Knudsen's company (Toft, 2021).

Corporate investigator Stig Rune Johnsen at PricewaterhouseCoopers examined the University of Bergen. The investigation was initiated by the university. Earlier in this book, the investigation was assigned the highest level of maturity as a value-oriented investigation, and Johnsen was introduced as a former special detective with 11 years of experience at the Norwegian national authority for investigation and prosecution of economic and environmental crime. Later he provided consulting services within anti-corruption.

The investigation at the University of Bergen was carried out by Stig Rune Johnsen, Marianne Pilgaard, Thor Dalhaug, Oda Renate Nødtvedt, Anni Terese

Haugen, Nora Gedde, and Ida-Sofie Sandvik at PricewaterhouseCoopers in Oslo, Norway. They conducted 18 interviews with 17 interviewees and reviewed 349 pages of documentation. Minutes from interviews made up 187 pages. Both suspects, Olsen and Knudsen, had the opportunity of contradiction when reviewing the draft manuscript for the statement of facts.

Corporate investigator Johnsen held a guest lecture at the Norwegian business school in March 2021, where he presented PwC's approach to internal investigation. He said that the mandate for an investigation should be formulated in such a way that it can be presented to interviewees as an explanation for the investigation. If the mandate is biased, then Johnsen refuses to take on the task. For example, if the client mandate says that investigators should find evidence to prove corporate innocence, then it is too biased for an investigator with integrity. The memory of an interviewee can be challenged in various ways, since memory is an active ongoing process that is under continuous influence. The most important part for a corporate investigator in an interview is to listen.

The mandate for the investigation by PwC (2021) at the University of Bergen was to assess Olsen's involvement in the development of internships for students. The case in question concerned a practice portal designed by Tom Knudsen that could focus on candidates from disciplinary subjects and with a match function specifically aimed at the private sector. Investigators were asked to review financial transactions, temporary employment, and potential procurements.

Examiners found that offering a large sum of university money for procurement of Knudsen's company did not make sense since the company had no business value. The company was based on an idea that had not been developed into any kind of functionality. Examiners found that the suggested matching functionality, that is, to connect interested parties, is the purpose of so many existing information and communication systems already.

Examiners draw the following conclusion (PwC, 2021: 62):

> As a state educational institution, it is particularly important that the University of Bergen manages to embrace good academic and scientific ideas under a secure administrative framework as it is committed to. The University of Bergen has not been able to do that in this case. The administration was involved too late. When they became involved, they announced that the premises laid down for the development of the idea through the purchase of the company Praktikk AS would under no circumstances be something a state institution could enter into. Despite this, the dean continued a process, partly outside the administration's control, which was intended for the University of Bergen to buy this company. The warnings were ignored. Instead, the dean focused on how the university could still buy the company. It was a misjudgment.

Examiners found no reason why the university should cover Knudsen's expenses. They were not related to university activities at all (PwC, 2021).

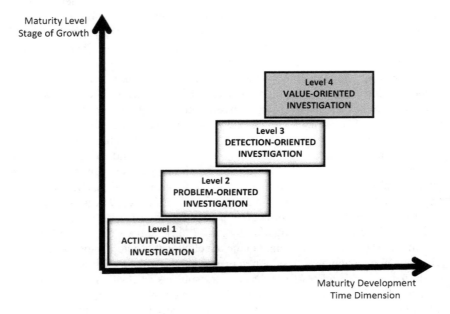

Figure 2.2 Maturity model for the PwC (2021) investigation at the university

Investigation Maturity Assessment

In Figure 2.2, the investigation is assigned the highest level of maturity as a value-oriented investigation. Examiners successfully reconstructed past events and sequences of events, assigned responsibility for deviant behavior to relevant persons, and drew substantiated conclusions regarding potential violations of rules and regulations regarding state universities. Examiners avoided drawing conclusions regarding violations of criminal laws by individuals, since this is the task of public police and prosecution rather than private detectives.

Generally, investigations at level 4 focus on value created by the examination, where the investigation is an investment by the client with an expectation of benefits exceeding costs. The ambition of the investigation is that the result will be valuable to the client. The value can lie in clean-up, change, simplification, renewal, and other measures for the future. The investigation also focuses on being justifiable. A number of explicit considerations are identified and practiced throughout the inquiry.

References

Agnew, R. (2014). Social concern and crime: Moving beyond the assumption of simple self-interest, *Criminology*, 52 (1), 1–32.

Arjoon, S. (2008). Slippery when wet: The real risk in business, *Journal of Markets & Morality*, 11 (1), 77–91.

Bao, D., Kim, Y., Mian, G.M. and Su, L. (2019). Do managers disclose or withhold bad news? Evidence from short interest, *The Accounting Review*, 94 (3), 1–26.

Bosse, D.A. and Phillips, R.A. (2016). Agency theory and bounded self-interest, *Academy of Management Review*, 41 (2), 276–297.

Davidson, R.H., Dey, A. and Smith, A.J. (2019). CEO materialism and corporate social responsibility, *The Accounting Review*, 94 (1), 101–126.

Eikefjord, E. (2021). Blir dette enda en alvorlig sak som fisler ut I noen "læringspunkter"? (Will this be another serious matter that gets bogged down into some "learning points"?), *Daily Norwegian Local Newspaper Bergens Tidende*, March 17, www.bt.no.

Ferraro, F., Pfeffer, J. and Sutton, R.I. (2005). Economics language and assumptions: How theories can become self-fulfilling, *Academy of Management Review*, 30 (1), 8–24.

Gamache, D.L. and McNamara, G. (2019). Responding to bad press: How CEO temporal focus influences the sensitivity to negative media coverage of acquisitions, *Academy of Management Journal*, 62 (3), 918–943.

Goncharov, I. and Peter, C.D. (2019). Does reporting transparency affect industry coordination? Evidence from the duration of international cartels, *The Accounting Review*, 94 (3), 149–175.

Gottfredson, M.R. and Hirschi, T. (1990). *A General Theory of Crime*, Stanford University Press, Stanford.

Grinde, E. (2021). Er den nye Tromsø-rektoren naiv eller egenrådig eller begge deler? (Is the new Tromsø president naive or headstrong or both?), *Daily Norwegian Business Newspaper Dagens Næringsliv*, March 23, www.dn.no.

Gupta, V.K., Mortal, S., Chakrabarty, B., Guo, X. and Turban, D.B. (2020). CFO gender and financial statement irregularities, *Academy of Management Journal*, 63 (3), 802–831.

Haga, A., Ramsvik, M. and Lindberg, P. (2020). UiB-avtale kunne gitt tidligere NHO-topp 20 millioner og fast stilling (University of Bergen deal could have given earlier business association top 20 million and permanent position), *Daily Norwegian Local Newspaper Bergens Tidende*, December 16, www.bt.no.

Hirschi, T. and Gottfredson, M. (1987). Causes of white-collar crime, *Criminology*, 25 (4), 949–974.

Holt, R. and Cornelissen, J. (2014). Sensemaking revisited, *Management Learning*, 45 (5), 525–539.

Hystad, J., Fanghol, T. and Strand, H. (2020). Tidligere NHO-topp ble ansatt ved UiB og fikk millionlønn, slev om avtale med UiB ble stoppet (Former business association executive was employed by the University of Bergen and received million salary, even though the agreement with the university was stopped), *Web-Based University Newspaper Khrono*, December 18, www.khrono.no.

Kakkar, H., Sivanathan, N. and Globel, M.S. (2020). Fall from grace: The role of dominance and prestige in punishment of high-status actors, *Academy of Management Journal*, 63 (2), 530–553.

Lindberg, P. (2021). Dette vil universitetsledelsen ha svar på (The university leadership will have answers to this), *Local Norwegian Newspaper Bergens Tidende*, www.bt.no, January 7.

Maslow, A.H. (1943). A theory of human motivation, *Psychological Review*, 50 (4), 370–396.

Mawritz, M.B., Greenbaum, R.L., Butts, M.M. and Graham, K.A. (2017). I just can't control myself: A self-regulation perspective on the abuse of deviant employees, *Academy of Management Journal*, 60 (4), 1482–1503.

Murphy, P.R. and Dacin, M.T. (2011). Psychological pathways to fraud: Understanding and preventing fraud in organizations, *Journal of Business Ethics*, 101, 601–618.

Obodaru, O. (2017). Forgone, but not forgotten: Toward a theory of forgone professional identities, *Academy of Management Journal*, 60 (2), 523–553.

Paternoster, R., Jaynes, C.M. and Wilson, T. (2018). Rational choice theory and interest in the "fortune of others", *Journal of Research in Crime and Delinquency*, 54 (6), 847–868.

Pettigrew, W.A. (2018). The changing place of fraud in seventeenth-century public debates about international trading corporations, *Business History*, 60 (3), 305–320.

Pillay, S. and Kluvers, R. (2014). An institutional theory perspective on corruption: The case of a developing democracy, *Financial Accountability & Management*, 30 (1), 95–119.

PwC. (2021). *Universitet i Bergen: Gjennomgang av "konseptet" (The University of Bergen: Review of "the concept")*, investigation report, PricewaterhouseCoopers, Oslo, March 11, p. 68.

Schnatterly, K., Gangloff, K.A. and Tuschke, A. (2018). CEO wrongdoing: A review of pressure, opportunity, and rationalization, *Journal of Management*, 44 (6), 2405–2432.

Schoultz, I. and Flyghed, J. (2020a). From "we didn't do it" to "we've learned our lesson": Development of a typology of neutralizations of corporate crime, *Critical Criminology*, 28, 739–757.

Schoultz, I. and Flyghed, J. (2020b). Denials and confessions: An analysis of the temporalization of neutralizations of corporate crime, *International Journal of Law, Crime and Justice*, doi: 10.1016/j.ijlcj.2020.100389.

Schoultz, I. and Flyghed, J. (2021). "We have been thrown under the bus": Corporate versus individual defense mechanisms against transnational corporate bribery charges, *Journal of White Collar and Corporate Crime*, 2 (1), 24–35.

Srivastava, S.B. and Goldberg, A. (2017). Language as a window into culture, *California Management Review*, 60 (1), 56–69.

Strand, H.K. (2021). Kritikk fra PwC: Brøt loven da Tom Knudsen ble ansatt (Critic from PwC: Violated the law when Tom Knudsen was hired), *Web-Based Newspaper Khrono*, March 13, www.khrono.no.

Svarstad, J. (2021). Tror ikke Dag Rune Olsen blir vraket som UiT-rektor (Do not think Dag Rune Olsen will be rejected as UiT rector), *Web-Based Magazine For Researchers Forskerforum*, March 11, www.forskerforum.no.

Toft, M. (2021). Gransking: Universitetet i Bergen braut lova (Investigation: The University of Bergen broke the law), *University Newspaper Universitetsavisa*, March 11, www.universitetsavisa.no.

Walburg, C. (2020). Chapter 21: White-collar and corporate crime: European perspectives, in: Rorie, M.L. (editor), *The Handbook of White-Collar Crime*, Wiley & Sons, Hoboken, pp. 337–346.

Weick, K.E. (1995). What theory is not, theorizing is, *Administrative Science Quarterly*, 40, 385–390.

Welsh, D.T. and Ordonez, L.D. (2014). The dark side of consecutive high performance goals: Linking goal setting, depletion, and unethical behavior, *Organizational Behavior and Human Decision Processes*, 123, 79–89.

Zysman-Quirós, D. (2020). Chapter 23: White-collar crime in South and Central America: Corporate-state crime, governance, and the high impact of the Odebrecht corruption case, in: Rorie, M.L. (editor), *The Handbook of White-Collar Crime*, Wiley & Sons, Hoboken, pp. 363–380.

3 University Coach Causing Donations

The coach at Yale, Rudolph Meredith, chose to cooperate with the FBI and further tipped off about Rick Singer – the man who orchestrated the scam that covered large parts of the scandal. Singer himself seized the opportunity to be early in the spotlight and collaborate by gathering evidence against the families and universities he had previously helped.

The college scandal was mainly about rich parents who bought college admissions for their children at prestigious universities in the United States, with payments hidden as donations. Test results and application forms were manipulated, and holes in the admissions systems were exploited to get the children admitted. As several of the cases occurred at the State University of California, an investigation was initiated into admission routines and processes, and whether those procedures could lead to exploitation for illegal acts. The schools investigators selected were four of the university campuses: UC Berkley, UC Los Angeles, UC San Diego, and UC Santa Barbara.

In 2019, it became public knowledge that the FBI was investigating the so-called college scandal under the code name "Operation Varsity Blues". The FBI was tipped off by a financier they questioned in another case, about a coach at Yale who asked for bribes (Katersky and Hutchinson, 2019). As reported by Pavlo (2021), Operation Varsity Blues "went public in March 2019 when it was revealed that government investigators (District of Massachusetts) had a cooperating witness who had uncovered a scheme whereby wealthy parents of college bound students paid bribes to get their offspring into the school of their choice" and "(t)he investigation involved some of the most prestigious schools in the country, a shifty middle-man, Rick Singer, wealthy parents eager to do whatever it took to get their kids into colleges and a lot of money". The cooperative witness was thus another case of a bottom-up approach to detection of white-collar convenience. The suspected fraud was concerned with the receipt of bribes by athlete managers to allow non-qualified students entry into the university.

The University of California was investigated by the auditor of the state of California. The California state auditor found that qualified students faced an inconsistent and unfair admissions system that had been improperly influence by relationships and monetary donations (State Auditor, 2020). Several rich and mighty people were involved in the corruption scandal.

DOI: 10.4324/9781003363934-4

On May 22, 2020, actress Lori Anne Loughlin in Hollywood pleaded guilty to one count of conspiracy to commit wire and mail fraud. Her husband Mossimo Giannulli, an American fashion designer, pleaded guilty to one count of conspiracy to commit wire and mail fraud and honest services wire and mail fraud. On August 21, 2020, Loughlin was sentenced to two months in prison while her husband was sentenced to five months. They had committed federal program corruption by bribing employees of the University of California to facilitate their children's admission. In exchange for the bribes, employees at the university designated the couple's children as athletic recruits with little or no regard for their athletic abilities. The bribed university officials did assess officially that their two daughters were qualified for the women's rowing team although none of them had trained in the sport of rowing nor had plans to do so. Loughlin and Giannulli paid $500,000 in bribes for the corrupt university service (Puente, 2020).

Offender Convenience Themes

Rudolph Meredith was Yale women's soccer coach. He pleaded guilty and helped build the case against other coaches at various universities (Schlabach, 2019). Figure 3.1 illustrates convenience themes in his case. As a coach, he was

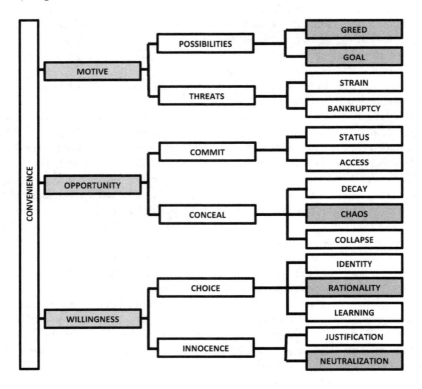

Figure 3.1 Convenience themes in the case of Rudolph Meredith at Yale University

responsible for securing funding to his team. The more funding and the more successful soccer games, the more money he would make for himself. It was thus a motive of possibilities both of the individual and the corporate types. Lack of oversight and guardianship at the university enabled concealment of the crime. It was a rational choice where guilt feelings could be neutralized by the claim of higher loyalty.

In the United States, it is great prestige to be a student at a highly ranked university. Admission assessment is based on the fact that there is a minimum requirement for grades and test results, but in addition, other factors are also assessed. In other words, it is not necessarily applicants with the best academic results that are accepted. Among the top universities, the heads of sports departments or coaches can make more money than university presidents. When economic factors and deficient processes are mixed, the result can be a major scandal.

The wealthy and influential actress Loughlin said in court that she acted out of love for her daughters. This is in line with the financial crime motive of social concern. Agnew (2014) introduced the motive of social concern and crime, where there is a desire to help others, and thus moving beyond the assumption of simple self-interest. However, as argued by Paternoster et al. (2018), helping others can be a self-interested, rational action that claims social concern. Social concern belongs to the convenience theme of motive-possibilities-individual as illustrated in Figure 3.2.

Agnew (2014) believes that social concern consists of four elements, namely that (1) individuals care about the welfare of others, (2) they want close ties with others, (3) they are likely to follow moral guidelines such as innocent people should not suffer harm, and (4) they tend to seek confirmation through other people's actions and norms. That a person puts others before oneself will initially lead to less crime. However, economic crime may be committed where the welfare of others and their success is the motive.

In the opportunity dimension of convenience theory, actress Loughlin had high social status as indicated in Figure 3.2. Status is an individual's social rank within a formal or informal hierarchy or the person's relative standing along a valued social dimension. Status is the extent to which an individual is respected and admired by others, and status is the outcome of a subjective assessment process (McClean et al., 2018). High-status individuals enjoy greater respect and deference from, as well as power and influence over, those who are positioned lower in the social hierarchy (Kakkar et al., 2020: 532):

> Status is a property that rests in the eyes of others and is conferred to individuals who are deemed to have a higher rank or social standing in a pecking order based on a mutually valued set of social attributes. Higher social status or rank grants its holder a host of tangible benefits in both professional and personal domains. For instance, high-status actors are sought by groups for advice, are paid higher, receive unsolicited help, and are credited disproportionately in joint tasks. In innumerable ways, our social ecosystem consistently rewards those with high status.

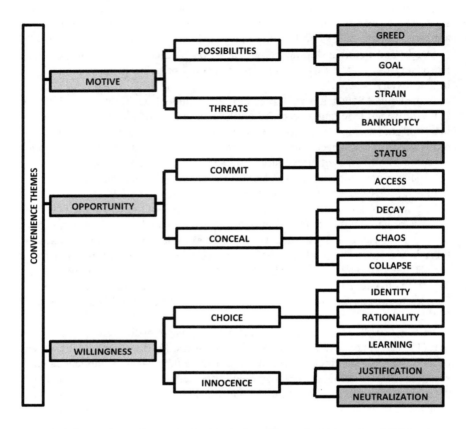

Figure 3.2 Convenience themes for Lori Anne Loughlin at the University of California

Especially individuals with high status based on prestige rather than dominance tend to be excused for whatever wrongdoing they commit. Individuals who attain and maintain high rank by behaving in ways that are assertive, controlling, and intimidating are characterized as dominant. Individuals who attain and maintain high rank through their set of skills, knowledge, expertise, and their willingness to share these with others are characterized as prestigious (Kakkar et al., 2020).

The willingness of actress Lori Anne Loughlin to bribe university officials might derive from an innocence perspective of both justification and neutralization. She found the act of wrongdoing morally justifiable (Schnatterly et al., 2018), probably based on upper-echelon information selection (Gamache and McNamara, 2019). She applied the neutralization technique number five presented earlier in this book – justify crime by higher loyalties: It was according to expectations. The offender denies the act was motivated by self-interest, claiming that it was instead done out of obedience to some moral obligation (Sykes and Matza, 1957). The offender appeals to higher loyalties. Those who feel they are in a dilemma employ this technique to indicate that the dilemma must be resolved at the cost of violating a law or policy. In the context of an organization, an employee may appeal to organizational values or hierarchies. For example, an executive could argue that he or she has to violate a policy in order to get things done and achieve strategic objectives for the enterprise. Similarly, the actress felt an obligation to help her daughters into a respectable educational institution.

Fraud Investigation Outcome

State Auditor (2020) found that campus staff took advantage of weaknesses in admissions processes to inappropriately admit 64 students as favors to donors, families, and friends. The majority of these applicants were white, and at least half had annual family incomes of $150,000 or more. Campus staff used the campuses' weak athletics admissions processes to admit 22 of these applicants, even though they possessed little athletic talent. In addition, the University of California at Berkley admitted 42 applicants through its regular admissions process based on their connections to donors and staff, while concurrently denying admissions to others who were better qualified.

Examiners found that the campuses' athletics admissions processes were open to abuse because they allowed for a large percentage of applicants to gain admission on the basis of many different considerations than the general applicant pool, and there was inadequate oversight of these admission processes (State Auditor, 2020: 18):

> For example, from academic year 20017–18 through 2019–20, UCLA's committee for reviewing student-athlete applicants admitted about 98 percent of the cases it reviewed for fall admission. The other campuses admitted a significant majority of student-athlete applicants as well. In contrast, the four campuses admitted from 14 percent to 32 percent of all applicants.

Examiners found that the reliance on donations to support university sport teams can put pressure on coaches to use their influence over admissions to falsify designated applicants as qualified athletes. For example, from 2014 through 2019, 75 percent of the UC Berkeley men's tennis team's budget came from donations (State Auditor, 2020: 19):

> Generally, coaches at the campuses are contractually responsible for fundraising for their teams and use that funding to pay for expenses such as team travel, athletic scholarships, and salaries for coaches and support staff. Their reliance on donations to support the continued existence of their teams can put pressure on coaches to use their significant influence over the admissions process to falsely designate applicants as qualified athletes to cultivate a positive relationship with prospective or existing donors.

Examiners found that the Berkeley campus in particular frequently gave preferential treatment to relatives and friends of faculty, staff, and donors. Multiple staff members in the campus admissions office were involved with admitting 42 additional applicants because of their special relationships. The leadership on the campus failed to uphold the principle of not giving preference to applicants based on non-scholarly criteria (State Auditor, 2020: 23):

> In one case, the development office referred a potential applicant to admissions staff so that they could meet with the applicant in person. An assistant director in the admissions office then informed the former admissions director that she would meet with the "VIP student . . . whose family is [a] potential donor." After the applicant applied to UC Berkeley, the former admissions director was the first person to read and rate the application, assigning it a rating of Strongly Recommend. The former admissions director then admitted the applicant, despite the fact that the second application reader gave the applicant the lowest possible rating of Do Not Recommend.

Examiners conclude that the university leadership failed to develop a campus culture to support a fair and merit-based admissions process. Responsibility for reinforcing the principles of fairness and merit-based decision-making lies primarily with campus leadership, who must communicate and visibly adhere to clear expectations that applicants will be evaluated and admitted based solely on their merit and achievement (State Auditor, 2020: 28):

> Instead of adhering to these principles, managers within the admissions office – including the former admissions director – participated in admitting these 42 applicants. Staff holding leadership positions in the admissions office communicated freely with UC Berkeley's development office and facilitated the admissions of donors' children. Staff from all over the campus advocated for their own relatives and friends. The former admissions director's open invitation to staff encouraged this inappropriate advocacy, modeling the idea that preferential treatment for relatives of staff was acceptable.

State Auditor (2020) recommended that the office of the president at the Berkeley campus should oversee the admissions process for at least three years. The office should require staff involved in making or informing admissions decisions to report all attempts to influence admissions decisions, regardless of source, to their supervisors or to the director of undergraduate admissions.

Review Information Sources

In the media, the name Rick William Singer was very frequently mentioned in coverage of the college scandal. He was the main architect of illegal admissions linked to donations. In the Netflix documentary *Operation Varsity Blues: The College Admissions* in 2021, the main focus is on Singer's active role in connection with the corruption scandal, in addition to shedding light on, among others, parents coaches, and universities. As a former high school coach, he had knowledge of the admission processes and the weaknesses around them. His company, "The

Key", ran counseling for wealthy families to help with admission tests and the like (Yan, 2019). The parents could pay large sums in donations directly to the university, called "the back door", while there was no guaranteed study allocation.

Singer took advantage of the market opportunity and offered a "side door", which involved bribes to employees at admissions offices and thus a guaranteed study allocation for a lower sum of money. He offered parents to manipulate pictures of their children playing various sports and paid Mark Riddell $10.000 to take admission tests, to some of the children's ignorance.

Reuters (2020) reported on the person who blew the whistle on the college fraud:

> A California businessman who tipped prosecutors off to a vast U.S. college admissions cheating, and fraud scheme was sentenced on Wednesday to one year in prison after admitting he participated in a stock fraud. U.S. District Judge Nathaniel Gorton in Boston said that under normal circumstances, Morrie Tobin, 57, would deserve eight years in prison for trying to deceive investors out of $15 million through "pump-and-dump" schemes. But he cited Tobin's "substantial assistance" in helping authorities probe not just that fraud but also an "infamous" scheme in which wealthy parents sought to fraudulently secure their children's admission to top universities. The scheme's mastermind, admissions consultant William "Rick" Singer, is cooperating after admitting he facilitated college entrance exam cheating and used bribery to help children gain admission to colleges as fake athletic recruits. To date, 55 people have been charged, including actress Lori Loughlin, who is to be sentenced next week after pleading guilty. Another defendant, test administrator Niki Williams, agreed to plead guilty Wednesday. Tobin's lawyer, Brian Kelly, said sending him to prison sends a "terrible message" to would-be cooperating witnesses. Tobin must also pay a $100,000 fine and forfeit $4 million. In court last year, assistant U.S. attorney Eric Rosen said the probe stemmed from an investigation into a California man's stock fraud. That man was Tobin, Kelly confirmed in court Wednesday.

Mark Edward Riddell is a Harvard graduate and former director of college entrance exam preparations at the IMG Academy in Bradenton, Florida. He was paid $10,000 for each of the standardized ACTs or SATs he edited for the children whose parents were eager for them to get into a prestigious undergraduate school. He pleaded guilty in court (Madani, 2019):

> A 36-year-old Harvard alumnus pleaded guilty Friday to taking college entrance exams for the children of wealthy parents as part of an alleged $25 million college admissions scam that has led to dozens of criminal charges. Mark Riddell pleaded guilty to charges of conspiracy to commit mail fraud and honest services mail fraud, as well as conspiracy to commit money laundering. He appeared in federal court in Boston and did not make any statements before his hearing. He could face up to 41 months in prison,

but prosecutors have said they will likely recommend 33 months instead, according to NBC Boston.

Lori Loughlin was released from prison in December 2020 (Associated Press, 2020):

> "Full House" actor Lori Loughlin was released from prison Monday after spending two months behind bars for paying half a million dollars in bribes to get her two daughters into college. Loughlin was released from the federal lockup in Dublin, California, where she had been serving her sentence for her role in the college admissions bribery scheme, the federal Bureau of Prisons said. Her husband, fashion designer Mossimo Giannulli, is serving his five-month sentence at a prison in Lompoc near Santa Barbara.

Lachenai (2021) reported on the former Yale coach Meredith:

> Operation Varsity Blues' Rudy Meredith is awaiting sentencing after plead-ing guilty. Meredith's part in the scandal involved leveraging his position as the head coach for the Yale women's soccer team, where he was the "win-ningest coach in Yale history", according to his faculty profile on the school's athletics website. He resigned his position in 2018, saying it was "time to explore new possibilities and begin a different chapter in my life". It would later emerge that, by that time, Meredith had already been cooperating with federal authorities in the Operation Varsity Blues investigation for roughly six months. A Yale spokesperson told the *New York Times* that the university only learned about the investigation after Meredith announced he was leav-ing; the day after he issued a press release about his departure, Yale received grand jury subpoena from the U.S. attorney in Massachusetts, seeking infor-mation about Meredith.

The fraud was called the college admissions bribery scandal. It was a criminal conspiracy to influence undergraduate admissions decisions at several top Ameri-can universities. The investigation into the conspiracy was code-named Operation Varsity Blues.

Fraud Investigation Evaluation

As a state-owned rather than private institution, the scandal required a public investigation. The authorities expressed their concern that the public universities are run using taxpayers' money and that, according to the scandal, the University of California has not fulfilled its duty as a professional and public institution. Among other things, the fraudulent admissions have caused an increase in the existing class divide. There was thus a strong and obvious motivation to start the state investigation. State auditors had to find out what happened, uncover short-comings, and make suggestions on how to improve the situation and eliminate the risk of illegalities. In response to the federal investigation, the university launched in March 2019 an internal audit of its system-wide and campus-specific admission processes, which they completed in February 2020. The audit, which the campuses mainly carried out themselves, showed weaknesses in several areas of the university's admissions processes, including processes related to athletic recruits and admissions.

The self-reporting from the university to the investigator is a problematic issue in terms of source credibility and information quality. However, the investigators have taken into account that the sources and the information they have used can be verified. Due to the variations in the source types, and because they are focused on the sources been proven to be usable, this means that even if one source has a few shortcomings, the others can still support the conclusion. Thus, the sources were suitable for the investigation. The credibility was strengthened through the wide range of sources, and information was confirmed by each other.

The auditors at State Auditor (2020) applied their managerial accounting knowledge to analyze and interpret accounting and financial transactions to reveal the magnitude of misconduct and fraud. Investigators applied legal knowledge to protect the privacy of involved persons and to draw the line between what is legal and what is illegal. Furthermore, digital competence was applied to search and interpret electronically available information regarding the scandal. In addition, the investigation employed other relevant knowledge workers as well, thereby indicating that the knowledge coverage was sufficiently wide to cover all relevant issues in the audit.

The result of the investigation can be evaluated in terms of the extent of clear answers to the issues in the mandate for the investigation. The mandate was to assess the risk of future wrongdoing and fraud in the admission processes on the various university campuses. While general in their assessments and recommendations, State Auditor (2020: 60) formulated the following recommendations:

> To better safeguard the integrity of the university's admissions processes, the Office of the President should, by July 21, begin conducting regular audits of the admissions processes at each of its undergraduate campuses, ensuring that it reviews each campus at least once every three years. These audits should be conducted by systemwide audit staff and include, but not be limited to, verification of special talents, communication between admissions staff and external parties regarding applicants, and other avenues for inappropriate influence on admissions discussed in this report. The audits should also endeavor to identify inappropriate admissions activity and deficiencies in the admissions process. The Office of the President should make the results of the audit public.

There is obvious value in the investigation outcome in terms of reviews of how fraudulent admissions could take place at several campuses belonging to the University of California. While federal investigators and prosecutors focused on the corruption side of the scandal to get both bribing individuals and bribed individuals convicted and incarcerated, State Auditor (2021) focused on the routines and lack of routines that enabled non-qualified students to be admitted to the prestigious university. Furthermore, there is some value to the recommendations, although they are vaguely formulated and mainly reactive to the form of fraud that occurred rather than proactive to potential other kinds of admission fraud that might happen in the future.

Investigation Maturity Assessment

In March 2019, federal prosecutors publicly announced their investigation into a college admission scheme that led to criminal charges against more than 50 people – including parents, college and university coaches, and a founder of a for-profit college counseling and preparation business – related to falsifying information to facilitate the admission of more than 30 students to more than ten different universities. The auditor of the state of California then conducted an audit of the University of California's admissions process. The review was to assess the risk for fraud and inappropriate admissions activities at four campuses, and examiners concluded that the university had allowed for improper influence in admissions decisions, and the university had not treated applicants fairly or consistently. The review was not to investigate Loughlin, Giannulli, or other offenders on the bribing side of the university admissions scandal.

The review by State Auditor (2020) is assigned the highest maturity level in Figure 3.3 since the investigation seems to be an investment. At maturity level 4,

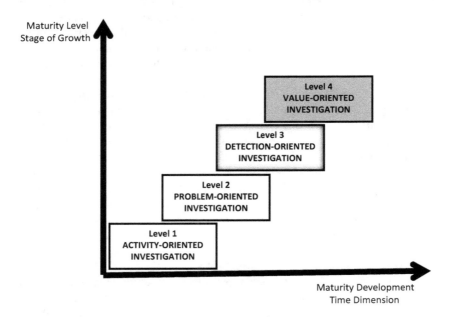

Figure 3.3 Maturity assessments for the State Auditor (2020) report

the investigation makes a valuable contribution to the client organization, where investigation benefits exceed investigation costs. The investigation is optimal, innovative, profitable, strategic, extraordinary, outstanding, provident, value-oriented, advanced, learning-focused, valuable, irreversible, truth-based, socially responsible, exceptional, excellent, perfect, and exemplary, and it is a profitable investment. The investigation is a masterpiece and enrichment for the client and society. The investigation is complete and influential. The investigation is strategically a success.

Of course, the complexity of this investigation was not very challenging. Witness statements from interviews and reviews of documents were readily available to examiners. Furthermore, several corrupt parents had already been prosecuted and convicted in court. The fraud scheme was thus well known when examiners started their review.

An estimate of the cost of the investigation that someone has presented is $444,600. This is a modest amount compared to many other corporate investigations. With limited resources, the auditors were thus nevertheless able to reconstruct past events and sequences of events as well as present some general recommendations for the future.

References

Agnew, R. (2014). Social concern and crime: Moving beyond the assumption of simple self-interest, *Criminology*, 52 (1), 1–32.

Associated Press. (2020). Lori Loughlin released after prison term for role in college scandal, *Los Angeles Times*, December 28, www.latimes.com.

Gamache, D.L. and McNamara, G. (2019). Responding to bad press: How CEO temporal focus influences the sensitivity to negative media coverage of acquisitions, *Academy of Management Journal*, 62 (3), 918–943.

Kakkar, H., Sivanathan, N. and Globel, M.S. (2020). Fall from grace: The role of dominance and prestige in punishment of high-status actors, *Academy of Management Journal*, 63 (2), 530–553.

Katersky, A. and Hutchinson, B. (2019). Federal agents uncovered the college admissions scandal by accident while working on unrelated case, *ABC News*, March 14, www.abcnews.go.com.

Lachenai, J. (2021). Operation Varsity Blues' Rudy Meredith is awaiting sentencing after pleading guilty, *Bustle*, March 16, www.bustle.com.

Madani, D. (2019). Mark Riddell, college admissions scandal test-taker, pleads guilty, *NBC News*, April 12, www.nbcnews.com.

McClean, E.J., Martin, S.R., Emich, K.J. and Woodruff, T. (2018). The social consequences of voice: An examination of voice type and gender on status and subsequent leader emergence, *Academy of Management Journal*, 61 (5), 1869–1891.

Paternoster, R., Jaynes, C.M. and Wilson, T. (2018). Rational choice theory and interest in the "fortune of others", *Journal of Research in Crime and Delinquency*, 54 (6), 847–868.

Pavlo, W. (2021). Operation "Varsity Blues" goes ut with perfect prosecution record and a reflection of how the system works, *Forbes*, December 16, www.forbes.com.

Puente, M. (2020). Lori Loughlin released from prison after serving 2-month sentence in college bribery scheme, *USA Today*, December 28, www.eu.usatoday.com.

Reuters. (2020). L.A. financier who tipped off feds to Rick Singer's college admissions scam when he was caught defrauding investors of more than $15 million gets one year in jail, *Daily Mail*, August 12. www.dailymail.co.uk.

Schlabach, M. (2019). Feds allege coaches bribed for school admission, *ESPN*, March 12, www.espn.com.

Schnatterly, K., Gangloff, K.A. and Tuschke, A. (2018). CEO wrongdoing: A review of pressure, opportunity, and rationalization, *Journal of Management*, 44 (6), 2405–2432.

State Auditor. (2020). *University of California, California State Auditor, 621 Capitol Mall,* report of investigation, Sacramento, p. 82.

Sykes, G. and Matza, D. (1957). Techniques of neutralization: A theory of delinquency, *American Sociological Review*, 22 (6), 664–670.

Yan, H. (2019). The CEO behind the college admissions cheating scam wanted to help the wealthy. But that's not all, *CNN*, March 12, www.edition.cnn.com.

4 Cruise Reluctance at Virus Outbreak

The events that led to the investigation of Hurtigruten Cruises by Wiersholm were the handling of Covid-19 outbreaks on two voyages from Tromsø to Svalbard with *MS Roald Amundsen* in July 2020. The outbreak led to 62 people testing positive for Corona, and 544 people who were on board the relevant voyages were exposed to a possible risk of infection. The suspected fraud was concerned with the violation of corona restrictions by cruise executives to ensure the flow of revenues into the company.

When the Corona virus caused lockdown of most activities, Norway's Hurtigruten cruises used its channels into political decision-makers to convince politicians to open up again for cruise activities. Hurtigruten management was successful, and they could quickly reopen their shipping activities. However, quarantine rules were not followed, suspected cases of the Corona virus were not followed up, and crew members felt their lives were in danger but were afraid of speaking out (Berglund, 2020a; Valderhaug et al., 2020). When the Coronavirus spread on Hurtigruten voyages, senior executives Daniel Skjeldam and Asta Lassesen attempted allegedly to suppress information and prevent disclosure of the scandal (Valderhaug, 2020a, 2020b).

When the Hurtigruten scandal became public, the board at the company hired Norwegian law firm Wiersholm (2020) to investigate the matter. Fraud examiners were to examine the shipping company's handling of passengers infected by the Covid-19 virus during cruise voyages. In 2022, the public prosecutor found the company guilty of negligence and made the company subject to a fine of one million Norwegian kroner (about 100,000 US dollars). In addition, the captain on the cruise ship received a fine of 30,000 Norwegian kroner and the medical doctor onboard the ship was fined 40,000 kroner (Ismail and Rydje, 2022).

Hurtigruten has long traditions dating back to 1893 to transport goods and passengers along the coast of Norway. Since the 1990s, the main activity has been tourist traffic. Hurtigruten ("Express Route") is still sailing from Bergen to Kirkenes on its route transporting passengers who travel locally, regionally, and between the ports of call, and also cargo between ports north of Tromsø. Today, Hurtigruten business is mostly exploration travel offering expedition cruises in Antarctica, Greenland, Iceland, Spitsbergen, Alaska, and more. From the very beginning, the shipping company has been private on a contract with the state and

DOI: 10.4324/9781003363934-5

with state subsidies. The company was on the verge of bankruptcy in 2007 but was saved by government grants and deferred repayments of loans (Sæbbe et al., 2014).

When the Corona crisis hit Norway and the rest of the world in the spring of 2020, Hurtigruten management hired public relations consultants at the firm First House, who were used to influence access to financial support from the Norwegian government. First House consultants were mostly former top politicians who used their network to influence the government in favor of their clients. The consultants were successful in obtaining government permission for Hurtigruten Cruises to sail again, while almost all other business activities in the country suffered from the lockdown (Lægland et al., 2020).

Deviance Convenience Themes

In the following application of convenience theory, it is assumed that the misconduct and wrongdoing were financially motivated. Management wanted the ships back into seas and oceans with passengers to secure revenues. There was a threat of a long-lasting lockdown that might have caused bankruptcy for Hurtigruten as indicated in Figure 4.1. Even though Hurtigruten, like many other companies in Norway, was financially supported by the government during the initial months of the Corona pandemic, it was obvious to the board and management that long-term survival would depend on revenues from transport of tourists, inhabitants, goods, and services. As a national symbol, it was important to rescue Hurtigruten. Many researchers have emphasized avoidance of corporate collapse and bankruptcy as an important motive for misconduct and wrongdoing (Brightman, 2009; Chattopadhyay et al., 2001; Downing et al., 2019; Geest et al., 2017; König et al., 2020).

The organizational opportunity to sail the ships without relevant protection against the virus for passengers and staff was a matter of status of decision makers versus staff members who were recruited from low-salary nations. There was power inequality between the elite and others in the company (Dearden, 2016, 2017, 2019; Friedrichs, 2010, 2020; Friedrichs et al., 2018; McClean et al., 2018; Patel and Cooper, 2014). The costs exceeded the benefits for whistleblowers (Keil et al., 2010; Mesmer-Magnus and Viswesvaran, 2005), leading to silence among staff members about what they had noticed. This was in sharp contrast to the Covid-19 outbreak prevention and response regulation aboard Hurtigruten ships (Wiersholm, 2020: 21):

> In the event of suspicion of the discovery of COVID-19 on board, the ship's Doctor must follow reporting directives as stated by the port authority where the vessel is destined and inform the Captain who shall inform the Company through the Operation Manager without delay.
>
> For ships operating in Norway, any case of suspicion of discovery of COVID-19, must immediately be reported by the Captain to the Norwegian Coastal Administration via Vardø Sjøtrafikksentral on telephone +47 78 98 98 98 as well as registered electronically in the portal SafeSeaNet Norway.

There was an ethical climate conflict (Murphy and Dacin, 2011; Murphy and Free, 2015), where the business was in a dilemma with safety. Another part of the opportunity structure might be found in rule complexity preventing compliance (Huisman, 2020; Lehman et al., 2020), where rules and guidelines concerning the pandemic were almost constantly changed by local and national officials.

Hurtigruten was in a crisis situation characterized by threats. The motive for management was to protect economic interests, mainly by:

- Fast access to personnel and avoidance of increased expenses in relation to quarantine periods. Quarantine rules were not complied with. It appeared in an email that the quarantine on land before boarding "will have an additional cost that budget owners must be informed about" (Wiersholm, 2020: 28).
- Avoidance of harm to corporate reputation and loss of income by stopping sailings. Documentation referred to fear of negative media coverage. An example of this is an email in which it "appeared that they managed to avoid the infection control doctor mentioning Hurtigruten in his press release" (Wiersholm, 2020: 31).

In the organizational dimension of convenience theory, CEO Daniel Skjeldam had a very high status in the company. Trygve Hegnar, who held the board chair position at Hurtigruten, was also the largest shareholder in the company for a while, personally headhunted Skjeldam to the position of CEO of the company in the autumn of 2012. That made Skjeldam the youngest leader of a listed Norwegian company as he was born in 1975 and thus 37 years at the time when he took on the position. When the virus scandal emerged, Hegnar quickly expressed complete confidence in Skjeldam, arguing that Skjeldam would be the best man to take the company out of its crisis (Berglund, 2020a):

> Skjeldam thus seems to have survived what's been described as one of the biggest scandals in Norwegian business history. A crushing internal report released Thursday on how Hurtigruten failed to ward off or control a Covid-19 outbreak on board its new ship MS Roald Amundsen points out plenty of mistakes, but none of them seems to have any consequences for the highly paid Skjeldam or others responsible.

High status as indicated in Figure 4.1 can enable the blame game by misleading attribution to others (Eberly et al., 2011) and scapegoating (Gangloff et al., 2016). Skjeldam's status made him almost too big to fail (Pontell et al., 2014), and to the extent someone was to blame for the scandal, and following the crisis, it was not him.

Foreign employees knew less about their rights when they were infected and obeyed whatever management told them. For example, even when infected, management told them to go back to work and not stay in quarantine.

The personal willingness dimension of convenience theory focuses on the willingness for deviant behavior among white-collar offenders. Personal willingness

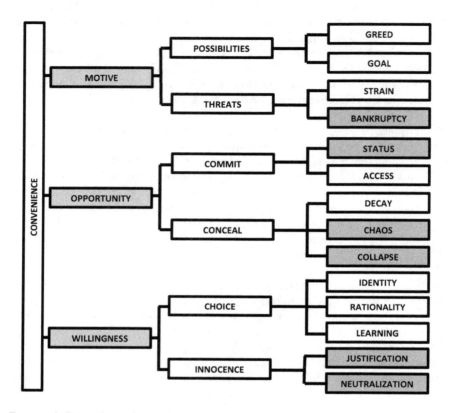

Figure 4.1 Convenience themes in the case of Skjeldam

for deviant behavior implies a positive attitude toward violating social norms, including formally enacted laws, rules, and regulations (Aguilera et al., 2018). "Deviance" is a term to describe behavior that contravenes accepted norms, values, and ethical standards (Smith and Raymen, 2018). Deviance is "the failure to obey group rules" (Becker, 1963: 8). Deviance is "a form of behavior that violates organizational norms and that consequently negatively impacts the well-being of the organization and its members" (Michalak and Ashkanasy, 2013: 20). Deviance is detrimental to organizational performance in several ways, including damaged reputation, exposure to lawsuits, and financial loss (Dilchert et al., 2007).

The willingness derives either from an active choice to commit and conceal offenses or from the perception of personal innocence when committing and concealing crime. There is little evidence of choice in this case. Rather, innocence is more visible in the case. Justification and neutralization seem visible as convenience themes. The justification by management was to sail ships to create revenues (Becker, 1963; Chen and Moosmayer, 2020; Schnatterly et al., 2018) and to compensate for negative events (Engdahl, 2015; Patel and Cooper, 2014). The justification by staff was to obey orders from peer pressure (Aguilera and Vadera, 2008; Gao and Zhang, 2019) and be loyal to higher authorities (Schoultz and Flyghed, 2016, 2020a, 2020b, 2021; Sykes and Matza, 1957).

Management at Hurtigruten found that the laws, rules, and regulations changed all the time. There was thus uncertainty as to what they were supposed to do and how they had to handle the matter. Rule complexity was thus a relevant reason for denial of wrongdoing. The investigation report mentions several times that government guidelines for handling Covid-19 changed all the time. Virus protection was thus perceived as an unclear matter, and management was unable to interpret constantly changing laws, regulations, and rules.

Yet another justification theme was the lack of government funding to keep the company alive. It was the government that had imposed sanctions on the company because of the pandemic. The company did not receive compensation for lost revenues, only for fixed and unavoidable costs.

Management demonstrated lack of self-control as they several times took employees out of quarantine to have them work. The employees were foreigners who knew little about their rights.

Investigation Report Outcome

The mandate for the investigation was approved by the board at Hurtigruten on August 6, 2020 (Wiersholm, 2020: 5):

Background

During the period 17–24 July 2020, MV "Roald Amundsen" undertook a cruise from the town of Tromsø, Norway, to Spitsbergen. A person, who later tested positive for Covid-19, was a passenger on this voyage. On 25 July, the ship once again left Tromsø to undertake another cruise to Spitsbergen. Status regarding the number of infected individuals on 4 August 2020 was 44. Most of these individuals have been on board the vessel during these two voyages. Any further voyages will be suspended until further notice. In a statement made on 3 August 2020, Hurtigruten's Group CEO, Daniel Skjeldam, said "we have failed, we have made a mistake". He communicated that an external investigation would be launched into Hurtigruten's handling of this matter. On 4 August 2020, law firm Wiersholm, represented by Jan Fougner, Attorney-at-Law, was retained and tasked with leading the investigation.

Client

Hurtigruten Group AS (the "Company") acts as client. The assignment is given by the Company's board of directors. Progress will be reported throughout and on completion of the matter to the Company's board of directors. If necessary, the retained investigators may communicate with other companies in the group and the Company's owners.

Assignment

Law firm Wiersholm represented by Jan Fougner, Attorney-at-Law, will examine the Subsidiary's handling of the incidence of the Covid-19 virus in connection with the voyages described above. The investigation will include a description of the applicable rules of law, including any internal guidelines applying to the voyages and identify to what extent such guidelines were followed before, during, and after the voyages. The investigation should provide a basis for understanding what happened and learning from the incident. The investigation will contain recommendations for any further action.

The client will ensure that Wiersholm and Wiersholm's aids are granted unlimited access to any records considered by them to be relevant to the execution of the assignment.

Aids

Classification company DNV GL is retained to assist Wiersholm in its work. Upon agreement with the Company, Wiersholm may retain other sub-suppliers on behalf of the Company, including technical expertise.

Method

The guidelines of the Norwegian Bar Association for private investigations will be followed to the extent appropriate.

Deadline

The investigation is to be carried out as swiftly as practically possible, in view of the need for a responsible and professional execution of the assignment.

Report

A written report will be prepared for subsequent submission to the Client. The report is to be submitted in a form suited for publication.

The report by Wiersholm (2020) provides information pointing to mistakes that were made in the preparation for the voyages and the handling of the outbreak. The investigation report by Wiersholm is 49 pages long. The report spends its ten first pages explaining guidelines for conducting internal investigations. Then it spends ten more pages on rules and regulations in shipping. The foreword is written by chairperson Hegnar, who removes the anonymity for top executives by listing "Leader 2" as CEO Skjeldam, "Leader 1" as operating executive Bent Martini, "Leader 3" as commercial executive Asta Lassesen, and "Leader 7" as chief financial officer Torleif Ernstsen. Other employees mentioned in the report remained anonymous.

The report by Wiersholm (2020) shows that Hurtigruten management was reluctant to implement effective Coronavirus controls. The company had set up a formal control system, but it was never implemented or followed up. Company officials failed to manage a virus control regime, and investigators concluded that management took far too many risks when they resumed cruises in July 2020. "Risk" is generally a term that relates to negative or undesirable outcomes (Wang, 2020: 1283):

> In everyday usage, a risk refers almost exclusively to a threat, hazard, danger or harm which should be avoided if at all possible.

The company was also criticized for poor communications both on board the vessel *Roald Amundsen* and with health authorities and for utterly failing to protect both passengers and crew despite repeated claims that they would do so. "The outbreak on the MS Roald Amundsen can't be blamed on any single incident or any one person's actions", concluded Jan Fougner, an attorney from Oslo law firm Wiersholm. The firm, along with classification and consulting firm DNV GL, led Hurtigruten's own investigation of how 71 passengers and crew members ended up testing positive for Covid-19 after the Amundsen's two cruises to Spitsbergen in July (Berglund, 2020a).

Chief investigator Fougner stressed at the press conference that "many have made mistakes", and it would not help to simply blame or fire various individuals (Berglund, 2020a):

> That alone seems to have saved Skjeldam from being dismissed or opting to step down himself, as many expected he would. Skjeldam claimed he and his harshly criticized management team are taking the report seriously, accepting responsibility and promising to do a better job in the future.

The report of investigation is structured around four key phases: preparation, embarkation, measures along the way, and handling of infection outbreaks. In terms of preparation, examiners found that Hurtigruten carried out preparations under demanding circumstances. The preparations meant that a number of new activities were to be carried out in a short time and with fewer employees. Hurtigruten Cruise had a risk assessment process that was not sufficient. No overall risk assessment was conducted for risks associated with Covid-19. This shortcoming has influenced the choice and implementation of preventive measures. No training related to the handling of Covid-19 incidents took place before the voyage. The organization of Hurtigruten in a hierarchical and corporate structure made executives reluctant to involve themselves in operational matters. Rather, executive management had simply no review of risks related to the pandemic when sailing ships with many passengers and crew. Examiners emphasize the lack of preparation at all levels of the organization including top management and the board.

At the embarkation phase, Hurtigruten ignored health authority requirements to test foreign crew members and potentially put them in quarantine before working with other crew members and providing service to passengers. There were no single rooms for crew members in case quarantine would become necessary. New crew members arriving from abroad went straight into contact with other crew members and passengers.

In terms of measures along the way, people with illness indications were treated as regular patients by the two doctors onboard. This implied some observation, but relatively fast discharge with improved health. There was suspicion of corona infection, but no testing was conducted by the two ship doctors. They communicated about the issue but did nothing to follow up on rumors regarding Covid-19 onboard the vessel. Ship management expected that the two doctors would follow up on any indications of infection. This expectation remained even after ship management first received information about crew members put in isolation with Covid-19 symptoms and need for testing, and then later learned that the information was withdrawn.

When it was discovered during the second voyage that a passenger from the first voyage had been identified with Covid-19, the passengers on the second voyage were not notified. A press release was withheld by agreement with a local doctor pending test results from the infected person's travel companions. The expectation of health authorities in Norway to notify passengers was not met, and warning passengers was no longer considered after the travel companions of the infected individual tested negative. The communication was characterized by a desire to disprove that the infection might be associated with Roald Amundsen, rather than considering the possibility of infection on board the ship. This is also evidenced by the lack of communication of infection suspicion from the local municipal doctor to public authorities in Norway registering all positive results, which prevented notification to passengers after the positive test result from the passenger sailing on the first voyage. There was no overall understanding of the pandemic. Rather, the relevant perspective was to keep business as usual before the pandemic occurred. When the ship arrived in the city of Tromsø with a confirmed infected person, the person was transported in a taxi, with a high risk of infecting the taxi driver.

The fourth phase of handling infection outbreaks was very slow. It took time before management reacted to positive test results. All passengers were informed 12 hours later than management. In the meantime, passengers moved freely around, and they were on planes and in other places with many people despite the high risk of infection. Management gathered all crew members for meetings at the same physical location without any restrictions concerning freedom of movement onboard the ship. Crisis management was not implemented according to the crisis management plan, and crisis actions differed and seemed random.

All crises are uncertain events that generate initial negative reactions. An effective response strategy should match external observers' situational attributions of the crisis to prevent cognitive dissonance among observers (Bundy and Pfarrer, 2015: 352):

> A higher situational attributions of responsibility should be matched with a
> response strategy that accepts more responsibility, and a crisis with lower

situational attributions of responsibility should be matched with a response strategy that accepts less responsibility. . . . An organization that is under-conforming by being defensive in response to a crisis with higher situational attributions risks being perceived as unethical and manipulative.

Hurtigruten management was perceived as unethical and manipulative at the disclosure of the scandal and the following crisis. They seemed not to accept responsibility. However, fraud examiners from Wiersholm (2020) did not blame them.

Review Information Sources

After the fraud investigation report was presented in public, Prime Minister Erna Solberg joined many others who were frustrated and angry with the Norwegian cruise and shipping line Hurtigruten, which is supposed to make daily calls at small ports all along the Norwegian coast. Hurtigruten's management had lobbied state officials hard to be allowed to resume cruising, and won their approval, only to violate quarantine rules for its low-paid crew. They were flown into Norway from the Philippines and put immediately to work on the cruise ship named Roald Amundsen, without going through mandatory ten-day quarantine. Some crew members fell ill during the first of two cruises, and a total of 71 passengers and crew ended up testing positive for the Coronavirus (Berglund, 2020b).

Chief examiner Jan Fougner criticized Hurtigruten for being "too eager" to start cruising again when Norwegian authorities reopened for it during the summer. Hurtigruten assumed way too much risk during a pandemic, Fougner said at the press conference, as he pointed to poor communication and, most of all, a culture of fear within the company (Berglund, 2020a).

Hurtigruten was established in 1893 by government contract to improve travel of persons and transport of goods along the coastline of Norway with its many isolated villages and towns. The Hurtigruten ships connect rural areas on a daily basis, which has enabled people to operate and live along the poorly chartered waters, where the voyage is especially difficult during the long and dark winters in the land of the midnight sun during summers. Until the 1940s most ports in the north could not be reached by road, so the sea was the only means of access.

Today, Hurtigruten is just as much a cruise line as a part of the infrastructure for communication in Norway. Ships are sailing along the Norwegian coastline, often deep into fjords with its breathtaking landscapes. In the summer, the midnight sun is a spectacular view to many passengers. The classic voyages offer one or two weeks options. The ultimate journey is from Bergen to Kirkenes and back again. The ports visited by night on the northbound cruise are revealed when visited in daylight on the southbound journey.

During the period July 17–24, 2020, Hurtigruten's vessel *Roald Amundsen* undertook a cruise from the town of Tromsø, Norway, to Spitsbergen. A person who later tested positive for Covid-19 was a passenger on this voyage. On July 25, the ship once again left Tromsø to undertake another cruise to Spitsbergen. Status regarding the number of infected individuals on August 4, 2020, was 44 passengers and crew members. A total of 544 individuals had been on board the vessel during these two voyages. Any further voyages were suspended until further notice (Wiersholm, 2020: 5):

> In a statement made on 3 August 2020, Hurtigruten's Group CEO, Daniel Skjeldam, said "we have failed, we have made a mistake". He communicated that an external investigation would be launched into Hurtigruten's handling of this matter.

The board claimed that it still had confidence in CEO Skjeldam and that both he and the rest of the top management at Hurtigruten needed to learn from all their potentially fatal mistakes (Berglund, 2020a):

> Trygve Hegnar, who leads Hurtigruten's board, has made a career out of criticizing and ridiculing other business executive's mistakes in the various media publications he owns. He nonetheless defended Hurtigruten's CEO here at Thursday's press conference, insisting Skjeldam was still the best person to restore public confidence in the historic shipping line that's run into serious problems with its international cruising.

Hurtigruten is still most known for its operation along Norway's western and northern coast between Bergen and Kirkenes with 34 ports. But as one of the world leaders in exploration travel on sea, the shipping company offers expedition cruises in Antarctica, Greenland, Iceland, Spitsbergen, Alaska, and other destinations. The company operates 11 ships and has more than 2,000 employees.

Hurtigruten was hit by a scandal and a following crisis. A scandal is a publicized instance of transgression that runs counter to social norms, typically resulting in condemnation and discredit and other consequences such as bad press, disengagement of key constituencies, the severance of network ties, and decrease in key performance indicators (Piazza and Jourdan, 2018). A scandal can be an act of elite deviance that might include financial, physical, and morally harmful behavior committed by privileged members of the organization and potentially in cooperation with the state (Rothe, 2020; Rothe and Medley, 2020). A crisis is an unexpected, publicly known, and harmful event that is associated with uncertainty. A crisis is a fundamental threat to a corporation. Ambiguity of cause, effect, and means of resolution often characterize a crisis. Most corporate crises originate from failures within the organization. Scholars denote that organizational crises require timely responses (König et al., 2020).

Prime Minister Solberg and Health Minister Bent Høie felt betrayed by the national symbol Hurtigruten's management who had pressured them into allowing the cruises. "The health minister and I have said that Hurtigruten deserves all the criticism it's getting", Solberg told NRK (Berglund, 2020b):

> Trade minister Iselin Nybø was also harsh in her assessment of Hurtigruten after its board's and leaders' apologetic press conference on Thursday: "Right now they don't have a very high star, but it's a strong brand, and they have

ambitions to rise up again", Nybø said. "Time will tell whether they manage to do so".

Norway's famed but now shamed shipping company announced the suspension of its leader of maritime operations early August while Wiersholm (2020) examiners were conducting their investigation. The virus scandal onboard *Roald Amundsen* was shaking public confidence in a company long viewed as part of the national heritage. When the fraud examination report was presented in September, it seemed that the top executive, CEO Skjeldam, survived disgrace as chairperson Hegnar expressed strong confidence in Skjeldam at a press conference (Berglund, 2020a).

As indicated in the references earlier, the media is an important information source in this case.

Corona Investigation Evaluation

Valderhaug (2021: 24) reported that Hurtigruten Cruises had paid law firm Wiersholm NOK 14 million for their 51-page report:

> The money runs fast when a company has to order an external investigation report. Hurtigruten experienced major outbreaks of corona during two voyages with MS Roald Amundsen at the end of July last year. A total of 42 crew members and 29 passengers were infected. Pretty soon it blew up to full storm around the way the shipping company handled the situation. The board of the shipping company therefore brought in external investigators at the beginning of August last year. The job went to the law firm Wiersholm and Veritas. Now the bill for the 51-page report is clear: It came to 14 million kroner. Attorney Jan Fougner presented the report on September 17 last year. It presents a lot of criticism of routines and processes. But the investigators avoided placing responsibility on someone in the management. Nevertheless, the operations executive resigned. This happened after a strong disagreement between him and CEO Daniel Skjeldam about the latter's involvement. The outbreak of infection also entailed other, direct costs.

- The company's financial costs for the outbreak at *MS Roald Amundsen* are around NOK 30 million. This includes overtime, follow-up of guests, travel coverage, other follow-up expenses, and the investigation. Thus writes press officer Øystein Knoph at Hurtigruten in an email.

What the outbreaks may have cost in the form of lost reputation and possible weaker future sales is probably impossible to estimate. However, Hurtigruten itself believes that the eruptions will have small financial consequences.

- The incident has had little, if any, effect on the company's finances in the long term, for example when it comes to cancelations or sales of future trips, says Knoph.

The police in Tromsø started early an investigation into the case. Hurtigruten is now waiting to see if a fine will be imposed through what is called a corporate penalty. The police had actually submitted a recommendation on this issue to the public prosecutor in Troms and Finnmark. But it was recently sent back to the police. The public prosecutor wants the police to assess what the outbreak has had to say for public health in Tromsø, according to the newspaper iTromsø. The board and management do not fear a fine.

• It is considered that any conclusion about the investigation will not have any significant financial effect on the group, the annual report for 2020 states.

Hurtigruten lost NOK 1.7 billion last year. And the losses will also be huge this year. Only the interest payments on the interest-bearing debt of approximately NOK 13 billion will be many hundreds of millions of kroner. Any conceivable fine will therefore not have much to say for the shipping company's already troubled finances.

Valderhaug (2021) compared the price of NOK 14 million for the law firm Wiersholm's (2020) report to Hurtigruten with the price of NOK 17 million for the audit firm Deloitte's (2016) report to Telenor regarding the telecom company's involvement in corruption in Uzbekistan through VimpelCom, the price of NOK 6 million for the law firm Hjort's (2016) report to the bank DNB regarding the bank's involvement in tax havens revealed by the Panama Papers, the price of NOK 100 million for the law firm Wiersholm's and other corporate investigators' reports in 2011 to fertilizer manufacturer Yara regarding the manufacturer's corruption in India and Libya, and the price of more than NOK 100 million for law firm Wiersholm and law firm Shearman Sterling's reports in 2008 to aluminum manufacturer Hydro regarding the manufacturer's corruption in Libya.

Investigation Maturity Assessment

Both Wiersholm and DNV GL have previously worked as paid consultants for Hurtigruten, raising questions about the impartiality of their report (Berglund, 2020a). Many crew members refused to talk to the investigators from Wiersholm (2020), fearing that they were not sufficiently independent of Hurtigruten management and board and that they could thus suffer harassment and reprisals. The fact that examiner Fougner and others at Wiersholm as well as DNV GL had other parallel roles and tasks paid for by Hurtigruten reduces the trust in their objectivity and independence, which in our perspective reduces the maturity level of the investigation report. The maturity level is further reduced by the fact that examiners failed in gaining trust sufficient to access many crew members as interviewees. Both in terms of process and in terms of outcome, the handling of interviewees has to be questioned, and the conclusions based on lacking information sources have to be questioned as well.

Examiners followed the guidelines for private investigations by the Norwegian Bar Association. The guidelines provide some suggestions regarding the examination process, but they lack criteria for examination outcome. The guidelines emphasize issues such as the right of contradiction for individuals, whose actions or opinions are subject to investigation.

Examiners avoided the issue of blaming someone for the scandal. While scapegoating is bad, responsibility should be assigned to someone. A scapegoat is a person who is blamed for the wrongdoings, mistakes, or faults of others (Gangloff et al., 2016). Scapegoating often occurs after initial denial of wrongdoing or obfuscation of wrongdoing. A scapegoat is a person burdened with the wrongdoing of others. Medical doctors are close to becoming scapegoats in the Wiersholm (2020) report, while top executives become excused by a bureaucratic structure in the Hurtigruten organization. While the blame game by misleading attribution to others is bad (Eberly et al., 2011; Lee and Robinson, 2000), examiners avoided the task of identifying responsible persons in management.

Ideally, an investigation should answer questions concerned with what happened, how it happened, when it happened, who did what to make it happen or not happen, and why it happened or not happened. The latter two questions concerned with responsibility and causality were avoided by fraud examiners from Wiersholm (2020) and DNV GL. Examiners avoided causality in terms of potential motives for the reluctance to consider the pandemic a serious matter for voyages by Hurtigruten. Here in this chapter, it is suggested that the motive was financial gain to avoid corporate collapse and bankruptcy.

As illustrated in Figure 4.2, Wiersholm (2020) conducted an activity-oriented investigation. The investigation focused on activities that were carried out in a

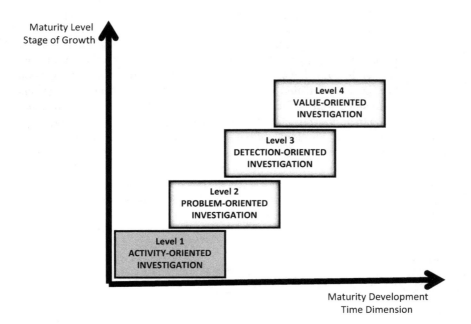

Figure 4.2 Maturity level for the Wiersholm (2020) investigation at Hurtigruten

reprehensible manner. The examiners looked for activities and prepared descriptions of these. Then examiners made up their minds regarding whether the activities were reprehensible or not.

A problematic issue in this case is that both Wiersholm and DNV GL had regular business relationships with Hurtigruten while conducting the investigation. Investigators were thus not independent of the client. Lawyers at Wiersholm were outside counsel handling legal matters for Hurtigruten. DNV GL were classifying and reviewing technical issues on Hurtigruten ships. Given lack of independence from the client, both the investigators' integrity and the investigation's objectivity can be questioned.

The Rise and Fall of Hurtigruten

This was the title of an article by Lervik-Olsen et al. (2021). They compared the Hurtigruten to Color Line, where the customers have their preference. They argued that Hurtigruten had for a long time a special place in many Norwegian hearts, and the cruise enterprise had established itself as a solid brand, both nationally and increasingly internationally. However, as argued by the authors, a good reputation and a strong brand must not be abused; it must be protected and managed.

Suddenly, the pandemic of Covid-19 hit the globe with outbreaks of ignored infection on *Roald Amundsen*, an investigation report by Wiersholm (2020), and following explanations, excuses, blame games, and strange versions of the wrongdoing. The survey numbers from the Norwegian research project Norwegian Customer Barometer at BI Norwegian Business School suggested that trust in Hurtigruten was disappearing. Customer satisfaction and loyalty dropped (Lervik-Olsen et al., 2021).

In 2007, 82 percent of passengers on Hurtigruten ships were satisfied with the product, while only 72 percent of passengers on Color Line ships were satisfied with the product. In 2021, it was the opposite, where 75 percent of passengers on Hurtigruten ships were satisfied with the product, while 80 percent of passengers on Color Line ships were satisfied with the product. The Norwegian Customer Barometer also measured customer loyalty, where passengers on Color Line ships have constantly been more loyal than passengers on Hurtigruten ships. In 2007, the difference was very small, with 82 percent loyalty among Hurtigruten passengers, and 83 percent loyalty among Color Line passengers. In 2021, the gap had increased substantially, where 73 percent loyalty reported among Hurtigruten passengers, and 90 percent loyalty among Color Line passengers (Lervik-Olsen et al., 2021).

References

Aguilera, R.V., Judge, W.Q. and Terjesen, S.A. (2018). Corporate governance deviance, *Academy of Management Review*, 43 (1), 87–109.

Aguilera, R.V. and Vadera, A.K. (2008). The dark side of authority: Antecedents, mechanisms, and outcomes of organizational corruption, *Journal of Business Ethics*, 77, 431–449.

Becker, H.S. (1963). *Outsiders: Studies in the Sociology of Deviance*, The Free Press, New York.

Berglund, N. (2020a). Hurtigruten boss survives disgrace, *News in English*, September 17, www.newsinenglish.no.

Berglund, N. (2020b). Government angry with Hurtigruten, *News in English*, September 18, www.newsinenglish.no.

Brightman, H.J. (2009). *Today's White-Collar Crime: Legal, Investigative, and Theoretical Perspectives*, Routledge, Taylor & Francis Group, New York.

Bundy, J. and Pfarrer, M.D. (2015). A burden of responsibility: The role of social approval at the onset of a crisis, *Academy of Management Review*, 40 (3), 345–369.

Chattopadhyay, P., Glick, W.H. and Huber, G.P. (2001). Organizational actions in response to threats and opportunities, *Academy of Management Journal*, 44 (5), 937–955.

Chen, Y. and Moosmayer, D.C. (2020). When guilt is not enough: Interdependent self-construal as moderator of the relationship between guilt and ethical consumption in a Confucian context, *Journal of Business Ethics*, 161, 551–572.

Dearden, T.E. (2016). Trust: The unwritten cost of white-collar crime, *Journal of Financial Crime*, 23 (1), 87–101.

Dearden, T.E. (2017). An assessment of adults' views on white-collar crime, *Journal of Financial Crime*, 24 (2), 309–21.

Dearden, T.E. (2019). How modern psychology can help us understand white-collar criminals, *Journal of Financial Crime*, 26 (1), 61–73.

Deloitte. (2016). *Review – Ownership at VimpelCom, Telenor*, audit firm Deloitte, Oslo, p. 54.

Dilchert, S., Ones, D.S., Davis, R.D. and Rostow, C.D. (2007). Cognitive ability predicts objectively measured counterproductive work behaviors, *Journal of Applied Psychology*, 92, 616–627.

Downing, S.T., Kang, J.S. and Markman, G.D. (2019). What you don't see can hurt you: Awareness cues to profile indirect competitors, *Academy of Management Journal*, 62 (6), 1872–1900.

Eberly, M.B., Holley, E.C., Johnson, M.D. and Mitchell, T.R. (2011). Beyond internal and external: A dyadic theory of relational attributions, *Academy of Management Review*, 36 (4), 731–753.

Engdahl, O. (2015). White-collar crime and first-time adult-onset offending: Explorations in the concept of negative life events as turning points, *International Journal of Law, Crime and Justice*, 43 (1), 1–16.

Friedrichs, D.O. (2010). Integrated theories of white-collar crime, in: Cullen, F.T. and Wilcox, P. (editors), *Encyclopedia of Criminological Theory* (Volume 1), Sage Publications, Los Angeles, pp. 479–486.

Friedrichs, D.O. (2020). Chapter 2: White collar crime: Definitional debates and the case for a typological approach, in: Rorie, M. (editor), *The Handbook of White-Collar Crime*, John Wiley & Sons, Hoboken, pp. 16–31.

Friedrichs, D.O., Schoultz, I. and Jordanoska, A. (2018). *Edwin H. Sutherland, Routledge Key Thinkers in Criminology*, Routledge, London.

Gangloff, K.A., Connelly, B.L. and Shook, C.L. (2016). Of scapegoats and signals: Investor reactions to CEO succession in the aftermath of wrongdoing, *Journal of Management*, 42, 1614–1634.

Gao, P. and Zhang, G. (2019). Accounting manipulation, peer pressure, and internal control, *The Accounting Review*, 94 (1), 127–151.

Geest, V.R., Weisburd, D. and Blokland, A.A.J. (2017). Developmental trajectories of offenders convicted of fraud: A follow-up to age 50 in a Dutch conviction cohort, *European Journal of Criminology*, 14 (5), 543–565.

Hjort. (2016). *Rapport til styret i DNB (Report to the Board at DNB)*, law firm Hjort, Oslo, p. 18.

Huisman, W. (2020). Chapter 10: Blurred lines: Collusions between legitimate and illegitimate organizations, in: Rorie, M.L. (editor), *The Handbook of White-Collar Crime*, Wiley & Sons, Hoboken, pp. 139–158.

Ismail, K. and Rydje, O.M. (2022). Får millionstraff for smitteutbrudd (Receives a million fine for outbreak of infection), *Daily Norwegian Business Newspaper Dagens Næringsliv*, January 29, pp. 26–27.

Keil, M., Tiwana, A., Sainsbury, R. and Sneha, S. (2010). Toward a theory of whistleblowing intentions: A benefit-cost differential perspective, *Decision Sciences*, 41 (4), 787–812.

König, A., Graf-Vlachy, L., Bundy, J. and Little, L.M. (2020). A blessing and a curse: How CEOs' trait empathy affects their management of organizational crisis, *Academy of Management Review*, 45 (1), 130–153.

Lægland, M., Ytreberg, R. and Johansen, R. (2020). Hurtigrutens innleide PR-rådgiver skaffet krisemøte med Venstre-kollega Iselin Nybø (Hurtigruten's hired PR adviser provided a crisis meeting with political party colleague Iselin Nybø), *Web-Based Business Newspaper E24*, May 11, www.e24.no.

Lee, F. and Robinson, R.J. (2000). An attributional analysis of social accounts: Implications of playing the blame game, *Journal of Applied Social Psychology*, 30 (9), 1853–1879.

Lehman, D.W., Cooil, B. and Ramanujam, R. (2020). The effects of rule complexity on organizational noncompliance and remediation: Evidence from restaurant health inspections, *Journal of Management*, 46 (8), 1436–1468.

Lervik-Olsen, L., Silseth, P.R. and Lorentzen, B.G. (2021). The rise and fall of Hurtigruten, *BI Business Review*, July 2, www.bi.no/forskning/business-review/.

McClean, E.J., Martin, S.R., Emich, K.J. and Woodruff, T. (2018). The social consequences of voice: An examination of voice type and gender on status and subsequent leader emergence, *Academy of Management Journal*, 61 (5), 1869–1891.

Mesmer-Magnus, J.R. and Viswesvaran, C. (2005). Whistleblowing in an organization: An examination of correlates of whistleblowing intentions, actions, and retaliation, *Journal of Business Ethics*, 62 (3), 266–297.

Michalak, R. and Ashkanasy, N.M. (2013). Emotions and deviances, in: Elias, S.M. (editor), *Deviant and Criminal Behavior in the Workplace*, New York University Press, New York.

Murphy, P.R. and Dacin, M.T. (2011). Psychological pathways to fraud: Understanding and preventing fraud in organizations, *Journal of Business Ethics*, 101, 601–618.

Murphy, P.R. and Free, C. (2015). Broadening the fraud triangle: Instrumental climate and fraud, *Behavioral Research in Accounting*, 28 (1), 41–56.

Patel, P.C. and Cooper, D. (2014). Structural power equality between family and nonfamily TMT members and the performance of family firms, *Academy of Management Journal*, 57 (6), 1624–1649.

Piazza, A. and Jourdan, J. (2018). When the dust settles: The consequences of scandals for organizational competition, *Academy of Management Journal*, 61 (1), 165–190.

Pontell, H.N., Black, W.K. and Geis, G. (2014). Too big to fail, too powerful to jail? On the absence of criminal prosecutions after the 2008 financial meltdown, *Crime, Law and Social Change*, 61 (1), 1–13.

Rothe, D.L. (2020). Moving beyond abstract typologies? Overview of state and state-corporate crime, *Journal of White-Collar and Corporate Crime*, 1 (1), 7–15.

Rothe, D.L. and Medley, C. (2020). Chapter 6: Beyond state and state-corporate crime typologies: The symbiotic nature, harm, and victimization of crimes of the powerful and their continuation, in: Rorie, M. (editor), *The Handbook of White-Collar Crime*, John Wiley & Sons, Hoboken, pp. 81–94.

Sæbbe, L.V., Endresen, R. and Holte, M.A. (2014). Vil kjøpe Hurtigruten – Hegnar tjener 500 millioner på handelen (Will buy Hurtigruten – Hegnar makes 500 million on the deal), *Nord24*, October 29, www.nord24.no.

Schnatterly, K., Gangloff, K.A. and Tuschke, A. (2018). CEO wrongdoing: A review of pressure, opportunity, and rationalization, *Journal of Management*, 44 (6), 2405–2432.

Schoultz, I. and Flyghed, J. (2016). Doing business for a 'higher loyalty' How Swedish transnational corporations neutralize allegations of crime, *Crime, Law and Social Change*, 66 (2), 183–198.

Schoultz, I. and Flyghed, J. (2020a). From "we didn't do it" to "we've learned our lesson": Development of a typology of neutralizations of corporate crime, *Critical Criminology*, 28, 739–757.

Schoultz, I. and Flyghed, J. (2020b). Denials and confessions: An analysis of the temporalization of neutralizations of corporate crime, *International Journal of Law, Crime and Justice*, doi: 10.1016/j.ijlcj.2020.100389.

Schoultz, I. and Flyghed, J. (2021). "We have been thrown under the bus": Corporate versus individual defense mechanisms against transnational corporate bribery charges, *Journal of White Collar and Corporate Crime*, 2 (1), 24–35.

Smith, O. and Raymen, T. (2018). Deviant leisure: A criminological perspective, *Theoretical Criminology*, 22 (1), 63–82.

Sykes, G. and Matza, D. (1957). Techniques of neutralization: A theory of delinquency, *American Sociological Review*, 22 (6), 664–670.

Valderhaug, R. (2020a). Hurtigruten-topper beskyldes for å ha undertrykket informasjon, *Daily Norwegian Newspaper Aftenposten*, September 19, p. 14.

Valderhaug, R. (2020b). –Vi har hele tiden vært åpne, og det skal vi fortsette med (-We have always been open, and we will continue to do so), *Daily Norwegian Newspaper Aftenposten*, October 29, p. 20.

Valderhaug, R. (2021). 14 millioner kroner for 51-siders rapport (NOK 14 million for a 51-page report), *Daily Norwegian Newspaper Aftenposten*, May 5, p. 24.

Valderhaug, R., Jordheim, H. and Christiansen, H. (2020). Rapport: Ikke rart at det gikk galt (Report: No surprise that it went wrong), *Daily Norwegian Newspaper Aftenposten*, September 18, p. 10.

Wang, P. (2020). How to engage in illegal transactions: Resolving risk and uncertainty in corrupt dealings, *British Journal of Criminology*, 60, 1282–1301.

Wiersholm. (2020). *Granskingsrapport: Utbrudd av covid-19 på Hurtigruten-skipet MS Roald Amundsen 17–31 juli 2020 (Investigation report: Outbreak of covid-19 on Hurtigruten ship MS Roald Amundsen July 17–31, 2020)*, law firm Wiersholm, Oslo, p. 51.

5   Russian Favors to Biathlon President

Anders Besseberg was president of the International Biathlon Union from 1992 until he was laid off in 2018 on the basis of accusations of wrongdoing. During those years, the sport of biathlon evolved from being a sport for people who were particularly interested to becoming one of the most popular winter sports on television. Besseberg is considered the architect of the various successful forms of competition in biathlon such as hunting start, joint start, and mixed relays. He lifted the sport of biathlon to new heights during his period as president. By being in the position of president for such a long time, he became a powerful individual with great influence internationally. There were no restrictions on being the union president and how many periods he could be in such a central position without being replaced. Besseberg has been a central figure in shaping the business, culture, ethics, structure, and compliance of right and wrong at IBU as an organization. The suspected fraud was concerned with the president receiving favors and bribes from Russian biathlon union officials.

The International Biathlon Union is headquartered in Salzburg in Austria (Ellingworth and Dunbar, 2018). Biathlon is a winter sport that combines cross-country skiing and rifle shooting. It is treated as a race, with contestants skiing through a cross-country trail whose distance is divided into shooting rounds. Major biathlon nations include France, Russia, Sweden, and Norway. Biathlon is a very popular sport among spectators, both present at shooting stadiums and in front of television screens all over the world. The business of biathlon events has grown significantly in recent decades, and rumors of both corruption and doping have flourished for several years in the media.

Russian doping whistleblower Grigory Rodchenkov told the media about organized doping of Russian athletes at the Sochi Winter Olympics (Ruiz and Schwirtz, 2016). He had been the head of Russia's national anti-doping laboratory (Pelley, 2018). Rodchenkov's allegations were confirmed by the independent McLaren report, leading to Russia's partial bans from the 2016 Summer Olympics and 2018 Winter Olympics. Rodchenkov's allegations and the McLaren findings led to an investigation particularly targeted at the management at the International Biathlon Union. When the IBU report was released (ERC, 2021), the *New York Times* wrote about it under the heading "Hunting trips, sex, and cash: How grooming biathlon's leader paid off for Russia: An investigation accuses biathlon's longtime

DOI: 10.4324/9781003363934-6

president of accepting gifts from Russians and then doing the country's bidding as a doping scandal swirled" (Panja, 2021):

> The president of the International Biathlon Union told the police that the young woman who had come to his hotel in Moscow was a prostitute, but he was hazy on the details. He did not remember the date or even who had paid for her services, he said, but it had assuredly not been him. The president, Anders Besseberg, had led biathlon's governing body for more than two decades by then, and he was accustomed to receiving gifts from his Russian hosts. Like a chocolate on his pillow or a gift bag placed on a chair in his hotel room, the company of a young woman during a trip to a World Cup biathlon event was not uncommon.
>
> And for decades, according to a report commissioned by biathlon's new leadership, Besseberg repaid the Russian favors by doing the country's bidding – defending its athletes, assailing its critics and even blocking efforts to root out doping by its teams. The yearlong effort to groom Besseberg, and later his top deputy, was so effective that at the height of Russia's state-run doping scandal one Russian official boasted to a colleague that the country had little to fear in biathlon – a grueling endurance sport that combines precision shooting with cross-country ski racing – because he had Besseberg "under his control".

The potential offender in this case study is Anders Besseberg, who appears in the view of the commission to have had no regard for ethical values and no real interest in protecting the sport from cheating. ERC (2021) claims that Besseberg was enabled by a complete lack of basic governance safeguards that left integrity decisions in the sole hands of himself and his allies on the IBU executive board, with no checks and balances, no transparency, and no accountability. Integrity is the quality of acting in accordance with the moral values, norms, and rules that are considered valid and relevant within the context in which the actor operates (Loyens et al., 2021). The external review commission found that Besseberg had been bribed by Russian officials by more than 300,000 Euros.

Motive Convenience Themes

Anders Besseberg's financial motive was based on the possibility to acquire wealth, free hunting trips, the availability of prostitutes, and the general treatment as a very important person. The investigation report describes how Besseberg was offered benefits by Russian officials. The Russian expected him in return to ignore rumors about doping of Russian biathletes as well as support Russian interests in general. According to the investigation report, Besseberg said that there was no uproar around the biathlon association before and that he wanted to keep it that way. It can be perceived as a convenient situation to say yes to benefits that would otherwise be unobtainable for him since his basic salary as president of the International Biathlon Union was very modest. By ignoring doping rumors, he felt that he contributed to progress and harmony in the biathlon family. Besseberg avoided the threats that could lead to riots around the sport, such as media attention about the sport being cunning, dirty, and full of doping scandals. His actions were convenient because they seemed like the best thing for both the union and the individual offender.

Besseberg contributed to concealing doping in Russia in order to receive benefits for his own gain. His behaviors and actions deprived pure and clean athletes of fair competitions, and he deprived them of honor, fame, and wealth. He was motivated to receive illegitimate benefits at the expense of others. It was rational self-interest focusing on incentives and benefits exceeding perceived detection risks and associated costs (Welsh et al., 2014). He was greedy and status-oriented, as illustrated by an incident related to a possible hunting trip in Canada (ERC, 2021: 64):

> Mr. Besseberg was unable to produce for the criminal authorities any evidence that he paid any of the expenses of these hunting trips himself. Jim Carrabre said that before the Vancouver Olympics in 2010, Anders Besseberg was in Canada and "since we knew that he is a passionate hunter, we offered to organize a hunt in Canada for him". Besseberg was extremely interested and asked us if we would pay for it. We said no, we (the Canadian Biathlon Union) would only organize the hunt. He would have to pay for the hunt himself. Besseberg then lost interest in the hunt.

As a very important person in the biathlon family, Besseberg was used to getting attention and expenses covered. He had climbed high up in Maslow's (1943) hierarchy of needs. Power, influence, and status were high and growing. This was a position he wanted to maintain and protect.

The investigation report places great emphasis on how he has favored Russia as a nation for a number of years. Russia is one of the largest nations economically that participates in biathlon, and it has been extremely important to have this nation onboard. By ignoring the suspicious blood values and blood passports of Russian biathletes for many years, Besseberg maintained a good relationship with the Russians both individually and at the organizational level. By dedicating World Cup events and a possible World Championship to Russia, the IBU and the sport were able to secure important financial support that came from Russia.

The investigation report claims that Besseberg received gifts from the former heads of the Russian Biathlon Federation (RBU), Alexander Kravtsov and Alexander Tikhonov, including a cash sum of up to $300,000, hunting trips, and services from prostitutes. In return Besseberg protected Russia – both public and private – by covering up positive doping results and blocking investigations that could disqualify Russian athletes (ERC, 2021: 60):

> Third, Dr Rodchenkov said he believed Alexander Kravtsov, who was head of the CSP throughout the relevant period, and president of the RBU from 2014 to 2018, was involved in the bribery of Mr Besseberg, based on

a conversation he witnessed when he went to see Mr Kravtsov at the CSP offices one day in approximately May or June of 2013. According to Dr Rodchenkov, when he arrived, Mr Kravtsov waved him into his office, where Kravtsov was in the middle of a conversation with Alexander Tikhonov (former IBU 1st Vice-President, who is a known close associate of Kravtsov). Dr Rodchenkov states:

Mr Kravstov and Mr Tikhonov were openly trying to recall how much money Mr Tikhonov had paid Mr Besseberg. . . . (They) openly discussed having paid Mr Besseberg somewhere between $200,000 USD and $300,000 USD in one-off payment. The cash for that payment had been held in a small diplomatic case. Tikhonov said the type of case they used could hold about $300,000 USD. Mr Kravstov disagreed and stated that this type of case could hold $400,000 USD. Mr Tikhonov said that Mr Besseberg was "under his control", which I understood to mean Mr Tikhonov had leverage over Mr Besseberg. I understood "under his control" to mean that Mr Besseberg was obligated to him and that Mr Tikhonov had leverage over him.

It could be argued that "under his control" represented a threat to Besseberg as a convenience theme. Over time, Besseberg felt probably pressured from several powerful individuals and institutions. Not only had Tikhonov control over Besseberg but Besseberg was also under pressure from others, such as the RBU and Russia, to accept whatever was going on among Russian biathletes (ERC, 2021: 59):

Dr Rodchenkov thought she was saying that they "had enough sensitive information to escape problems in the future" but did not know what that sensitive information might have been. He only noted that Dr Rodionova appeared to be unconcerned about doped Russian biathletes being caught through IBU testing (including ABP testing), from which he inferred that she understood X had made an arrangement with Mr Besseberg to prevent such exposure.

Irina Rodionova had told Rodchenkov on several occasions between 2010 and 2011 that they had built relations with Besseberg in order to directly solve problems between the RBU and IBU. She was the one who said that they had enough sensitive information about Besseberg to escape problems in the future. The threat occurred as Besseberg did not do what was expected of him after receiving several hundred thousand dollars in bribe (ERC, 2021: 60):

In sum and substance, Mr Kravtsov and Mr Tikhonov were discussing that they had paid Mr Besseberg to do something specific and he had not fulfilled his part of the bargain. They were clear that they had given him enough money to be sure that he would do this particular thing.

Besseberg was exposed to pressure and threats from Russian officials after he had received money, trips, and services in a corruption scheme. Initially, in his contact with the Russians, he had received no bribes from Russia and was thus not exposed

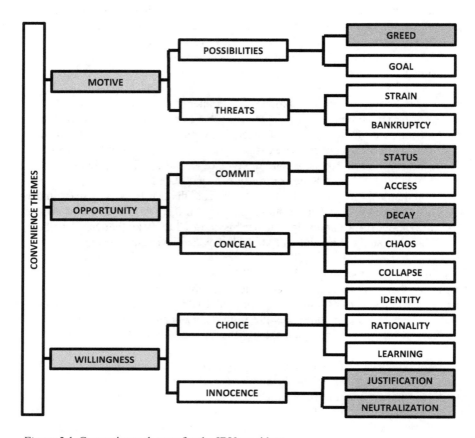

Figure 5.1 Convenience themes for the IBU president

to pressures and threats. Pressures and threats were a result of the relationship with the Russians entered into by Besseberg. Therefore, it would be a misleading application of the convenience theme in the motive dimension to suggest threat as a motive. Initially, there was no threat. Threat became only a consequence of misconduct. This is why the convenience theme along the axis of motive-threat-individual is not relevant as illustrated in Figure 5.1. Besseberg's initial motive to involve himself with the Russians was not based on threats from the Russians. The initial motive was along the axis of motive-possibilities-individual to receive favors and services that only later lead to threats against him.

In the financial motive dimension of convenience theory, Besseberg was interested in hunting trips and sex paid for by others, in addition to cash (ERC, 2021: 63):

> The police also seized thirteen watches at Mr Besseberg's home. Four of them were from specific sporting events, the other nine watches being luxury

brands like RAM (2), Omega Broad Arrow, Ulysee Nardin (2), Huboldt Geneve, Poljot, and two unknown brands (both probably Russian). Mr Besseberg confirmed that he had received the Omega watch (worth about Euro 20,000) as a personal present in March 2011 in Khanty-Mansysk, to mark the occasion of the 100th IBU Executive Board meeting and his 65th birthday. He said a blue watch (brand unknown, probably *Naprer') was given to him by Alexander Tikhonov, but he could not provide the occasion or the date of the gift, just that it was at an IBU World Cup event at Holmenkollen. That leaves seven watches of unclear provenance. Mr Besseberg himself did not state that he had bought them or indicate how he had obtained them.

Besseberg climbed the hierarchy of needs for status and success (Maslow, 1943). He had contributed to the success of the biathlon sport and probably wanted to satisfy the need for acclaim as a narcissist (Chatterjee and Pollock, 2017). He was greedy as well (Goldstraw-White, 2012). The motive was individual possibilities, as indicated in Figure 5.1.

Yet another potential threat motive is prevention of a corporate scandal. If people learned about extensive doping of athletes in international biathlon competitions, the public as well as sponsors and television channels could become less interested in the sports events. It might thus be argued that Besseberg's motive was not only individual but also corporate on behalf of the International Biathlon Union. However, based on the information provided in the ERC (2021) report, Besseberg acted as an individual without regard to the organization he represented and was responsible for.

Opportunity Convenience Themes

There seems to be two dominating convenience themes for organizational opportunity in the case of Besseberg. The two themes, status and decay, are illustrated in Figure 5.1. In addition, it might be argued that access and chaos were convenience themes as well in the case.

As president at IBU for a long time, and as entrepreneurial creator of modern biathlon events, he enjoyed a very high status. Besseberg had considerable freedom of action in his position as IBU president. There were great opportunities for him for deviant behavior without any reactions from potential observers. Besseberg served as president of IBU for 26 years, and during that time he had developed a personal network of influential individuals. This is reflected in the IBU presidential election in 2014, when both Carrabre and Tikhonov ran for the office. Several of the key members of the IBU organization did not want any of these candidates and therefore advised Besseberg to run as a counter-candidate (ERC, 2021: 94):

At the Congress meeting the next day, Mr Besseberg was re-elected as IBU President in the first round, winning 33 of the 50 votes cast. Messrs. Leistner, Carrabre, Taschler and Lehotan, and Ms Kim were re-elected to the Executive

Board without opposition; Thomas Pfüller was re-elected as VP Marketing; and Olle Dahlin was elected VP Development.

Besseberg's status, power, and influence can be exemplified by how he told others that the world cup events in Russia in 2018 could not be moved elsewhere (ERC, 2021: 153):

> Three IBU events were scheduled to be held in Russia in the 2017/18 season, namely the last two IBU Cup events (in Uvat on 9–11 March and Khanty-Mansiysk on 13–17 March) and the final IBU World Cup event, which was scheduled to be held in Tyumen on 22–25 March 2018. Following the Schmid Report and the IOC's decision to exclude the ROC from the 2018 Olympic Games, there was significant pressure from many different stakeholders, not least the biathletes for the IBU to move those events out of Russia . . .
>
> On 8 December 2017, Biathlon Canada wrote an open letter to the IBU Executive Board, saying that not moving the two IBU Cups and the IBU World Cup event that had been allocated to Russia for season 2017/18 was inconsistent with the IOC's decision to disallow participation by the Russian team at the 2018 Olympic Games, expressed its frustration, and said it would not be sending a team to those events . . . On 9–10 December 2017, the IBU Executive Board met in Leogang . . .
>
> The Commission agrees with Nicole Resch's view that Mr Besseberg's actions were clearly pro-Russia to a remarkable degree in this period. Rather than bow to the wishes of the national federations and athletes who wanted him to move the three IBU events in 2018 out of Russia, he insisted that they must remain there, and used his double vote to ensure they did. He then apparently lied to a member of the IBU Athletes' Committee about why he did so, falsely suggesting that WADA had said he should keep the events in Russia.

Decay and chaos are convenience themes that enable deviance between principal and agent in an agency relationship. Besseberg as an agent had been delegated authority, responsibility, and tasks that were performed in such a way that the agent found suitable and most appropriate. In the terminology of principal–agent perspectives, the corporation might be defined as the principal, while executives are agents. The principal–agent theory suggests that the organization is a nexus of contracts. A corporation is a web of contractual relationships consisting of individuals who band together for their mutual economic benefit. The theory argues that a principal is often unable to control an agent who does work for the principal, while at the same time being responsible for the agent's behavior. The agency perspective assumes narrow self-interest among both principals and agents. The interests of principal and agent tend to diverge, they may have different risk willingness or risk aversion, there is knowledge asymmetry between the two parties, and the principal has imperfect information about the agent's contribution (Bosse and Phillips, 2016; Chrisman et al., 2007; Pillay and Kluvers, 2014; Williams, 2008).

In the opportunity dimension of convenience theory, ERC (2021: 1) argue that Besseberg's corrupt behavior was enabled by a complete lack of basic governance safeguards that left integrity decisions in the sole hands of the president and his allies on the IBU Executive Board:

> The final report of the independent IBU External Review Commission (the Commission) identifies what the Commission considers to be evidence of systematic corrupt and unethical conduct at the very top of the IBU for a decade (2008 to 2018) and more, by a president (Anders Besseberg, IBU President 1993 to 2018) who appears, in the view of the Commission, to have had no regard for ethical values and no real interest in protecting the sport from cheating. Enabled by a complete lack of basic governance safeguards that left integrity decisions in the sole hands of the President and his allies on the IBU Executive Board, with no checks and balances, no transparency, and no accountability whatsoever to keep them honest, Mr Besseberg's proclaimed commitment to clean sport was, in the Commission's view, a charade. He and his allies recounted by rote their supposed "zero tolerance for doping" but did only the absolute minimum that was necessary to preserve a veneer of respectability for the sport.

As indicated in Figure 5.1, there was a combination of status and decay that made wrongdoing convenient. While status enabled the commitment of wrongdoing (Patel and Cooper, 2014; Pontell et al., 2014), decay enabled the concealment of wrongdoing (Crosina and Pratt, 2019; Eberl et al., 2015; Rooij and Fine, 2020). The president of the Biathlon Union in the United States, Max Cobb, claimed that Besseberg behaved like and had the status of a king (Christiansen et al., 2021).

Generally, a deviant culture both in the mind of Anders Besseberg and at IBU has created a convenient structure for misconduct and potential corruption. He has operated in a gray zone for a long period of time and mixed with people who first provided illegitimate benefits and then pressured him in various situations to ignore warnings of doping and to argue for World Cup events in Russia.

Willingness Convenience Themes

Besseberg himself has persistently claimed his innocence, saying that he has never done anything wrong and that he does not understand the accusations against him. He has also been strongly critical of one of the whistleblowers, Grigory Rodchenkov. He claims his innocence by denying Rodchenkov's allegations. Neutralization of potential guilt feelings and justification of actions has been a recurring theme where Besseberg has stated that the hunts, for example, were only in connection with meetings and other work-related events. Many of these statements and interviews with Besseberg have shown clear signs of classical neutralization techniques. Through the willingness to deviate that developed for Besseberg, his boundaries for self-control became somewhat distant.

His identity probably changed with so much power over a long period of time. He might also have developed a learning pattern over time, where one constantly develops an inner acceptance of what one can get away with. This is not the same as the learning theme in convenience theory, which suggests learning from others as an explanation for the initial willingness for deviant behavior. The learning suggested here suggests more the slippery-slope perspective where the offender gradually increases the extent of deviance. However, acceptance by learning is not typical for slippery slope where the unconscious sliding is an important characteristic.

Besseberg confirmed to the police that he had received several invitations from members of the Russian Biathlon Union (ERC, 2021: 63):

> Mr Besseberg confirmed to the police that he had received various hunting and fishing invitations and trophies from Russian officials, including invitations to hunt in Khanty-Mansiysk (3–4 timer) and Tyumen (2–3 times). He admitted that he never paid for the equipment or accommodation or for the trophies from these trips but said this was not bribery or anything else improper, since these invitations "more or less" took place only in connection with official meetings and IBU World Cup events, as part of the normal program of events in which he participated in his official capacity as IBU President.

As quoted earlier, investigators found that Besseberg had no regard for ethical values and no real interest in protecting the sport from cheating. The foregoing quote suggests that Besseberg disclaims wrongdoing and justifies his actions by claiming that his actions were normal and that it was completely normal and natural to behave in this way.

There was a sense of rationality in accepting bribes from Russians, on the one hand, and protecting Russian interests, on the other hand (ERC, 2021: 160):

> The Commission agrees with Nicole Resch's view that Mr Besseberg's actions were clearly pro-Russia to a remarkable degree in this period. Rather than bow to the wishes of the national federations and athletes who wanted him to move the three IBU events in 2018 out of Russia, he insisted that they must remain there, and used his double vote to ensure they did . . . The Commission therefore considers that Mr Besseberg has a case to answer for breaches of his duty under the IBU Ethics Code of the time to behave and act with complete credibility and integrity.

Investigators found evidence to suggest that Besseberg tried his best to downplay the scandals surrounding Russian athletes' doping efforts and hindered the efforts of others who tried to introduce and enforce anti-doping rules. Investigators believe that Besseberg's actions were very clearly on Russia's side in particular in the years 2017 and 2018. Among other things, he lied to a member of the IBU's athletes' committee about why Russia should remain the host of the World Cup and other events by blaming WADA (ERC, 2021: 160):

He then apparently lied to a member of the IBU Athletes' Committee about why he did so, falsely suggesting that WADA had said he should keep the events in Russia.

Rationality is about making conscious choices based on assessments of pros and cons to achieve goals and ambitions. It is a cost-benefit assessment where the offender assesses the benefits (profit, services, admiration, attention, etc.) against the costs (possible detection leading to bad press, dismissal, punishment, etc.). If the benefits exceed costs, it will appear rational to commit white-collar crime. Besseberg has used his position as IBU president to receive bribes (cash, watches, hunting trips, and prostitutes) without any costs until recently that he probably did not expect. His subjective perception of detection risk and punishment severity was apparently very low as he did not perceive wrongdoing.

In addition to assuming that Besseberg had low morals and poor ethics in addition to little self-control, it can be argued that Besseberg performed his pro-Russian actions due to pressure from Tikhonov and others in Russia. He had to follow orders; otherwise, it could lead to negative consequences for him. This argument is in line with the obedience perspective where a follower is obedient to a leader. This concept is about obedience as a form of social influence, which involves performing an action under the command of an authority figure. However, as argued earlier, the initial situation for Besseberg did not require obedience as long as he did not accept bribes. It was his acceptance of gifts and services that lead him into a situation depending on the will of Russian officials. In convenience theory, the willingness for deviant behavior is a matter of the initial willingness to accept illegitimate favors and not a matter of the consequences of actually accepting those favors.

Besseberg used the neutralization technique of claiming legal mistake: This should never pop up as illegal in the first place. An offender using this technique to remove a potential feeling of guilt argues that the law is wrong and that what the person did should indeed not pop up as illegal. One may therefore break the law since the law is unreasonable, unfair, and unjust. An offender may argue that lawmakers sometimes criminalize behaviors and sometimes decriminalize more or less randomly over time. For example, monetary benefits involved in bribing people were treated as legal expenses in accounting as marketing costs some decades ago, while corruption today is considered misconduct and therefore is criminalized. An offender may also argue that what is illegal at home is legal somewhere else, and vice versa. The following incident illustrates Besseberg's application of this neutralization technique (ERC, 2021: 87):

In a second, separate incident, in March 2013 at the IBU World Cup event in Holmenkollen, Mr. Tikhonov gave the president of a national biathlon federation a small wallet as a present. Back in his room, the person discovered that there was a €500 note in the wallet. Immediately, he went downstairs and handed the wallet back. He told the Commission that the next morning Anders Besseberg called him and asked him to come and meet with him and Mr Tikhonov. At the meeting, Mr Besseberg said that it is a normal custom in Russia to put some coins in a wallet as a present for someone. Mr Tikhonov also said that it is normal in Russia to put in some coins. The national president insisted that €500 is a lot more than some coins and not acceptable. Mr Besseberg said to him: "usually you should have accepted the gift because this is a normal way to do things in Russia".

When interviewed, investigators asked Tikhonov about this incident. He did not deny it but claimed that he had given the wallet to the person as a birthday present. However, the person told investigators that he had no birthday at that time. Tikhonov said that he put €500 in the wallet because that was the smallest note he had available. He said it was no bribe since it was such a small amount of money. Investigators did not agree with Tikhonov (ERC, 2021: 87):

> It is a well-known technique for corruptors, to start with small favors, in order to draw the subject in and make them feel indebted and complicit, so that they are then susceptible to further approaches. Once again, therefore, it considers this to be an improper approach by Mr Tikhonov, even if not as blatant as the approach to Ms Resch and it regards Mr Besseberg's acquiescence in the practice as highly improper, again irrespective of the precise motivation, and a breach of his duties as IBU President.

Besseberg's behavior seems to be in accordance with the differential association perspective, where an offender associates with those who agree with him and distances himself from those who are critical to his activities (Sutherland, 1983). It is a matter of learning from others, who in this case are Russian officials. It was a rational choice, where perception of benefits exceeded perceptions of costs (Pratt and Cullen, 2005). Probably behavioral reinforcement of deviance occurred over time (Benartzi et al., 2017). Besseberg may have been sliding on the slippery slope (Welsh et al., 2014) toward more serious corruption with a lack of self-control (Gottfredson and Hirschi, 1990).

Anders Besseberg's actions as IBU president in relation to Russia's interests in biathlon seem to be deviant based on willingness to participate in a corruption scheme. There seems to be no reason why he should protect Russian interests without accepting the gifts he denies having received as bribes. Besseberg has not yet been convicted, and he denies all criminal charges through his lawyer. Therefore, it is difficult to get a full picture of the situation. In addition, he refused to appear for an interview with the investigators, so the current picture is certainly incomplete.

Review Commission Mandate

A   In late 2017, the Intelligence & Investigations Department of the World Anti-Doping Agency (WADA) issued a confidential report, outlining allegations of corruption within the International Biathlon Union (the IBU), including that the then IBU President had covered up anti-doping rule violations by

Russian biathletes, with the assistance of the then IBU Secretary General, and that delegates of IBU member federations at the 2016 IBU Congress had been bribed to vote in favor of the 2021 World Championships being held in Tyumen, Russia.

B The criminal authorities in Austria and Norway subsequently opened formal criminal investigations into potential doping fraud, corruption, and/or financial crimes. They conducted surveillance of communications by the then IBU President and Secretary General, and in April 2018 they searched their private residences, as well as the IBU's offices.

C The investigations of WADA and the criminal authorities in Austria and Norway are continuing. In the meantime, the IBU President and Secretary General have both stepped down from their respective positions at the IBU, and they have since been replaced as IBU President and Secretary General respectively and no longer hold any positions with the IBU.

D The new IBU President and Executive Board elected at the 2018 IBU Congress are committed to the proper investigation of any and all alleged wrongdoing, in accordance with the IBU's obligations as a signatory to the World Anti-Doping Code (the Code), and in cooperation with WADA and the criminal authorities, to ensure that any and all past wrongdoing is uncovered and properly sanctioned. They are also committed to updating and strengthening the constitution of the IBU (the IBU Constitution) and the IBU's governance practices moving forward in line with international best practice, to minimize the chances of recurrence.

E On 12 June 2018, the Executive Board of the International Olympic Committee (IOC) suspended all direct financial payments from the IOC to the IBU pending election of a new IBU President and confirmation of improvements in the IBU's Code of Ethics and Ethics Commission, and in the IBU's anti-doping operations, and an update on the work done by the IBU to follow up on evidence of Russian doping provided by WADA to the IBU. On 4 October 2018, the IOC Executive Board "noted the positive steps taken by the IBU to address the actions required by the IOC earlier this year, but also highlighted the importance of the further assurances for implementation in order to take biathlon into an era of greater transparency and good governance . . .". On 2 November 2018, the IOC Executive Board decided that financial payments should be resumed after receiving "a strong undertaking from the new IBU President to see those reforms through to implementation".

THEREFORE, at its meeting in Lausanne on 3/4 November 2018, the new IBU Executive Board decided as follows:

1 Appointment and mandate of the Commission

1.1 An independent external commission (the External Review Commission or Commission) shall be constituted, consisting of English lawyer Jonathan Taylor QC (the Chair), Austrian lawyer Dr Christian Dorda,

German lawyer Dr Tanja Haug (replacing her law partner Dr Anja Martinas of 20 January 2020, due to personal commitments), and a former biathlete nominated by the IBU Athletes Committee, Vincent Defrasne, to carry out the following mandate on the basis set out in these Terms of Reference:

1.1.1   an internal IBU Constitution Working group is conducting, in a first step, a comprehensive review of the IBU Constitution, the IBU's rules of conduct (ethical, anti-doping and otherwise) and related disciplinary rules and regulations. In a second step, the External Review Commission examines the working group proposal, taking into account the IBU's governance structures, practices, policies and procedures, by making recommendations as to any reforms or amendments that the Commission considers necessary or appropriate to ensure that these legal instruments, structures, practices, policies and procedures reflect the highest standards of integrity and transparency, and that the IBU is operating in accordance with international best practice in this area, and has a strengthened ability to prevent and to respond robustly to any future breaches of its rules; and

1.1.2   to that end, as well as to ensure that the IBU fulfils its investigatory obligations under Article 20.3.10 of the World Anti-Doping Code, and its commitment to cooperation with WADA under Article 4.2 of the IBU Constitution, to conduct a full and unfettered investigation into all anti-doping, compliance, ethical and other disciplinary matters arising from the ongoing investigation by WADA and various national and international criminal authorities, as well as into any further issues of concern that arise in relation to IBU governance or ethical matters within the IBU and/or otherwise in the sport of biathlon that are identified in the course of the investigation (together, the Matters), in order:

(a)   to establish all of the relevant facts in relation to the Matters;

(b)   to determine whether any person or member or other body that is subject to the jurisdiction of the IBU has a case to answer for breach of their obligations to the IBU in relation to any of the Matters, whether by contract, under the IBU rules and regulations, or otherwise, including but not limited to:

(i)   determining whether the IBU anti-doping rules and disciplinary rules, as well as all applicable World Anti-Doping Code provisions, have been properly applied, leading to appropriate adjudication and subsequent consequences, or alternatively whether any anti-doping rule violations have been covered up or otherwise improperly handled (by the IBU and/or others);

    (ii) determining whether any breaches of the IBU code of ethics and/or other rules of conduct have occurred; and

    (iii) determining whether the Russian Biathlon Union was given any preferential treatment by the IBU with respect to the hosting of events, either generally or in particular in relation to the vote for Tyumen to host the 2021 World Championships, and whether the voting for Tyumen was tainted by corruption; and . . .

Investigation Report Outcome

In view of the commission, the evidentiary record that the commission has gathered establishes that both Besseberg and Secretary General Nicole Resch have a case to answer for breach of their duties under the IBU constitution, IBU disciplinary rules, and/or the IBU code of ethics. These regulations require people at IBU to act at all times with the utmost integrity, to protect the rights of clean athletes, and to not undertake any actions that are contrary to the interests of the biathlon sport. In the commission's view, the evidence uncovered suggests that IBU president Anders Besseberg consistently preferred and protected Russian interests in virtually everything that he did. The commission claims that they have identified provision of bribes and extensive favors by the Russians to Besseberg, particularly in the form of free hunting trips and the services of prostitutes (ERC, 2021: 64):

> Another way of gaining improper influence over someone is by obtaining compromising material that can be used to blackmail them. In this regard, the Commission notes that there is evidence of Mr Besseberg's use of prostitutes in Russia, some or all of them arranged for him by his hosts. It was notorious within IBU circles that Mr Besseberg's hosts would often provide him with the services of a young, female "interpreter" when he visited Russia. An IBU Board Member stated to the Commission: "in this regard Anders was a special man. It was well known that when he was in Russia, he had an interpreter on his side". The interpreter indeed translated speeches and other conversation, but "what kind of the role of the interpreters of Mr Besseberg are doing later after official events, I don't know, if it was a double role". He understood that "the RBU hired these interpreters". Nicole Resch said to the police: "Because of the way Anders Besseberg treated these women, I got the impression of an intimate relationship". But she could not say definitively if these women were paid or who paid them.

Examiners exemplify how Besseberg protected Russian interests in the case of the 2018 IBU World Cup event in Tuymen in Russia. In advance it had been agreed to move the event away from Russia if further Russian doping cases were detected (ERC, 2021: 160):

> When interviewed by the Commission, Max Cobb and Ivor Lehotan were both very clear in their recollection that the agreement of the IBU Executive

Board was that if the new LIMS evidence that WADA had obtained led to any further cases against Russian biathletes (beyond the four already pending: Glazyrina, Romanova, Vilukhina, and Zaitseva), the 2018 IBU World Cup Final event would be moved from Tyumen. In contrast, Dr Leistner said he could not really remember any such discussion. However, a press release issued by the IBU stated that "all members of the Association of the International Olympic Winter Sports Federations (AIOWF) agreed at a conference call on 9 December 2017 that all competitions in Russia will be conducted as planned for the ongoing season 2017/2018, unless new important and legally backed evidence is brought up".

The Commission also has evidence that Mr Besseberg was well aware of the situation and was also apparently himself of the view that there had been a conspiracy between the Moscow laboratory and the Ministry of Sports. On 9 January 2018, Mr Besseberg met with athletes and coaches at the IBU World Cup event in Rupholding, and they expressed significant concern about competing in Russia. In addition, the IBU Athletes' Committee passed on to the IBU Executive Board a letter setting out their position that it was simply wrong to have the final 2018 IBU World Cup event and two IBU Cups in Russia, noting that there had even been threats of physical harm made to athletes who travelled to Russia, and that they were also worried about dope tests being tampered with . . .

According to Max Cobb: "During the discussion Mr Besseberg threatened that if the World Cup in Tyumen would not take place, we all could be held liable with our private assets". Mr Besseberg told the criminal prosecutors that it was not him who said that. Rather, as far as he could recall, "noted that there is a risk that in the event of a withdrawal the board members could be liable with their private assets".

ERC (2021) concluded that both Anders Besseberg and Nicole Resch improperly favored Russian interests, in breach of their duties to the IBU and to the sport.

Investigation Maturity Assessment

The IBU external review commission was chaired by Jonathan Taylor. He was a lawyer and a partner at the law firm Bird & Bird in the UK. He was head of the sports group in London, where he advised governing bodies, event organizers, and others active in the sector. He appeared regularly before the Court of Arbitration for Sport in Lausanne on doping and other matters. The review committee included Vincent Defrasne (former French biathlete), Christian Dorda (Austrian lawyer), Tanja Haug (German lawyer), Anja Martin (German lawyer), and Lauren Pagé (legal secretary). The mandate for the work by commission had three items:

1   Assist WADA and the criminal authorities with their investigations. Allegations that triggered the investigations: Anders Besseberg covered up anti-doping rule violations by Russian biathletes, with the assistance of Nicole

Resch; vote in favor of 2021 IBU world cup in Tyumen in Russia was corrupted. Wada handed over its investigation to the external review commission, with close cooperation ever since. The external review commission has provided support to Austrian criminal authorities and offered its support to Norwegian criminal authorities regarding biathlon investigations. The commission has also been in contact with the German and Austrian authorities involved in Operation Aderlass (blood doping in different sports).

2   Support the updating and strengthening of the IBU governance system in accordance with best practice. Next steps are criminal investigations in Austria and Norway that are ongoing. Austrian and Norwegian authorities have set up a joint investigation team that Europol has joined. At IBU, the Biathlon Integrity Unit will take over responsibility to support the criminal authorities as necessary from the IBU's side.

3   Determine whether anyone has a case to answer for breach of the IBU rules. Both substantive rules as well as procedural rules apply. Is there admissible and credible evidence that would be sufficient, if accepted by the hearing panel, to prove each element of the rule breach charged to the requisite standard (comfortable satisfaction/balance of probabilities)? In corruption cases, unlikely to be much direct evidence, but use indirect/circumstantial evidence and inferences that strand together to create a strong enough cable to sustain charges. The Biathlon Integrity Unit may bring charges before the CAS.

The commission compiled more than 70,000 documents and electronic files. They interviewed 60 people, and they accessed anti-doping evidence from criminal proceedings in Austria. The commission failed in interviewing Anders Besseberg as well as Nicole Resch. This is an obvious shortcoming in the investigation that reduces investigation report maturity, since Besseberg and Resch are important information sources as well as persons entitled to correct allegations against them and also to contradict conclusions drawn by examiners. While Besseberg denied cooperation with the examiners with an excuse that criminal investigations against him were pending in both Norway and Austria, Resch denied cooperation citing health-related reasons. An important skill for examiners is to approach suspects as information sources in a manner that makes potential interviewees motivated for questioning. Obviously, Taylor and his colleagues on the commission failed in their approach.

As argued by King (2020), an important element in determining investigation maturity is the applied maturity level of financial fraud investigative interviewing since interviewing is at the heart of the investigation process. The aim of an investigative interview is to elicit an accurate and detailed account of an incident for the purpose of reconstructing past events and sequences of events. An investigative interview should be carried out in a manner that does not place significant stress or strain on the interviewee.

Both Besseberg and Resch declined the opportunity to comment substantially on the allegations and evidence set out in the commission report. However, in accordance with Austrian law, the commission was granted access to the Austrian criminal investigation file and therefore had copies of the statements that Besseberg and Resch respectively made to the police and which they both referred the commission to as explanation of their respective positions. Such files represent secondary information compared to primary information in an interview, which reduces their value. The files are of less value also because the purpose of crime interviews is different from the purpose of rule-breaking interviews.

The investigation report seems biased toward wrongdoing. For example, examiners claim that all interpreters for Besseberg were prostitutes. While Besseberg had admitted to the police that he received the service of a prostitute on one single occasion between 2010 and 2014 in Moscow, he denied that interpreters were prostitutes.

Similarly, examiners jump to the conclusion of corruption (ERC, 2021: 68):

> Although the Commission has not found direct evidence that Mr Besseberg received cash bribes from Russian parties, there are significant apparent gaps in his explanation of his personal finances, as well as direct evidence that he received expensive hunting trips paid for by his Russian hosts.

In most civilized and democratic countries, this kind of evidence would not be sufficient to cause conviction in criminal court. Any doubt must always benefit defendants, and here there is doubt left for insights into the context. In civil court, where some apply the rule of more-likely than less-likely incident, with a probability of 50 percent and above being sufficient, the outcome might be different. The threshold of 50 percent should not be sufficient for IBU constitution, rules, and ethics. In fair proceedings, and especially in criminal courts, an incident should be documented beyond any reasonable doubt before conviction.

Based on these shortcomings, the IBU investigation is allocated at level 2 as a problem-oriented investigation in Figure 5.2. At this level, the investigation focused on issues that needed clarification. Examiners were looking for answers. Once examiners believed they had found answers, the investigation was terminated. The client had an unresolved problem, and the client regulated premises for the investigation. There was apparently no room for investigators to pursue other paths than those that addressed the predefined problem. Lawyers are typically in charge of investigations at this level, where they map the facts. They find out what happened and how it happened, but they are reluctant to find out why it happened.

The low level of investigative maturity contrasts reactions in the media and elsewhere. After the release of the report, nobody would have read the 220 pages but rather relied on the press conference presentation by commission leader Jonathan Taylor. Nobody questioned, for example, the commission's suggestion and indication that because the interpreters helping Besseberg understand Russian in talks in Russia were young Russian females, they were probably all prostitutes.

After the report, Besseberg was facing punishment from four different actors (Christiansen, 2021): (1) Austrian police, where doping in legal terms is considered fraud; (2) Norwegian police, where improper favors, gifts, and services are considered corruption; (3) IBU Integrity Group, where violations of rules and

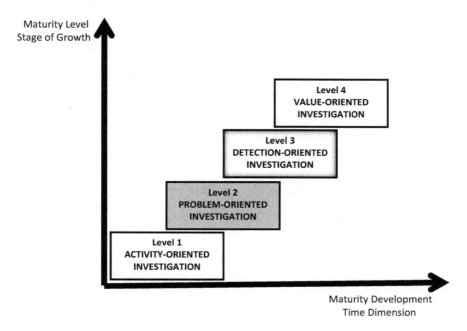

Figure 5.2 Maturity assessments for the ERC (2021) report

regulations can cause dismissal, and (4) Norwegian Sports Association, where violations of rules and regulations can cause dismissal as well as revocation of honorary award.

References

Benartzi, S., Beshears, J., Milkman, K.L., Sunstein, C.R., Thaler, R.H., Shankar, M., Tucker-Ray, W., Congdon, W.J. and Galing, S. (2017). Should governments invest more in nudging? *Psychological Science*, 28 (8), 1041–1055.

Bosse, D.A. and Phillips, R.A. (2016). Agency theory and bounded self-interest, *Academy of Management Review*, 41 (2), 276–297.

Chatterjee, A. and Pollock, T.G. (2017). Master of puppets: How narcissistic CEOs construct their professional worlds, *Academy of Management Review*, 42 (4), 703–725.

Chrisman, J.J., Chua, J.H., Kellermanns, F.W. and Chang, E.P.C. (2007). Are family managers agents or stewards? An exploratory study in privately held family firms, *Journal of Business Research*, 60 (10), 1030–1038.

Christiansen, A.K. (2021). Skiskyttertoppen risikerer straff fra 4 kanter (The Biathlon President risks Punishment from 4 sides), *Norwegian Daily Newspaper Aftenposten*, February 3, p. 39.

Christiansen, A.K., Friberg, J. and Asbjørnsen, M. (2021). IBU-topp om Besseberg: -Han var som en valgt konge (IBU top about Besseberg: -He was like an elected king), daily Norwegian newspaper *VG*, January 29, www.vg.no.

Crosina, E. and Pratt, M.G. (2019). Toward a model of organizational mourning: The case of former Lehman Brothers bankers, *Academy of Management Journal*, 62 (1), 66–98.

Eberl, P., Geiger, D. and Assländer, M.S. (2015). Repairing trust in an organization after integrity violations. The ambivalence of organizational rule adjustments, *Organization Studies*, 36 (9), 1205–35.

Ellingworth, J. and Dunbar, G. (2018). Biathlon president steps down after police raid in Austria, *AP News*, April 12, www.apnews.com.

ERC. (2021). *Final Report of the IBU External Review Commission, ERC (External Review Commission)*, International Biathlon Union, Austria, 28 January, p. 220.

Goldstraw-White, J. (2012). *White-Collar Crime: Accounts of Offending Behavior*, Palgrave Macmillan, London.

Gottfredson, M.R. and Hirschi, T. (1990). *A General Theory of Crime*, Stanford University Press, Stanford.

King, M. (2020). Private investigation into economic crime: Regulation of a multidisciplinary field, *Journal of Applied Security Research*, doi: 10.1080/19361610.2020.1832018.

Loyens, K., Claringbould, I., Heres-van Rossem, L. and Eekeren, Frank van. (2021). The social construction of integrity: A qualitative case study in Dutch football, *Sports in Society*, doi: 10.1080/17430437.2021.1877661.

Maslow, A.H. (1943). A theory of human motivation, *Psychological Review*, 50 (4), 370–396.

Panja, T. (2021). Hunting trips, sex and cash: How grooming biathlon's leader paid off for Russia – An investigation accuses biathlon's longtime president of accepting gifts from Russians and then doing the country's bidding as a doping scandal swirled, *The New York Times*, January 28, www.nytimes.com.

Patel, P.C. and Cooper, D. (2014). Structural power equality between family and nonfamily TMT members and the performance of family firms, *Academy of Management Journal*, 57 (6), 1624–1649.

Pelley, S. (2018). The Russian doping mastermind on the run, *CBS News*, February 11, www.cbsnews.com.

Pillay, S. and Kluvers, R. (2014). An institutional theory perspective on corruption: The case of a developing democracy, *Financial Accountability & Management*, 30 (1), 95–119.

Pontell, H.N., Black, W.K. and Geis, G. (2014). Too big to fail, too powerful to jail? On the absence of criminal prosecutions after the 2008 financial meltdown, *Crime, Law and Social Change*, 61 (1), 1–13.

Pratt, T.C. and Cullen, F.T. (2005). Assessing macro-level predictors and theories of crime: A meta-analysis, *Crime and Justice*, 32, 373–450.

Rooij, B. and Fine, A. (2020). Chapter 15: Preventing corporate crime from within: Compliance management, whistleblowing, and internal monitoring, in: Rorie, M.L. (editor), *The Handbook of White-Collar Crime*, Wiley & Sons, Hoboken, pp. 229–245.

Ruiz, R.R. and Schwirtz, M. (2016). Russian insider says state-run doping fueled Olympic gold, *The New York Times*, May 12, www.nytimes.com.

Sutherland, E.H. (1983). *White Collar Crime – The Uncut Version*, Yale University Press, New Haven.

Welsh, D.T., Ordonez, L.D., Snyder, D.G. and Christian, M.S. (2014). The slippery slope: How small ethical transgressions pave the way for larger future transgressions, *Journal of Applied Psychology*, 100 (1), 114–127.

Williams, J.W. (2008). The lessons of 'Enron' – Media accounts, corporate crimes, and financial markets, *Theoretical Criminology*, 12 (4), 471–499.

6 Foreign Aid Local Kickback Schemes

The methodological approach applied by corporate investigators in this case combined the collection of primary data with a review of secondary data. Primary data was collected almost exclusively during field research through semi-structured interviews, focus group discussions, a problem-description and solution-identification workshop, and observation. A shortcoming in their approach was the selection of experts and victims, but no offenders. Statements from experts, stakeholders, and especially victims can become biased in the direction of over-stating problems to make their statements more interesting. Offenders are an important source of information as they know more about motive, opportunity, and willingness.

A total of 402 interviewees were consulted during the review. However, their responses are in no way systematized and presented in the report. Rather, the information sources seem more or less ignored by reviewers.

Furthermore, the report itself is problematic, as it confuses findings with recommendations. Sometimes findings are presented, while suddenly normative statements about how it should be are in the text.

Corruption and other forms of financial crime are widespread in development cooperation and foreign aid by religious and other non-government organizations (Holland, 2020; Kleinfeld, 2020a, 2020b, 2020c, Kleinfeld and Dodds, 2020; Norad, 2020; Reuters, 2020). Henze et al. (2020) reviewed the exposure to corrupt practices in humanitarian aid implementation mechanisms in the Democratic Republic of Congo (DRC) after the humanitarian aid organization Mercy Corps noticed systemic and massive fraud in their development and aid projects.

Mercy Corps is a charity. The international non-government organization experienced a scam in the Democratic Republic of Congo. The scam involved corrupt aid workers, business owners, and community leaders (Kleinfeld, 2020a):

> Together they zeroed in on the humanitarian sector's flagship rapid response programmes – the main mechanism for helping displaced people in Congo, where hundreds of millions of dollars of foreign aid are spent every year.

The suspected fraud was concerned with corruption in foreign aid projects. Some $636,000 was lost by Mercy Corps and partners in just a few months. It was

DOI: 10.4324/9781003363934-7

estimated that the charity had lost $6 million in about two years. Kleinfeld (2020a) describes the modus operandi in some of the wrongdoing:

> When a conflict or natural disaster occurred, aid groups would receive reports from local community leaders that exaggerated the number of people who had fled their homes. Businesspeople would then pay kickbacks to corrupt aid workers to register hundreds of additional people for cash support who were not actually displaced. The merchants would then receive the aid payments and share with the local leaders. Of the nineteen Mercy Corps aid workers alleged to be involved in the scam, some were using the extra cash to buy new cars, Armani glasses, and iPhones, according to several of their colleagues who spoke to The New Humanitarian (TNH). One even started building a hotel, colleagues said.

UN agencies and aid groups in Congo created an anti-fraud task to conduct an operational review after the NGO Mercy Corps discovered the fraud scheme. The investigating team consisted of three international consultants and two Congolese researchers contracted by Adam Smith International, an aid consultancy. The anti-fraud task was funded with a grant from the UK government (Henze et al., 2020).

Motive Convenience Themes

Assuming that the allegations against local charity aid workers regarding corruption are correct, convenience themes can be identified for this group of offenders in the Mercy Corps case as illustrated in Figure 6.1. A potential motive is the need to restore the perception of equity and equality (Leigh et al., 2010). Being an aid worker is a job, but aid organizations tend to believe that their employees are idealists who do not necessarily need a decent salary.

The equity perspective suggests that an individual compares his or her work efforts to another person or group of persons chosen as reference. A situation evaluated as being without equity will initiate behavior to remove the feeling of discomfort (Huseman et al., 1987; Kamerdze et al., 2014; Martin and Peterson, 1987; Roehling et al., 2010).

The equity perspective is linked to the social exchange perspective, where there is a norm of reciprocity. Social exchange considers trusted employees as partners with the employer, who exchange valued contributions. The organization provides trusted employees material and socio-emotional rewards in exchange for their work effort and loyalty (Cropanzano and Mitchell, 2005). If a trusted employee perceives that the norm of reciprocity is violated, then the retaliation principle implies that the emphasis is placed both on the return of benefits and on the return of injuries (Caesens et al., 2019). Disloyalty is to defect from supporting someone. A trusted individual who feels mistreated might reciprocate by behaving in a manner that harms the source of this mistreatment (Gibney et al., 2009). Restoring the perception of equity and equality might also be a matter of responding to dehumanization, which is a feeling of being a tool or an instrument

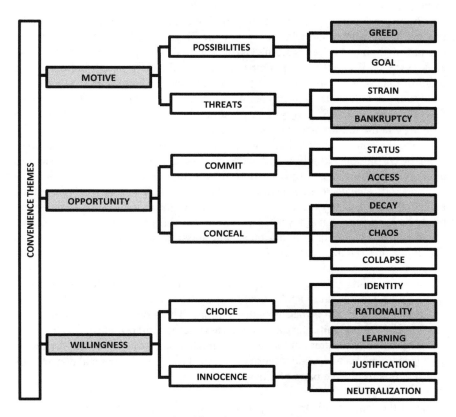

Figure 6.1 Convenience themes for aid workers at Mercy Corps

based on a perception of a treatment as lesser than or different from others (Bell and Khoury, 2016; Väyrynen and Laari-Salmela, 2015).

Foreign aid workers are paid very differently in various countries during their assignments, and financial compensation by placement in the field varies among non-government aid organizations and their countries of origin. International aid workers come from a number of different professions and areas of expertise, many work on contracts, and they do not form a homogeneous group where it is easy to say something about a common driving force for working in the foreign aid sector.

Along the convenience axis of motive-possibility-individual in Figure 6.1, some aid workers – especially locally employed people – use corrupt methods to cover their own basic needs. At the same time, it is important to understand that even the local employees who make good money beyond covering basic needs, by participating in or being a driving force of kickback systems revealed by the investigation, live in societies where the survival mindset is dominant. The situation is unpredictable, and poverty is everywhere. Obtaining as much as possible to be prepared for worse times is incorporated in peoples' minds. Aid workers who have the opportunity to move away from the local situation by changing jobs and travel elsewhere, and who do not use the illegitimate funds they acquire via corrupt methods to cover basic needs for survival, also participate in the kickback systems. Without their participation the fraud cannot be carried out in the order of magnitude revealed by the Mercy Corps and Adam Smith investigation. According to colleagues, employees who have been detected have spent money on, among other things, luxury goods and real estate that enabled them to climb higher up in the hierarchy of needs (Maslow, 1943).

Along the convenience axis of motive-threat-corporate in Figure 6.1, involvement in corruption is motivated by the need to avoid the threat of barriers to aid activities. By distancing oneself from or refusing to participate in the corrupt methods, one can create security problems for employees beyond oneself, be excluded from access to refugee camps and other locations, and be harmed and hindered in carrying out aid work. Threats can come from local leaders and others in positions of power or armed groups, and pressure can come from local actors and colleagues (Henze et al., 2020: 11):

> The day-to-day management of the coexistence with armed forces of widely varying natures and capabilities, ranging from the Monusco military component, Fardc and armed non-state groups. This normally implies complex systems of humanitarian diplomacy where access and presence often must be negotiated with interlocutors able to threaten organizations and individuals. This is an area where aid integrity is often at stake, with financial demands or requests to receive parts of the assistance.

Some of the most dominant convenience themes identified here in the financial motive dimension are:

- Rational self-interest: You become suspicious if you do not receive or participate, following pressure from local leaders, partners, or corrupt colleagues (Henze et al., 2020: 21):

  > One procurement officer described receiving unsolicited envelopes of money when collecting goods; when he refused the payment, the supplier explained that someone had to take the money to avoid problems with future purchases. While the money went to a colleague, he noted if you refuse, "People will look at you suspiciously".

- Management by objectives: Employees seek to demonstrate results to other units, donors, and sponsors in order to secure financial support and their own position. There is pressure from government donors and others concerning efficient implementation, rapid distribution of funds, quick results, and fixed project cycles. There is a great risk that goals are not reached, or not reached in time, when not participating in corruption. The goals thus justify the means.

- Avoidance of stress and strain: Failure to use common corrupt methods and shortcuts can lead to difficult and dangerous working conditions. Bribes can buy physical security for employees in unstable and dangerous environments (Henze et al., 2020: 12):

> Interviewees during this review have already pointed out that they are being pressured by armed movements to use paid escorts and that refusal can lead to security incidents. Furthermore, the new reality of community members asking for payment to provide information about humanitarian needs in their community, and new staff candidates expecting sky-high salaries is already affecting aid organizations in North Kivu.

- By refusing to participate, one can lose contracts and resources (Henze et al., 2020: 24):

> NGO actors provided examples of how reporting or refusing corrupt behavior can result in reprisals to their organization and ultimately hinder their ability to serve their communities. The most common form of reprisal described was being blocked from funding opportunities not only from the target aid organization but other agencies. Suppliers described similar experiences, which primarily involve failing to be considered for future contracts.

Therefore, the decision not to react negatively to corruption by blowing the whistle but rather adapt to the system and participate as a silent partner in crime makes the motive move from possibility to threat at the individual level.

Opportunity Convenience Themes

The organizational opportunity structure is mainly a result of trust-based management typically found in charities. Uygur (2020) studied fraud in the charity sector in England and Wales. He analyzed 42 fraud and 42 no-fraud charities. His findings suggest that excessive trust toward charities creates the opportunity for fraud to take place.

Trust is an important contribution to the convenience of white-collar crime. Dearden (2016) argues that violation of trust is at the core of white-collar crime opportunity. Trust implies that vulnerability is accepted based upon positive expectations of the motives and actions of another. Controlling a trusted person is often considered both unnecessary and a signal of mistrust. In many cultures, the opposite of showing trust is to monitor and question what a person is doing. For example, a board can tell management what to do, but they do not tell them how to do it. The board shows trust that management will do it in an acceptable manner. If the board would move from only controlling what management has done to how management did it, then it might be perceived as mistrust. Kim et al. (2009: 401) define trust as "a psychological state comprising the intention to accept vulnerability based on positive expectations of the intentions or behavior of another". The positive expectations can relate to what another does, how it is done, and when it is done. The positive expectations can relate to the reaction of another, where it is expected that the reaction will be understandable, acceptable, and favorable. Vulnerability means that trust can easily be violated without detection or correction of deviant behavior. Trust is associated with dependence and risk (Chan et al., 2020: 3):

> The trustor depends on something or someone (the trustee or object of trust), and there is a possibility that expectations or hopes will not be satisfied, and that things will go wrong. Trust is not absolute, but conditional and contextual.

Just like the concept of trust is relational, such that trust inherently requires a target, so too is the concept of felt trust relational. It is the felt trust that can influence an individual's tendency to crime, while it is the actual trust that is part of the opportunity structure for crime.

The gap between the two represents how accurately people understand others' perceptions of them (Campagna et al., 2020: 994):

> The concept of felt trust reflects what the more general interpersonal perception literature refers to as a dyadic meta-perception – one person's belief about the thought, attitude, or perception held by another person.

Control is replaced by trust in principal–agent relationships creating chaos in terms of guardianship as indicated in Figure 6.1. Chaos in humanitarian assistance often results from the pressure to act quickly in emergencies not only because human life may be at risk but also because fundraising and media pressure demand fast action (Maxwell et al., 2008: 8):

> Operations are sometimes conducted in completely unfamiliar environments or may involve massive scale-up (and speed-up) to existing programs. And the normal physical, administrative, legal, and financial infrastructure and services have often been substantially or entirely damaged or destroyed.

In the organizational opportunity dimension of convenience theory, the investigation by Henze et al. (2020) identified, made visible, and summarized the risks and weaknesses in the system that enable corruption to take place. The same risks constitute organizational opportunities for those who either want to exploit the system for their own gain or take the path of least resistance to achieve the organization's goals and respond to or avoid threats. Systemic weaknesses create organizational opportunities.

Along the convenience axis of opportunity-commit-access, there seem to be some convenience themes in particular:

- The employees are senior or independent persons in the situation they work: They are not necessarily senior in their own organizational structure, but senior people locally and thus persons with the opportunity to manage resources for the right and the wrong purposes. Often, they are in independent positions only loosely coupled to their employers with little or no peer control. Typically, the same field workers are responsible for allocating funds as well as for implementing projects. These are not always people with relevant socio-economic knowledge of the local area.

- The employees have access to systems and tools for information retrieval and storage that can be manipulated and modified during, afterward, or in the event of an audit. Some of the practices in Congo were referred to by sources as audit-safe that can withstand scrutiny by auditors without corruption being revealed (Henze et al., 2020: 36):

  > Most interviewees expect an internal audit to be able to discover ongoing fraud but some of the corrupt practices in DRC were described as "audit proof" in the sense that they presumably persisted undetected despite the operation of internal audits. This includes for example the addition of ghost beneficiaries who meet the criteria of eligibility or behaviors such as intimidation and coercion of colleagues or other stakeholders.

- The employees have access to strategic resources, such as colleagues working in the same system that has accepted the methods, local actors collaborating, and cash flows to be distributed as aid (Henze et al., 2020: 11):

  > The increased introduction of cash and voucher assistance in various forms. This ranges from financial transfers via banks and telephone networks to the use of electronic or paper-based vouchers, or, in some cases, direct cash distribution to recipients.

Along the convenience axis of opportunity-conceal-decay, there seem to be some convenience themes in particular:

- Social dissolution is where offenders take advantage of opportunities that arise due to lacking transparency. People are typically on short-term contracts, which make the situation confusing. Internal investigations are often abandoned if the suspected individual has left the organization, with little regard to whether the persona acted alone. A useful and operational definition of corruption is often lacking in non-governmental organizations. There is a lack of training in anti-corruption, where the focus of identity tends to be on victims rather than offenders. Training programs tend to be centralized, often digital and online, with lack of real cases involving current employees and executives. Trust comes at the expense of transparency and weaknesses in systems. Gaps in systems are not closed despite repeated abuses. When bad apples leave aid projects, there is no efforts to find out how they did it. Aid funds continue to be redirected and abused. Knowledge of gaps in systems and reporting routines are quickly learned by new project workers.
- Institutional decline can happen quickly as there is corruption in the local business community. Bribes and kickbacks of varying sizes and scope are

expected and normal. There is generally a confusing situation with great poverty, lack of control mechanisms, and a desire to help vulnerable people rather than to manage operations. There are typically conflicts in geographically remote locations. Little or no communication or coordination efforts occur around corruption issues due to organizations' fear of losing reputation, and the issue of corruption is sometimes considered a taboo topic.

- Concealing poor performance in aids projects based on fear of losing funding and reputation if disclosure should occur. Corrupt methods can enable continued financial support for non-performing aid organizations.

Corruption reports from government agencies for foreign aid tend to have stakeholders such as their own politicians as target groups and not people in the field. For example, the Norwegian agency for development cooperation publishes an annual report from their fraud and integrity unit. The report states that zero tolerance for corruption and other types of financial irregularities is a general principle of Norwegian development assistance (Norad, 2020). However, the agency suffers from the urgency of and distance from disaster areas. Rather than being specific about corruption incidents, the agency in their annual reports only presents statistics of whistleblowing cases, from which there is little to learn. The lack of knowledge of offenders and modes of crime makes it convenient for offenders to continue with corruption and other forms of financial crime.

Along the convenience axis of opportunity-conceal-chaos, there seem to be some convenience themes in particular:

- Principal–agent problems of deviance in objectives, preferences, risks, and information cause inability of principals to monitor activities. Senior people with extensive experience and employees with only loose ties to communities do not know what is going on locally (Henze et al., 2020: 26):

  This lack of experienced staff is explained by the often-cited general difficulty in attracting staff to work in remote and insecure areas. Furthermore, INGOs also regret a reduction in funding for these positions. Finally, aid organizations have different approaches to the ratio of national to international staff and the locations in the country where international staff will be based.

- There is seldom any presence of agencies for development cooperation who are supposed to do quality-assurance of foreign aid projects (Henze et al., 2020: 27):

  Issues related to effectively discovering corrupt practices during monitoring activities arose throughout discussions on project implementation, resource management, and local partnerships during this review. A common concern is ensuring the discovery of corruption while it is underway and taking corrective action, rather than long after the end of a project. Many monitoring activities do not appear to be leveraged to their full potential in supporting the discovery of red flags and/or corrupt practices, especially during needs assessment and program implementation.

- Activities occur in routines that are never questioned or reviewed because of the urgency in crisis situations (Henze et al., 2020: 37):

  The repetition of the displacements in some areas and homogeneity of ensuing responses creates pull and push factors. People learn that displacements induce access to resources and even begin to understand the most appropriate answers to questionnaires when seeking assistance. Once identified as recipients, people will wait for their assistance to arrive, when they may otherwise have been able to return home.

- Few or no random controls are taking place along the way that allow for detection (Henze et al., 2020: 27):

  The main risks identified during the monitoring stage are the manipulation of monitoring reports and the failure to detect corrupt practices through existing complaint mechanisms. Monitoring reports were reported as being manipulated by paying bribes to monitoring officers as part of efforts to hide corruption and/or poor project implementation, with aid staff who receive, and review monitoring reports being implicated.

- Stable routines with their gaps and shortcomings imply that people learn how the development assistance business responds to various messages. The predictability of responses can be exploited by deviant individuals (Henze et al., 2020: 2):

  Community participation across the entire project cycle appears largely passive. Contributing to this is a mutual lack of trust between recipient communities and aid organizations. Related to this, predefined response mechanisms, short-funding cycles and time pressure leave insufficient room to adequately consult with communities and plan appropriate responses, increasing the opportunity for decisions to be misappropriated and for corruption to occur.

- In an internal review, Mercy Corps interviewed more than 220 aid workers, local leaders, business owners, recipients of emergency aid, and members of armed groups. The common denominator they told was the main opportunity for corruption was rapid response programs. This frequently opens up for overpricing and cartel activity, which help maintain the level of corruption (Henze et al., 2020: 21):

  Interviews highlighted specific factors that facilitate the risk for corruption, which include the nature and scope of tender processes, collusion, and difficulties in reporting kickback demands and overall market conditions. Kickbacks may be solicited or unsolicited by the purchaser;

indeed, interviewees explained that suppliers expect to have to remit a commission or kickback as part of purchases or contracting even if not formally arranged.

- Lack of due diligence makes partners, participating organizations, and subcontractors appear to be legitimate. However, conflicts of interest and other problematic issues are seldom checked due to lack of time or resources. This happens despite the fact that low trust is often reported between aid organizations and local communities. In addition, there are low levels of transparency in and between organizations, and exposing corruption is considered an internal matter.
- Lack of understanding of local cultural and socio-economic factors is yet another theme in the chaos perspective (Henze et al., 2020: 16):

Lastly, the often-insufficient knowledge of the context, socio-economic factors, and local power dynamics further exacerbate the risks of corrupt practices.

- The risk of corruption is stated to be greater in projects that lack the support of the local population than those that are considered relevant (Henze et al., 2020: 3):

    Unfortunately, an overarching consequence of these dynamics is the lack of trust that persists between aid organizations, communities, and authorities, as well as among certain aid organizations. Moreover, how appropriate and relevant a program is, has a direct effect on exposure to risk of corruption, sexual exploitation, and abuse. In other words, if a program is not seen as relevant by the host community, there will be greater motivation to establish corrupt practices.

- Organizations lacking decentralized field offices are stated to have greater risk of pressure and corruption, and this can be partly explained by worse insight into local conditions and power dynamics (Henze et al., 2020: 26):

    KI of aid organizations with a tendency to have decentralized field offices report not only better oversight but also understanding of local power dynamics and socio-economic factors and therefore decreasing constant payment demands.

- Available tools against corruption are not adapted to the situation and local requirements. Ethical guidelines tend to be general in their formulations and considered practically not feasible in the field or are primarily adapted to donor requirements or the organization's country of origin. Guidelines for remotely managed projects are not implemented since efforts in Congo are not considered remotely managed, even though efforts have many of the characteristics of such projects (Henze et al., 2020: 17):

    Intervention methods appear to be largely predefined and are based on the type of funding provided as well as the preference and structure of the implementing organization. The question of access and security define generally "the when" rather than "the how" of intervention. Some interviewees point out that such decisions can be taken with insufficient knowledge of the field reality.

- Projects that are classified as remotely managed often have a more comprehensive risk assessment against corruption. There is little use of information technology that can help control functions. Some of the technology used is open to manipulation and not easily accessible when used in remote areas. Corruption risk is often not included in projects' risk assessments, and organizations do not share information and experience (Henze et al., 2020: 30):

> Specifically, evaluations should probe more deeply the quality control and compliance measures used by contracting agencies, particularly for managing risk of potential down-stream-corruption (. . .) Where the field presence of some donors is limited, donor coordination and information-sharing can be important.

Market failure is a relevant convenience theme but not considered dominant in terms of the convenience model applied to the Congo case. Without inadequate control mechanisms and the themes described earlier, cartel activities and risk in connection with obtaining tenders would not constitute an equally important source of corruption.

In addition to aid workers joining kickback schemes for their own financial gain, sometimes as a result of threats or to avoid adverse incidents, there is a danger associated with reporting suspicions of corruption for their own safety and security and their own position if they disturb the system or disrupt the corruption scheme (Henze et al., 2020: 24):

> Reporting of corrupt practices by NNGOs and suppliers is perceived to result in reprisals to their organization or business. As one aid actor explained, the overall climate in the DRC generally dissuades people from reporting corruption. NNGO actors provided examples of how reporting or refusing corrupt behavior can result in reprisals to their organization and ultimately hinder their ability to serve their communities. The most common form of reprisal described was being blocked from funding opportunities not only from the target aid organization but other agencies. Suppliers described similar experiences, which primarily involve failing to be considered for future contracts. Based on their experience, both NNGOs and suppliers described suspecting collusion amongst individuals within a group of agencies (most often citing UN agencies), who together will exclude NNGOs or suppliers who refuse, report or otherwise "disturb the system".

Therefore, whistleblowing is usually non-existent since whistleblowers tend to suffer retaliation and reprisals. In the minds of corrupt individuals, the lack of whistleblowing makes corruption convenient. Local employees experience threats to their own position in the local community if they attempt to blow the whistle on financial crime. In a society with strong social roles in hierarchies and networks, local survival mechanisms are crucial for the individual, and historically, standing up to authorities has often led to punishment in countries such as Congo (Henze et al., 2020: 13):

> Specifically, in a context where personal relations and networks of solidarity play a central role, the price of accusing an individual of corruption can be high. Indeed, some political elites at power during various periods have used anti-corruption rhetoric to cement control of state institutions and eliminate political rivals and opponents. With a socio-cultural history of deferring to authority and a battle for survival against a background of extreme poverty, the local population is routinely subjected to, tolerates or is complicit in corrupt practices, often with collective resignation. Civil society actors represent a constituency that actively speaks out against abuses, but with few resources and under constant threat from local authorities.

Aid workers are being relocated. An example is employees who wanted to report corruption during the Ebola epidemic (Freudenthal, 2020):

> Attempts by some whistle-blowers to denounce certain practices have at best been stifled and at worst have resulted in death, such as the case of Dr Richard Valery Mouzoko Kiboung, an epidemiologist who was killed on 19 April in a militia attack in Butembo while chairing a meeting with members of the Ebola response team.

Whistleblowing by notifying of perceived corruption is not only associated with personal risk for the whistleblower but there is also widespread failure of control in reporting corruption allegations. The practical aspects of notification make this an inaccessible avenue for many, as there might be no access to a phone, long waiting times and no one answering, or a long travel distance to executive offices. Whistleblowers are uncertain about which organization is the correct recipient, and many cannot read. There is also a cultural barrier against talking about difficult subjects with strangers. The routines are considered to be very ineffective, and complaints lead to nothing. Sometimes those who are accused of wrongdoing are put in a position of reviewing allegations against themselves. The current practice is that no one is punished. Corrupt aid workers can quit, notices against them are filed, and they go on to other jobs in other organizations without consequence (Henze et al., 2020: 29):

> Failures to follow-up with complaints perpetuate low levels of confidence in the aid sector, and little faith in the value of these mechanisms. Multiple interviewees expressed frustration with the absence of follow-up or sanctions once suspicions of fraud are reported. Some perceive aid organizations to be too concerned with protecting staff and/or the reputation of the organization,

while others stated that these mechanisms are ineffective because they operate through the very same actors involved in corruption.

In those rare cases where a government agency in a sponsoring nation detects fraud in projects they have financed, money transfers are stopped, contracts can be terminated, and all or part of the funds are demanded to be repaid. If and when the sum is returned, the case is considered closed. Organizations are expected to take care of their own corrupt employees, but in most instances, there are no individual consequences. There is thus a widespread perception that notification will normally lead to no change at all, and the whistleblowing itself may cause more harm that may outweigh the harm of the corrupt practice.

Willingness Convenience Themes

The final dimension in convenience theory is individual willingness for deviant behavior. Learning from others by differential association is a possible explanation as indicated in Figure 6.1. The differential association perspective suggests that offenders associate with those who agree with them and distance themselves from those who disagree. The choice of crime is thus caused by social learning from others with whom offenders associate (Sutherland, 1983).

The final dimension in convenience theory is personal willingness for deviant behavior. Rationality is one such convenience theme:

- Offenders weigh different considerations where local conditions are seen as requirements and local practices are seen as normal. The desire to achieve results exceeds the aversion to violating rules.
- Offenders defend the necessity by claiming that the security situation is such that corruption is the justifiable solution, that a quick response was crucial, and that it was necessary to resolve the situation and get things done or avoid serious threats.
- Offenders perceive deterrence as weak where detection risk is low, especially along the way, as controls occur long time after project completion. People have left when misconduct is detected. Nothing is detected during project implementation, and there is thus nothing suitable for correcting practice. Punishment is unlikely in cases of detection, and investigations are often shelved if the employee quits (Henze et al., 2020: 15):

  > While individuals might act alone, it is more likely that members of communities and/or authorities collude with the staff of aid organizations, who may initiate or be pressured to comply with such behavior.

- If someone is found responsible and guilty, the punishment is low. One can lose the job, but the lack of coordination and transparency, and the fact that foreign aid organizations are reluctant to talk about corruption in their own ranks means that many get jobs in other organizations in the same area or industry. There is very little risk of criminal conviction because of varying jurisdictions with low or very low law enforcement capabilities. Deterrence works poorly as a tool in all stages. Initially in an aid effort, there is urgency. During the aid effort, results have to be reported to secure continued funding. After completion of an aid effort, there is a new urgent project somewhere else on the globe.

Learning is another convenience theme in the dimension of personal willingness for deviant behavior:

- The perspective of slippery slope implies that aid workers are coming in to help adapt over time to what is considered normal in the local environment. Minor, insignificant violations initially are replaced over time by more serious and significant violations. The offender does not notice that the seriousness increases as the rise in misconduct occurs in very small steps. The offender participates in and supports the endemic corruption in the system. Emergency aid and long-term aid have become integral parts of the war economy in Congo and being present in a war zone requires adaptation to the local situation.
- The perspective of conformity pressure implies loyalty to both local colleagues and local partners, with an excuse that everyone else does it, and it is done everywhere (Henze et al., 2020: 19):

    As local actors explained, "in over 20 years of experience, it is frequent that a percentage is required to be paid to receive a contract as a local NGO". The amount most cited was 10–12 percent of the full contract amount, which is expected to be returned out of the initial disbursement.

- Obedience implies that employees protect each other and the local management, either out of loyalty or fear of disclosure consequences (Henze et al., 2020: 24):

    Pressure to add non-eligible persons can be exerted by local authorities (e.g., village chief, IDP President), armed groups, and host/resident community members. Equally, staff members of aid organizations might add non-eligible persons.

The convenience theme of innocence may not be defined as dominant in this case, as rational choices, assessments, and priorities explain how corruption in the development assistance system takes place in practice. The choice of offending is claimed to be based on realities locally and not based on naivety or ignorance. Thus, innocence seems to be no relevant convenience theme is this case.

Investigation Report Outcome

The report by Henze et al. (2020) is not examining the Mercy Corps scam. However, the investigation was triggered by the scam that raised the alarm about widespread corruption and problems with the systems designed to root it out. The two main objectives of the operational review were to:

- Produce an analysis of the risks related to corruption and fraud along all stages of the project cycle as well as supply chains common to the humanitarian sector in DRC that is also gender-sensitive and protection oriented.
- Examine which existing prevention and mitigation measures are effective and indispensable to curb the risks of corruption. Further identify potential solutions to decrease corruption risks within specific program modalities and emergency response systems. These would be actionable and affordable operational and strategic recommendations for the humanitarian community in DRC.

Reviewers found that corruption in DRC is endemic, and no sector in the country is immune from the diversity of modes with which corruption is practiced, including humanitarian aid. As well as routine bribery, corruption practices in the country extend to nepotism, abuses of budgets, embezzlement, and other forms of misappropriation. Nepotism is a form of favoritism that is granted to relatives.

Reviewers found that corruption starts early in the project cycle. When an aid project is designed, both people with good intentions and people with bad intentions present their views on the scope of the emerging project. At the next stage of resource mobilization, corruption is frequent when selecting partner organizations. Kickback payments, diversion, favoritism, and nepotism appear common (Henze et al., 2020: 22):

> Many interviewees cited recruitment of national staff as an entry point for corruption, though a few reported not having issues of this nature. Similar to kickbacks in procurement, there is a strong perception amongst interviewees that corruption in recruitment in the aid sector is the norm or at the very least expected. Corruption practices may be initiated from within the organization or by the jobseeker. Corruption practices described by interviewees included: actors internal to the organization will coach external candidates on how to orient their CVs in accordance with the terms of reference; insiders provide questions and answers prepared for job tests to their preferred candidates. This facilitation is rewarded with kickbacks by successful candidates. The practice of procuring sex in recruitment was acknowledged as widely practiced in the DRC.

At the next stage of project implementation, examiners found that the main risk in this area of the project cycle is the inclusion of persons who are not eligible to receive aid according to set criteria. This might be in addition to eligible recipients or instead of them.

The main risks identified during the monitoring stage are the manipulation of monitoring reports and the failure to detect wrongdoing through traditional complaint mechanisms. Potential whistleblowers can be bribed together with monitoring officers as part of efforts to hide poor project performance and corruption.

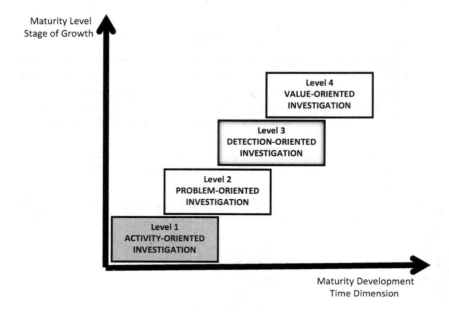

Figure 6.2 Maturity assessments for the Henze et al. (2020) report

Investigation Maturity Assessment

The most important criticism is that there is nothing previously unknown presented in the report. There is no reconstruction of past events and sequences of events. Therefore, there are no insights to be gained from the report by Henze et al. (2020). Accordingly, the investigation is at the lowest level of maturity as indicated in Figure 6.2. It was an activity-oriented investigation, where the reviewers interviewed a substantial number of people about well-known corrupt activities. The examiners made up their minds that the activities were reprehensible. They describe what is going on, but they do not reveal key enablers and barriers of corruption. They do not analyze causal relationships in terms of causes and effects of corruption.

Corrupt Aid Humanitarians

Mercy Corps presents itself as a global team of humanitarians working together on the front lines of today's biggest crises to create a future of possibilities, where everyone can prosper. The mission of the organization is to alleviate suffering, poverty, and oppression by helping people build secure, productive, and just communities. In more than 40 countries, over 5,000 team members work side by side with people living through poverty, disaster, and violent conflicts, according to the website www.mercycorps.org.

Fleckenstein and Bowes (2000) phrased the question: Do members often betray trust in terms of white-collar crime in religious institutions? Similarly, it is relevant to ask the question: Do humanitarians in global teams of humanitarians often betray trust in terms of financial crime in foreign aid organizations? According to Owens and Shores (2010), most white-collar crime incidents are exploitations of trust, where trust may originate from a shared religious identity between the victim and the perpetrator. Similarly, trust among aid workers may originate from a shared aid identity between the victim and the perpetrator. Shores (2010) phrased the questions: Are social religious networks an attractive arena for white-collar criminals? Is the morale of not acting illegally blinded from a chance when an attractive opportunity arises? While shared religious beliefs may lead to less acceptability of white-collar crime, the extent of opportunity for white-collar offenders may be greater in religious settings, mainly because of the trust-based culture found in religious institutions (Fleckenstein and Bowes, 2000; Owens and Shores, 2010; Shores, 2010).

Maxwell et al. (2008: 7) found that the majority of humanitarian aid workers interviewed across several aid agencies did not rate prevention of corruption particularly high on the priorities of the agency:

Corruption was generally perceived as an unavoidable part of the emergency environment, and the prevention of corruption was often considered as just another routine part of doing business. Whether this reflects justified confidence or complacency remains to be seen, but what is clear is that there are few incentives within the systems of reporting and accountability that currently exist for corruption to be uncovered or reported.

While the general perception of foreign aid workers might be individuals with high moral and ethical standards, the opposite can be the case. Both in recruiting aid workers and in learning from other aid workers, the tendency to accept law violations such as corruption benefiting oneself might be stronger than commonly known. While most studies focus on situational factors such as corrupt countries with no public authorities in place, the Mercy Corps scam documents that local executives from the aid organization can be involved in corruption as well, for example in the form of kickbacks.

References

Bell, C.M. and Khoury, C. (2016). Organizational powerlessness, dehumanization, and gendered effects of procedural justice, *Journal of Managerial Psychology*, 31, 570–585.

Caesens, G., Nguyen, N. and Stinglhamber, F. (2019). Abusive supervision and organizational dehumanization, *Journal of Business and Psychology*, 34, 709–728.

Campagna, R.L., Dirks, K.T., Knight, A.P., Crossley, C. and Robinson, S.L. (2020). On the relation between felt trust and actual trust: Examining pathways to and implications of leader trust meta-accuracy, *Journal of Applied Psychology*, 105 (9), 994–1012.

Chan, J., Logan, S. and Moses, L.B. (2020). Rules in information sharing for security, *Criminology & Criminal Justice*, pp. 1–19, doi: 10.1177/1748895820960199.

Cropanzano, R. and Mitchell, M.S. (2005). Social exchange theory: An interdisciplinary review, *Journal of Management*, 31 (6), 874–900.

Dearden, T.E. (2016). Trust: The unwritten cost of white-collar crime, *Journal of Financial Crime*, 23 (1), 87–101.

Fleckenstein, M.P. and Bowes, J.C. (2000). When trust is betrayed: Religious institutions and white collar crime, *Journal of Business Ethics*, 23 (1), 111–115.

Freudenthal, E. (2020). How "Ebola business" threatens aid operations in Congo, *The New Humanitarian*, June 18, www.thenewhumanitarian.org.

Gibney, R., Zagenczyk, T.J. and Masters, M.F. (2009). The negative aspects of social exchange: An introduction to perceived organizational obstruction, *Group and Organization Management*, 34, 665–697.

Henze, N., Grünewald, F. and Parmar, S. (2020). *Operational Review of Exposure to Corrupt Practices in Humanitarian Aid Implementation Mechanisms in the DRC*, Adam Smith International, London, p. 88.

Holland, H. (2020). Mercy Corps says more than $600,000 lost in Congo aid scam, *Nasdaq*, June 11, www.nasdaq.com.

Huseman, R.C., Hatfield, J.D. and Miles, E.W. (1987). A new perspective on equity theory: The equity sensitivity construct, *Academy of Management Review*, 12 (2), 222–234.

Kamerdze, S., Loughran, T., Paternoster, R. and Sohoni, T. (2014). The role of affect in intended rule breaking: Extending the rational choice perspective, *Journal of Research in Crime and Delinquency*, 51 (5), 620–654.

Kim, P.H., Dirks, K.T. and Cooper, C.D. (2009). The repair of trust: A dynamic bilateral perspective and multilevel conceptualization, *Academy of Management Review*, 34 (3), 401–422.

Kleinfeld, P. (2020a). Exclusive: Congo aid scam triggers sector-wide alarm, *The New Humanitarian*, June 11, www.thenewhumanitarian.org.

Kleinfeld, P. (2020b). UN wows to "maintain trust" in Congo aid effort after damning review leaked, *The New Humanitarian*, June 12, www.thenewhumanitarian.org.

Kleinfeld, P. (2020c). Language changed as leaked report into Congo aid corruption made public, *The New Humanitarian*, July 22, www.thenewhumanitarian.org.

Kleinfeld, P. and Dodds, P. (2020). Exclusive: Leaked review exposes scale of aid and abuse in Congo, *The New Humanitarian*, June 12, www.thenewhumanitarian.org.

Leigh, A.C., Foote, D.A., Clark, W.R. and Lewis, J.L. (2010). Equity sensitivity: A triadic measure and outcome/input perspectives, *Journal of Managerial Issues*, 22 (3), 286–305.

Martin, J. and Peterson, M.M. (1987). Two-tier wage structures: Implications for equity theory, *Academy of Management Journal*, 30 (2), 297–315.

Maslow, A.H. (1943). A theory of human motivation, *Psychological Review*, 50 (4), 370–396.

Maxwell, D., Walker, P., Church, C., Harvey, P., Savage, K. and Bailey, S. (2008). *Preventing Corruption in Humanitarian Assistance*, Transparency International, Berlin, www.transparency.org.

Norad. (2020). Annual report from the Fraud and integrity unit for 2019, *Norwegian Agency for Development Cooperation*, March 20, p. 17, www.norad.no.

Owens, E.G. and Shores, M. (2010). Informal networks and white collar crime: Evidence from the Madoff Scandal, *Social Science Research Network*, p. 54, www.pars.ssm.com.

Reuters. (2020). Mercy Corps says more than $600.000 lost in Congo aid scam, *Reuters*, June 11, www.reuters.com.

Roehling, M.V., Roehling, P. and Boswell, W.R. (2010). The potential role of organizational setting in creating 'entitled' employees: An investigation of the antecedents of equity sensitivity, *Employee Responsibilities & Rights Journal*, 22, 133–145.

Shores, M. (2010). *Informal Networks and White Collar Crime: An Extended Analysis of the Madoff Scandal*, www.dspace.library.cornell.edu.

Sutherland, E.H. (1983). *White Collar Crime – The Uncut Version*, Yale University Press, New Haven.

Uygur, S.A. (2020). *Fraud in the Charity Sector in England and Wales: Accountability and Stakeholder Oversight*, A thesis submitted in fulfillment of the requirement for the degree of Doctor of Philosophy of Royal Holloway, University of London, London.

Väyrynen, T. and Laari-Salmela, S. (2015). Men, mammals, or machines? Dehumanization embedded in organizational practices, *Journal of Business Ethics*, 147, 1–19.

7 Camaraderie in Peninsula Business

The peninsula of Hove is an extremely attractive resort for recreational purposes. There is strict national regulation that nobody can build anything in the 100-meter belt along the shoreline on the Norwegian coast. The shoreline is a limited public good that many nations protect and preserve for the recreation and benefit of all its inhabitants and visitors. Privatization of the shoreline, especially in the form of vacation resorts, is thus illegal. Nevertheless, some rich and mighty people are able to violate the law, and they build and expand their vacation homes on the shoreline. With the help of architects, builders, attorneys, and relationships to community planners, they use their resources to get what they want.

Hove is a peninsula outside the city of Arendal on the south coast of Norway. The peninsula is owned by the municipality of Arendal. In 2002, the municipality introduced a corporate structure for their ownership, where the corporation Hove should focus on recreational activities on the peninsula (Danielsen, 2020; Gulbrandsen, 2020; Haugerud and Fasting, 2020; Mehl, 2020a, 2020b; Sandberg, 2020a; Tvermyr, 2020).

Rumors of financial misconduct and business activities that did not promote but rather hindered recreational activities caused an investigation in 2019. Aust-Agder (2019) examined activities and Hove. Examiners interviewed people on the board and management people at Hove. They reviewed documents and visited areas on the peninsula that had been transformed into profitable business activities.

In addition, the law firm DLA Piper (2019) was hired to review the processes of developments on the Hove peninsula. They focused on several issues including Hove Camping, which had been established as a business enterprise on the peninsula. They suggested that all further developments on the peninsula should be terminated until a thorough review of legal arrangements at Hove had taken place. One of the legal issues was registered encumbrances on the peninsula (Sandefjord, 2020).

Sandberg versus Fasting

Two important public figures in the debate about Hove included Alf Sandberg and Jan Fasting. They presented their allegations against each other in the local newspaper Agderposten. Sandberg (2020a) argued that the purpose of a national park

DOI: 10.4324/9781003363934-8

is to take care of nature and not to make money. Haugerud and Fasting (2020) argued that the only reason Sandberg was so involved in the Hove case was that he lived there and wanted the peninsula for himself. The city councilor in Arendal supported Fasting's views (Danielsen, 2020: 16):

> The vast majority can see for themselves that Hove appears in far better con-dition than 20 years ago. Alf M. Sandberg seems to think that everything that has happened at Hove in recent years has been negative for both nature and the local population. Sandberg uses strong words such as corruption and camaraderie and goes so far as to suggest that the named persons have been involved in illegal activities. The councilor will strongly refute this. In the article, Sandberg goes one step further concerning who he criticizes in rela-tion to everything he has written before. Among others, he has mentioned Arendal Sailing Club, Hove's Friends, the Gjensidige Foundation, and the Church's City Mission, in addition to politicians and employees in the admin-istration. Everything seems to be based on Sandberg's understanding, that everyone who for one reason or another has taken a positive view of the municipal company Hove Operation and Development Company (HDU) and of Canvas Hove or the company's employees, are doing something that does not deserve the light of day.

Danielsen (2020) argued that everything that has taken place in recent years is positive, while Sandberg (2020a) argued that all incidents are negative. Danielsen (2020) emphasized that the nature areas are taken care of much better now that HDU, in collaboration with Hove's Friends, ensures access, that the trails get bet-ter year by year, and that Hove Camping has been opened up and made accessible to everyone after Canvas Hove took over.

Two more public figures were Kristina Stenlund Larsen and Tomm W. Chris-tiansen. They supported Alf Sandberg in his struggle to avoid business activities on the peninsula. They were both members of the municipal council in Arendal and switch political party in November 2020 to find more support for their views in the new party that they joined (Mehl, 2020b).

Offender Convenience Themes

Assuming that allegations of corruption and camaraderie are relevant in the case of Hove (Danielsen, 2020; Larsen, 2020; Sandberg, 2020a, 2020b, 2020c), con-venience theory can be applied to the Hove phenomenon in terms of motive, opportunity, and willingness as indicated in Figure 7.1.

The motive was corporate opportunities for an enterprise such as Hove Can-vas and Hove Developments to expand and make profits through mutual benefits in exchange relationships (Cropanzano and Mitchell, 2005; Huang and Knight, 2017; Pillay and Kluvers, 2014).

In the opportunity perspective, the companies had access to resources in the form of delegated authority from the municipality as well as funding from the

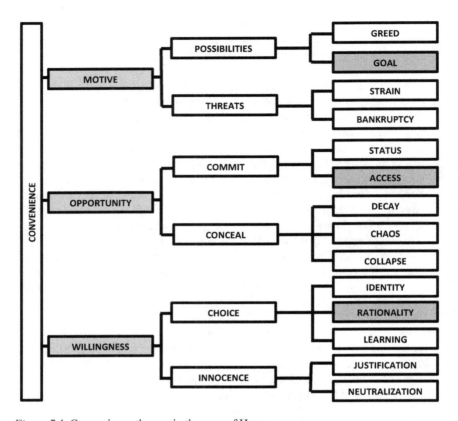

Figure 7.1 Convenience themes in the case of Hove

municipality (Adler and Kwon, 2002; Benson and Simpson, 2018; Cohen and Felson, 1979). Entrepreneurial individuals were associated with the enterprises that could create opportunities for deviant behavior (Ramoglou and Tsang, 2016). The entrepreneurship perspective emphasizes that entrepreneurs discover and create innovative and entrepreneurial opportunities (Smith, 2009; Tonoyan et al., 2010; Welter et al., 2017). Criminal entrepreneurs actualize illegal opportunities in the shadow economy (McElwee and Smith, 2015).

In the willingness dimension, there was a rational decision to explore and exploit the peninsula for corporate gain that might also benefit the municipality in the long run. There were perceptions of benefits exceeding costs (Pratt and Cullen, 2005), and behavioral reinforcement of deviance occurred over time (Benartzi et al., 2017). There were no perceived deterrence effect (Comey, 2009), and developers were sensation seeking to experience adventure (Craig and Piquero, 2017).

Fraud Investigation Outcome

Auditors at Aust-Agder (2019) were to review agreements and decision processes related to the Hove case. In particular, they were to review whether Hove Operation and Development Company (HDU), wholly owned by the municipality, were following intentions and guidelines from the politicians. The auditors found that the owner, through the development plan and HDU's articles of association, tells HDU to operate like a regular business. Based on the activities HDU refers to through its annual reports from establishment until today, the auditors consider that the HDU board's self-assessment of being in line with expectations is not unreasonable.

The auditors also found no basis for assessing that the activities which appear from the HDU's annual reports are not in line with the assumptions contained in the HDU's management documents. However, the auditors considered that the goals for HDU which appear in the development plan and the goals in the company-specific ownership strategy from 2018 might be perceived as different from each other. This seemed particularly challenging when the development plan as the most central management document was adopted in 2001. This discrepancy could create unclear expectations for the HDU's activities, both from the ownership body and from the public in general.

The auditors assessed that there were in principle no restrictions in the board's authority either under the statutes of the association or the HDU act to make such purchases or enter into such agreements that HDU had made DHT, Lowcamp, and Canvas Hove. Even if the sale of some properties in the main area of the peninsula were canceled, the fact that the HDU had the authority to act as seller in the procurement, at the same time as Arendal municipality was actually the legal owner, could cast doubt on whether there was sufficient independence between HDU and owner.

Based on the criteria used by the audit, the auditors considered that HDU in connection with the aforementioned contractual processes was covered by the public access to information act and the public procurement act. Nor could the auditors see that there was illegal public funding related to the processes. However, the auditors considered that the planned sale of property from HDU to Canvas Hove, which was canceled, might have led to a different conclusion.

The auditors criticize that the Hove processes have not ensured openness, transparency, and publicity in line with municipality's ownership principle. By choosing to present various business plans to political and political bodies rather than to HDU bodies, the process caused to blur the public's perceptions of the boundaries between the municipality, where politicians rule the scene, and HDU, where business people rule the scene. This blurring might in turn create different expectations and unclear understandings both at the owner's municipal council and among inhabitants concerning HDU's independence in relation to the municipality.

Investigation Report Maturity

Auditors from Aust-Agder (2019) based their conclusions mainly on reviews of documents. They had an initial meeting with the chairperson and the chief executive at the HDU to gain an overview of available documentation. The auditors conducted no further interviews and used no other information sources than documents. Larsen (2020: 21) characterized the audit in her remarks:

> The audit report's inadequate evaluation of the process is used to claim that illegalities have not occurred. I argue that the audit report, in addition to incorrect application of the law and a deficient document base, has been founded on incorrect assumptions. The audit believes that HDU was in its right to develop the campsite on Hove, without affecting the encumbrances that explain the Hove peninsula's role and purpose.
>
> If the councilor continues to claim that the liens have been automatically reset when two property numbers at Hove were merged, then it is clearly in violation of the book on real estate law. The councilor's non-answer to Sandberg's relevant questions is not trustworthy. Trust can also not be restored by Tvermyr, Koren Pedersen or Stalleland's attempts to obscure what the main issue is all about.

Since most relevant information is in the heads of individuals who were involved in the processes, which was ignored by the auditors, the investigation report is located at the lowest maturity level as indicated in Figure 7.2.

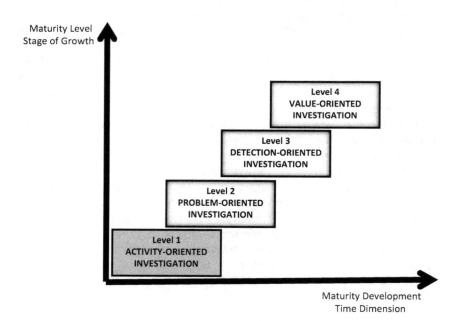

Figure 7.2 Maturity level for the Aust-Agder (2019) investigation at Hove

Environmental Crime Allegations

Local politicians who wanted to preserve Hove peninsula argued that the peninsula was suffering from environmental crime by Canvas Hove and others, including dredging, sand filling, various buildings, and piers for boats (Ellingsen, 2020). Environmental harm and crime have received increased attention in recent years (Böhm, 2020; Gibbs and Boratto, 2017; Huisman and Erp, 2013; Lynch, 2020). Traditionally, white-collar crime cases have focused on non-violent financial crime. Recently, with increased environmentalism, researchers have focused on white-collar crime that can impose physical harm on people (Benson and Simpson, 2018: 129):

> These offenses are potentially much more serious in that they can and often do impose physical costs on individuals. This is not to say that the perpetrators deliberately set out to harm other people. They do not. The physical harms that they cause are unintended in the sense that they are not what the offender is trying to achieve. The motivation for the offense is not to impose harm on others but rather to gain a financial advantage.

For example, Wingerde and Lord (2020: 478) argue that the waste industry is a criminogenic industry that is vulnerable to environmental crime:

> First, this concerns the waste product itself. Waste is a product that has a negative value attached to it. . . . Second, the industry in itself also has some characteristics that are considered to be criminogenic.

A convicted white-collar offender presented in the following had her summerhouse close to the city of Grimstad, which is north of the city of Arendal. She is the first convicted environmental criminal in Norway for violations of the 100-meter belt regulations. Agder court of appeals wrote in its verdict (Aust-Agder, 2019: 20):

> There is a strong development pressure in the beach zone and individuals spend very high amounts of money to gain access to this limited good. Effective enforcement of established rules and guidelines is therefore necessary, and material and serious violations must result in tangible reactions. Often, purely economic reactions in terms of fines will have less deterrent effect.

This is interesting, as imposing fines so far was the rule in Norway. However, rich people have no problems paying substantial fines, and then they tend to continue as before. Going to jail is another matter (Dhami, 2007; Logan, 2015; Logan et al., 2019; Stadler et al., 2013). The white-collar crime convict, the rich heir Hanne Madsen, received a verdict of 45 days in jail by the court.

Hanne Madsen had taken over a business enterprise from her father. She had also inherited the family summerhouse. She bought a property behind the summerhouse, which was within the 100-meter belt as well. When acquiring the land, she told the municipality that she would do nothing to it, so that the public could continue walking across into a public beach nearby. However, few years later, she had expanded the summerhouse and an annex. She had built an underground hallway from the summerhouse to the annex. On the acquired property, she built a tennis court. The leading Norwegian business newspaper *Dagens Næringsliv* wrote in its editorial (DN, 2019: 2):

> This case is particularly serious, therefore a severe punishment. The violations of the Planning and Building Act included, among other things, blasting and construction of a 500 square meter concrete deck with artificial turf for a tennis court at the newly expanded summerhouse. A violation the municipality found that the owner had not even attempted or bothered to apply for a permit. The summerhouse owner has defended herself with a lack of knowledge of the illegal construction work. That may well be the case, but ignorance does not relieve guilt in the opinion of the law.

In court, Hanne Madsen presented herself almost as a victim of law violations, as she had trusted the architect, the attorney, the carpenter, the plumber, and all others involved in developing her vacation resort. Being a victim is a neutralization technique where the offender has a perception of victimization by an incident where others have ruined her life. The perception of being a victim increases as the media pressure and coverage become more personal. It is thus not at all obvious that she sees herself as a white-collar offender who has committed an environmental crime.

References

Adler, P.S. and Kwon, S.W. (2002). Social capital: Prospects for a new concept, *Academy of Management Review*, 27 (1), 17–40.

Aust-Agder. (2019). *Avtaler og beslutningsprosesser knyttet til Hove-saken (Agreements and decision-making processes related to the Hove case)*, audit firm Aust-Agder Revisjon, Arendal, September, p. 61.

Benartzi, S., Beshears, J., Milkman, K.L., Sunstein, C.R., Thaler, R.H., Shankar, M., Tucker-Ray, W., Congdon, W.J. and Galing, S. (2017). Should governments invest more in nudging? *Psychological Science*, 28 (8), 1041–1055.

Benson, M.L. and Simpson, S.S. (2018). *White-Collar Crime: An Opportunity Perspective*, (3rd Edition), Routledge, New York,.

Böhm, M.L. (2020). Criminal business relationships between commodity regions and industrialized countries: The hard road from raw material to new technology, *Journal of White Collar and Corporate Crime*, 1 (1), 34–49.

Cohen, L.E. and Felson, M. (1979). Social change and crime rate trends: A routine activity approach. *American Sociological Review*, 44, 588–608.

Comey, J.B. (2009). Go directly to prison: White collar sentencing after the Sarbanes-Oxley act, *Harvard Law Review*, 122, 1728–1749.

Craig, J.M. and Piquero, N.L. (2017). Sensational offending: An application of sensation seeking to white-collar and conventional crimes, *Crime & Delinquency*, 63 (11), 1363–1382.

Cropanzano, R. and Mitchell, M.S. (2005). Social exchange theory: An interdisciplinary review, *Journal of Management*, 31 (6), 874–900.

Danielsen, H. (2020). De aller fleste kan selv se at Hove fremstår i en langt bedre forfatning enn for 20 år siden (The vast majority can see for themselves that Hove appears in a far better condition than 20 years ago), *Local Norwegian Newspaper Agderposten*, October 24, p. 16.

Dhami, M.K. (2007). White-collar prisoners' perceptions of audience reaction, *Deviant Behavior*, 28, 57–77.

DLA Piper. (2019). *Vurdering av prosess i forbindelse med utvikling av Hoveodden (Assessment of the process in connection with the development of the Hove peninsula)*, law firm DLA Piper, March 28, Oslo, p. 13.

DN. (2019). Ny dom kan skremme pengesterke hytteeiere fra ulovlig bygging – Ny dom gir god hjelp til kommuner som vil stoppe ulovlige byggearbeider i strandsonen (New court sentence might scare money-rich cottage owners from illegal construction building – New court sentence provides good help to municipalities who want to stop illegal construction work in the beach zone), *Daily Norwegian Business Newspaper Dagens Næringsliv*, September 21, p. 2.

Ellingsen, T. (2020). Fikk svar fem måneder etter alt var ferdig (Received an answer five months after everything was done), *Local Norwegian Newspaper Agderposten*, November 18, pp. 2–3.

Gibbs, C. and Boratto, R. (2017). Environmental crime, in: Pontell, H.N. (editor), *Oxford Encyclopedia of Criminology and Criminal Justice*, oxfordre.com/criminology.

Gulbrandsen, J.M. (2020). "Har aldri opplevd at man uttaler og får publisert anklager og spekulasjoner uten begrunnelse" ("Have never experienced that statements and accusations are made and published without justification"), *Daily Local Newspaper Agderposten*, October 30, pp. 18–19.

Haugerud, V.T. and Fasting, J. (2020). En suppe av rykter, fakta og meninger (A soup of rumors, facts and opinions), *Local Norwegian Newspaper Agderposten*, October 23, p. 17.

Huang, L. and Knight, A.P. (2017). Resources and relationships in entrepreneurship: An exchange theory of the development and effects of the entrepreneur-investor relationship, *Academy of Management Review*, 42 (1), 80–102.

Huisman, W. and Erp, J. (2013). Opportunities for environmental crime, *British Journal of Criminology*, 53, 1178–1200.

Larsen, K.S. (2020). Å sette Arendal på kartet (To put Arendal on the map), *Local Norwegian Newspaper Agderposten*, October 29, p. 21.

Logan, M.W. (2015). *Coping with Imprisonment: Testing the Special Sensitivity Hypothesis for White-Collar Offenders*. A dissertation to the Graduate School of the University of Cincinnati in partial fulfillment of the requirements for the degree of Doctor of Philosophy in the Department of Criminal Justice, Cincinnati, OH.

Logan, M.W., Morgan, M.A., Benson, M.L. and Cullen, F.T. (2019). Coping with imprisonment: Testing the special sensitivity hypothesis for white-collar offenders, *Justice Quarterly*, 36 (2), 225–254.

Lynch, M.J. (2020). Green criminology and environmental crime: Criminology that matters in the age of global ecological collapse, *Journal of White Collar and Corporate Crime*, 1 (1), 50–61.

McElwee, G. and Smith, R. (2015). Towards a nuanced typology of illegal entrepreneurship: A theoretical and conceptual overview, in: McElwee, G. and Smith, R. (editors), *Exploring Criminal and Illegal Enterprise: New Perspectives on Research, Policy &*

Practice: Contemporary Issues in Entrepreneurship Research Volume 5, Emerald, Bingley.

Mehl, S.H. (2020a). Gir en halv million til HDU i koronastøtte (Gives half a million to HDU as corona support), *Daily Local Norwegian Newspaper Agderposten*, October 17, p. 8.

Mehl, S.H. (2020b). Hove-utbrytere har meldt seg inn i Sp (Hove-leavers have signed up for the center party), *Daily Local Norwegian Newspaper Agderposten*, November 14, p. 17.

Pillay, S. and Kluvers, R. (2014). An institutional theory perspective on corruption: The case of a developing democracy, *Financial Accountability & Management*, 30 (1), 95–119.

Pratt, T.C. and Cullen, F.T. (2005). Assessing macro-level predictors and theories of crime: A meta-analysis, *Crime and Justice*, 32, 373–450.

Ramoglou, S. and Tsang, E.W.K. (2016). A realist perspective of entrepreneurship: Opportunities as propensities, *Academy of Management Review*, 41, 410–434.

Sandberg, A.M. (2020a). Hove-spørsmål – mens vi venter på reguleringsplanen (Hove questions – while we are waiting for the regulation plan), *Local Norwegian Newspaper Agderposten*, October 23, p. 17.

Sandberg, A.M. (2020b). Jeg bruker sterke ord for å bli hørt (I use strong words to get heard), *Local Norwegian Newspaper Agderposten*, October 29, p. 20.

Sandberg, A.M. (2020c). Folk i offentlige roller vil ha skryt fremfor kritikk – men jeg kan ikke skryte av dere i Hove-saken (People in public roles would like praise rather than criticism – but I cannot praise you in the Hove case), *Local Norwegian Newspaper Agderposten*, November 3, p. 19.

Sandefjord. (2020). *Viktige tinglyste heftelser på eiendommen Hove-odden i Arendal (Important registered encumbrances on the Hove peninsula)*, law firm Sandefjord, February 1, Sandefjord, Norway, p. 4.

Smith, R. (2009). Understanding entrepreneurial behavior in organized criminals, *Journal of Enterprising Communities: People and Places in the Global Economy*, 3 (3), 256–268.

Stadler, W.A., Benson, M.L. and Cullen, E.T. (2013). Revisiting the special sensitivity hypothesis: The prison experience of white-collar inmates, *Justice Quarterly*, 30 (6), 1090–1114.

Tonoyan, V., Strohmeyer, R., Habib, M. and Perlitz, M. (2010). Corruption and entrepreneurship: How formal and informal institutions shape small firm behavior in transition and mature market economies, *Entrepreneurship: Theory & Practice*, 34 (5), 803–831.

Tvermyr, O.G. (2020). Vi må snakke hverandre og kommunen opp. Sandberg bedriver det stikk motsatte (We have to talk each other and the municipality up. Sandberg does the exact opposite), *Daily Local Newspaper Agderposten*, October 28, p. 17.

Welter, F., Baker, T., Audretsch, D.B. and Gartner, W.B. (2017). Everyday entrepreneurship: A call for entrepreneurship research to embrace entrepreneurial diversity, *Entrepreneurship: Theory and Practice*, 41 (3), 323–347.

Wingerde, K. and Lord, N. (2020). Chapter 29: The elusiveness of white-collar and corporate crime in a globalized economy, in: Rorie, M.L. (editor), *The Handbook of White-Collar Crime*, Wiley & Sons, Hoboken, p. 469–483.

8 Mayor Reprisal against Employee

The mayor in the municipality of Ørland in the middle of Norway was in 2020 accused of violating the Norwegian working environment act. Local media reported that a midwife had blown the whistle on the mayor. Hilde Kristin Sandvik was the accuser, while Tom Myrvold was the accused. Sandvik was a midwife in the municipality of Ørland, while Myrvold was the mayor. Sandvik and Myrvold had relationships at several levels: personal, political, and professional. The personal relationship was a love affair that lasted for some months following a veteran championship in handball for both women and men. The political relationship was a membership in the same conservative party, where they both had positions in the municipal council at Ørland. The professional relationship was his role as mayor and her role as employed midwife in the municipality. In 2022, Tom Myrvold had to resign from the position of mayor in the municipality of Ørland. The reason was plagiarism, where he had taken text from other persons into his own articles without proper citations.

Law firm Simonsen (2020) was hired to investigate the allegations on behalf of the councilor in the municipality. Local media reported after presentation of the investigation report: "Delivered notice against Tom Myrvold: The municipality's lawyer believes the mayor acted unfortunate" (Fosna, 2020).

When Myrvold dropped the sexual relationship with Sandvik, he entered into a sexual relationship with another midwife. At the same time, he asked municipal employees to monitor Sandvik's behavior and check her working hours. When Sandvik applied for leave of absence to get away from the municipality for a while, he interfered by questioning whether she could leave without any replacement being recruited.

The investigation was carried out by lawyers Marianne Kartum and Nils Håkon Risberg at the law firm Simonsen Vogt Wiig in the city of Trondheim in Norway. Kartum specialized in labor law, compliance, risk assessment, procedures, and solutions. Risberg specialized in restructuring, insolvency, compliance, risk assessment, tax, and fees.

DOI: 10.4324/9781003363934-9

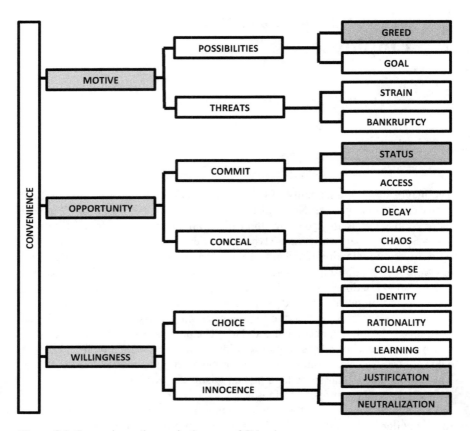

Figure 8.1 Convenience themes in the case of Ørland

Offender Convenience Themes

In this case study, there is no financial benefit in the motive dimension. Nevertheless, the theory of convenience can be applied to the case when assuming that Myrvold explored and exploited his position as mayor for benefits other than financial gain. As illustrated in Figure 8.1, Tom Myrvold's motive was individual possibilities. He climbed the hierarchy of needs for status and success (Maslow, 1943) and wanted to satisfy the need for acclaim as a narcissist (Chatterjee and Pollock, 2017).

In the opportunity dimension of convenience theory, he enjoyed a very high status. He was a trained air force pilot and had a very high rank in the Norwegian armed forces. The main air force base in Norway is located in the municipality of Ørland where fighter planes such as F45 are stationed. High social status in privileged positions creates power inequality compared to those without any or lower status in their positions. Status is an individual's social rank within a formal or informal hierarchy or the person's relative standing along a valued social dimension. Status is the extent to which an individual is respected and admired by others, and status is the outcome of a subjective assessment process (McClean et al., 2018). High-status individuals enjoy greater respect and deference from, as well as power and influence over, those who are positioned lower in the social hierarchy (Kakkar et al., 2020: 532):

> Status is a property that rests in the eyes of others and is conferred to individuals who are deemed to have a higher rank or social standing in a pecking order based on a mutually valued set of social attributes. Higher social status or rank grants its holder a host of tangible benefits in both professional and personal domains. For instance, high-status actors are sought by groups for advice, are paid higher, receive unsolicited help, and are credited disproportionately in joint tasks. In innumerable ways, our social ecosystem consistently rewards those with high status.

In the willingness dimension of convenience theory, Myrvold might justify his actions by claiming to be entitled to involve himself in municipal affairs and claiming to be entitled to a private life of his choice. As suggested by Nichol (2019), empathy deficit can imply that the offender possesses a sense of entitlement. The offender finds one's own actions morally justifiable (Schnatterly, et al., 2018). By neutralizing potential guilt feelings, an offender does not feel accountable for, ashamed of, or responsible for negative consequences (Chen and Moosmayer, 2020).

Deviance Investigation Outcome

Examiners Kartum and Risberg at Simonsen (2020) addressed four issues emphasized by whistleblower Sandvik against Myrvold. Point 1 in the notice concerns Sandvik's temporal leave application. It had to be assessed whether there were aspects of the employer's or the mayor's behaviors and possible involvement in Sandvik's application for temporal leave from the municipal position of midwife that deserved criticism. Examiners needed to look for a basis for establishing that there was a breach of provisions in the working environment act, internal guidelines, or other matters covered by the employer's liability. Midwife Sandvik claimed that Mayor Myrvold at the end of 2016 and early 2017 got involved and raised questions about Sandvik's application for leave from the position in Ørland municipality. Examiners suggest that one of the mayor's tasks is to be a link between politics and administration. In light of this, a mayor must be able to have an open dialogue with the councilor and the municipal chiefs related to the follow-up and implementation of political decisions. However, the mayor should not interfere in personnel matters. The employment responsibility is assigned to the councilor. Examiners found no written documentation of Myrvold's direct involvement in Sandvik's application. Based on these perspectives, examiners found no evidence to suggest that Myrvold had been directly involved in Sandvik's leave application.

Point 2 in the notice concerns interference in the way Sandvik carried out work in 2018. It had to be assessed whether there were aspects of the employer's or the mayor's behaviors and possible involvement in the way midwife Sandvik carried out her job that deserved criticism. Examiners needed again to look for a basis for establishing that there was a breach of provisions in the working environment act, internal guidelines, or other matters covered by the employer's liability. Sandvik had explained that her closest manager, Karin Stærseth, informed Sandvik in early 2018 that Myrvold, via municipal manager Ervik, had made a request about how Sandvik performed her work as a midwife. Størseth has in an interview confirmed that she raised this issue with Sandvik, but she could not remember for sure what caused it. She was quite certain that the inquiry came via Marit Ervik from Tom Myrvold. Marit Ervik did not specifically remember that Tom Myrvold contacted her in 2018 with an inquiry about how Sandvik performed her work. However, she could not rule out such an inquiry had been made, and her follow-up would then have been that she took this matter further with Karin Størseth. Examiners found evidence that Myrvold's involvement in the midwifery service, by leading individuals in the municipal administration, had in fact been perceived as unfortunate and untidy. This negative reaction was based partly on the fact that Sandvik was the only one employed in the midwife service and that she would consequently very easily be identified with the performance in the service. Nevertheless, examiners claim they did not find any evidentiary basis for ascertaining that Myrvold had directly interfered with the way Sandvik carried out her work.

Point 3 in the notice concerns the liberal party's newspaper article. Both Sandvik and Myrvold belonged to the liberal party. The newspaper article expressed concern about the midwife service in the municipality. Some of the information in the article was leaked to the author of the article. Sandvik was convinced that the leakage came from Myrvold. However, examiners found no evidence of such wrongdoing by the mayor.

Point 4 in the notice concerns her sick leave in 2019. The sick leave was caused by psychosocial conditions at work. Sandvik accused Myrvold of having contributed to the deterioration in her psychosocial working environment. Examiners found no evidence that could support Sandvik's accusation against Myrvold.

Simonsen (2020: 36) thus draws the following conclusion:

> After an overall assessment of Hilde Kristin Sandvik's psychosocial work environment, our conclusion is that there is no evidentiary basis for concluding that there is a breach of the Work Environment Act § 4–1 compared § 4–3. Furthermore, it is our conclusion that Tom Myrvold's involvement in the midwifery service in Ørland municipality is, in isolation, within what he, as mayor, can discuss with the head of administration and the municipal manager. Finally, it is our conclusion that there is neither a breach of the impartiality provisions in the Public Administration Act nor the municipality's ethical guidelines. It is nevertheless our assessment that Tom Myrvold's extensive involvement in the midwifery service has appeared to be unfortunate. It is our recommendation that Tom Myrvold be communicated the

conclusions in this report. Beyond this, in our opinion, there is no need to implement further measures.

Investigation Report Maturity

The evaluation of an investigation might apply as core criteria the extent of feasible strategies in the examination, such as knowledge, information, configuration, method, and system strategies:

- Knowledge strategy: Only legal knowledge; no knowledge in psychology, sociology, organization, or management.
- Information strategy: Random chat-like interviews without focus. Random emails reviewed. Very few sources of information, and they were used randomly.
- Configuration strategy: Sequential check of information in relation to notices, reports, and paragraphs (value chain), no iterative search for the essence of the issues (value shop).
- Method strategy: Lack of explicit interpretation of interviews, jumps from interview quotes to examination conclusions. Interpretation should involve a systematic approach in the form of content analysis.
- System strategy: Not used digital aids or access to computer information systems, neither to search for information nor to analyze findings and visualize them.

Furthermore, if focused, the examiners should have addressed the following questions: Is Myrvold an abuser? Is Sandvik a victim? If so, is it crime? Crime is characterized by the fact that (1) it is wrong to do, and (2) it should be punished. There was asymmetry in the relationship between Myrvold and Sandvik. Myrvold exploits his position, first in relation to one midwife, then in relation to another midwife. So he is an abuser. Sandvik was subjected to surveillance by Myrvold. So she is a victim. What Myrvold did is wrong to do. It should be punished, for example, by a financial compensation and reparation of several hundred thousand kroner from Myrvold to Sandvik.

Based on this evaluation, the investigation by Simonsen (2020) is assigned level 2 of problem-oriented investigation in Figure 8.2. The investigation focused on activities that may have been carried out in a reprehensible manner. The examiners looked for activities and prepared descriptions of these. They broke down the investigation into single issues from the whistleblowers. The examiners never attempted to understand the psychological, sociological, or criminological issues in the case. They only conducted a fragmented legal assessment.

A psychology professor commented saying he could "well understand that at a psychological level it feels like there is retaliation and sanctions" (Holseth, 2020):

- They have talked to a large number of people and tried to put this information into a legal framework. The question is whether they have gone far enough into the matter from a psychological point of view, says Berge Matthiesen.

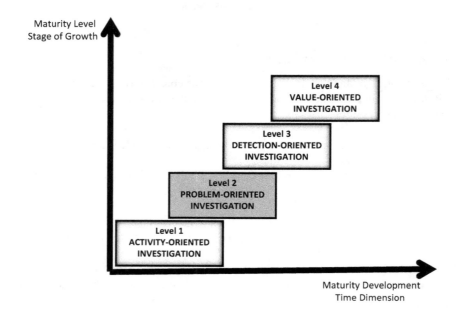

Figure 8.2 Maturity level for the Simonsen (2020) investigation at Ørland municipality

Attorney and one of Norway's leading experts on whistleblowing issues is Birthe Eriksen, who says the following about the report (Holseth, 2020):

• To me it seems that some kind of abuse of power has taken place that in my assessment is more serious that what is communicated in the report.

In March 2022, Tom Myrvold had to resign from the position of mayor in the municipality of Ørland. The reason was plagiarism, where he had taken text from other persons into his own articles without proper citations. Myrvold made the following press statement at his resignation (Svendsen and Sørbø, 2022):

In recent days, there have been several cases exposed where I have taken text from others and used them in my own posts without providing a source. I will once again give an unreserved apology to all those I have taken text from and the editors who have printed this. I would like to apologize to those I have had as co-authors in posts, who have not been aware that these may have contained text I have taken from others. I have had the pleasure of being mayor of Ørland municipality since 2015; a role that has given me a unique opportunity to take part in the development of Norway's foremost defense municipality. This has been a great privilege for me, and I want to thank both the inhabitants of Ørland and my party for giving me this opportunity. I have been in tough political processes before and with a straight back resisted personal attacks and attempts to hit me as a person. What has emerged in the last couple of days is as a result of mistakes I have made myself, and this has challenged my integrity as mayor and human being. For me, this is a much more important consideration to take. Therefore, I will take the consequence of this and ask the municipal council in Ørland municipality for exemption from the position as mayor and other elected positions at the first opportunity. I think this is correct both for the municipality that I love so much, but also for my own family and good colleagues in the party.

References

Chatterjee, A. and Pollock, T.G. (2017). Master of puppets: How narcissistic CEOs construct their professional worlds, *Academy of Management Review*, 42 (4), 703–725.

Chen, Y. and Moosmayer, D.C. (2020). When guilt is not enough: Interdependent self-construal as moderator of the relationship between guilt and ethical consumption in a Confucian context, *Journal of Business Ethics*, 161, 551–572.

Fosna. (2020). Leverte varsel mot Tom Myrvold: Kommunens advokat mener ordføreren opptrådte uheldig (Delivered notice against Tom Myrvold: The municipality's lawyer believes the mayor acted unfortunate), *Local Norwegian Newspaper Fosna-Folket*, July 16, www.fosna-folket.no.

Holseth, I.M. (2020). Ekspert om rapport: Kan godt forstå at det på et psykologisk plan føles som at det er gjegjeldelse og sanksjoner (Expert on report: -Can well understand that at a psychological level it feels like there is retaliation and sanctions), *Local Norwegian Newspaper Fosna-Folket*, November 19, www.fosna-folket.no.

Kakkar, H., Sivanathan, N. and Globel, M.S. (2020). Fall from grace: The role of dominance and prestige in punishment of high-status actors, *Academy of Management Journal*, 63 (2), 530–553.

Maslow, A.H. (1943). A theory of human motivation, *Psychological Review*, 50 (4), 370–396.

McClean, E.J., Martin, S.R., Emich, K.J. and Woodruff, T. (2018). The social consequences of voice: An examination of voice type and gender on status and subsequent leader emergence, *Academy of Management Journal*, 61 (5), 1869–1891.

Nichol, J.E. (2019). The effects of contract framing on misconduct and entitlement, *The Accounting Review*, 94 (3), 329–344.

Schnatterly, K., Gangloff, K.A. and Tuschke, A. (2018). CEO wrongdoing: A review of pressure, opportunity, and rationalization, *Journal of Management*, 44 (6), 2405–2432.

Simonsen. (2020). *Rapport om mottatt varsel vedrørende forhold ved jordmortjenesten i Ørland kommune (Report on notification received regarding conditions at the midwifery service in Ørland municipality)*, report of investigation, law firm Simonsen Vogt Wiig, May 20, Oslo, p. 36.

Svendsen, M. and Sørbø, K. (2022). Ordfører går av etter avsløringer om omfattende plagiering (Mayor resigns after revelations about extensive plagiarism), *Norwegian Public Broadcasting NRK*, March 20, www.nrk.no.

9   Municipal Benefits to Relatives

The examination represents a value-oriented investigation. The examination was a clarification. The investigation focused on value created by the examination, where the investigation is an investment by the client with an expectation of benefits exceeding costs. The ambition of the investigation was that the result would be valuable to the client. The report provides solid evidence in terms of pictures of drainage work on private property.

The report did not suggest crime or police reporting. This is in line with recommendations and guidelines for private investigations, where examiners should constrain themselves to reconstruct events and sequences of events. As the major political party decided to pursue the matter despite reluctance in the municipal council, it was not difficult to turn findings in the examination report into a police report. By adding legal elements, a lawyer helped transform information into a document directing the police toward handling the case in the criminal justice system.

There was suspicion of corruption in the municipality of Alver, which is located on the west coast of Norway. Auditing firm Nordhordland (2019) was hired to investigate the matter. A whistleblower had notified the control committee in the municipality that invoices had been paid by the municipality that seemed to be of a private nature for a municipal official (Fjeld, 2020). Anny Bastesen admitted that she approved two invoices that were not related to municipal activity (Nordpoll, 2020). She was technical manager in the municipality (Nydal, 2020a). Neither the control committee nor the municipal council at Alver wanted to report the case to the police. Therefore, a major political party in the municipality decided to do it on their own. They reported the case to the police on September 14, 2020, where they argued that fraud, corruption, and financial misconduct should be investigated.

Offender Convenience Themes

Assuming that technical manager Anny Bastesen made the municipality pay for drainage work that was done on the private property of close relatives then her behavior is relevant to study based on the theory of convenience as illustrated in Figure 9.1. The misconduct is a form of corruption, where she abuses her position

DOI: 10.4324/9781003363934-10

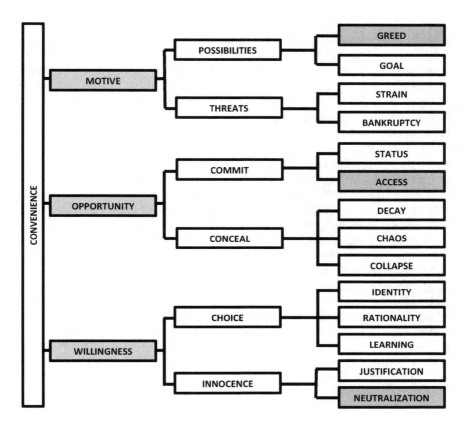

Figure 9.1 Convenience themes in the case of Alver

to provide an illegitimate benefit to close relatives. The benefit for her consists of gratefulness and respect. Agnew (2014) introduced the motive of social concern and crime, where there is a desire to help others, and thus moving beyond the assumption of simple self-interest. However, as argued by Paternoster et al. (2018), helping others can be a self-interested, rational action that claims social concern. The self-interest or self-regarding preference and rationality can imply interest in other's materialistic well-being. While the economic model of rational self-interest focuses on incentives and detection risks and associated costs (Welsh et al., 2014), Agnew (2014) suggests that economic crime can also be committed when individuals think more of others than of themselves.

Agnew (2014) believes that social concern consists of four elements, namely that 1) individuals care about the welfare of others, 2) they want close ties with others, 3) they are likely to follow moral guidelines such as innocent people should not suffer harm, and 4) they tend to seek confirmation through other people's actions and norms. That a person puts others before oneself will initially lead to less crime. However, economic crime may be committed where the welfare of others and their success is the motive.

In the organizational opportunity dimension of convenience theory, technical manager Anny Bastesen had access to resources to commit misconduct as she was legally able to approve invoices. A white-collar offender has typically legitimate and convenient access to resources to commit crime (Adler and Kwon, 2002; Füss and Hecker, 2008; Huisman and Erp, 2013; Lange, 2008; Pinto et al., 2008; Reyns, 2013). A resource is an enabler applied and used to satisfy human and organizational needs. A resource has utility and limited availability. According to Petrocelli et al. (2003), access to resources equates access to power. Other organizational members are losers in the competition for resources (Wheelock et al., 2011). In the conflict perspective suggested by Petrocelli et al. (2003), the upper class in society exercises its power and controls the resources. Valuable resources are typically scarce, unique, not imitable, not transferrable, combinable, exploitable, and not substitutable.

In the perspective of personal willingness for deviant behavior in convenience theory, lack of self-control might characterize the offender. As argued by Gottfredson and Hirschi (1990), human behavior finds innocence in the self-centered quest for satisfaction and avoidance of suffering. Self-control is the blockade that stands between the individual and criminal activity. Lack of self-control is lack of such a blockade, making the short-term pleasure seeking dominate the mind. Lack of self-control implies that the offender lacks the ability and tendency to consider potential implications of a deviant action (Kroneberg and Schultz, 2018), as they are impulsive and unstable (Craig and Piquero, 2016; Jones et al., 2015). Those lacking self-control will typically have a short-term focus and be adventuresome, risk-willing, and indifferent.

Fraud Investigation Outcome

The investigation case concerned municipal drainage work that was carried out on the site of a sister of the technical manager in the former Meland municipality that became part of Alver municipality. The drainage work was carried out by a contractor with a family relationship to the technical manager. The technical manager approved the invoice related to the drainage project that ended with a price tag of NOK 240,000 (about USD 24,000). A municipal employee blew the whistle on the drainage case. The control committee in Meland municipality processed the case, and commissioned examiners from Nordhordland (2019) to review the entire case. The audit firm concluded with the following findings (Nydal, 2020b):

- The requirement for impartiality is violated in several cases by payments from the municipality and in the municipal process.
- The administration has implemented an activity, without obtaining a price for the work performed, and there is no price assessment of the activity.
- The auditor has requested, but not received, written documentation on assessments of municipal responsibility or benefit for own facilities by incurring costs in the activity.

• There are no written agreements that mention costs, which the municipality is to cover for a private party, nor has a written agreement been entered into that the municipality has the right to facilities built on private land.

The case was then processed further by the control committee in Alver municipality, which chose to end the processing of the case. The municipal council in the municipality also did not want to pursue the matter. Councilor in Alver Municipality, Ørjan Raknes Forthun, claimed that the technical manager was a victim of failing internal control. The technical manager Anne Bastesen herself claimed that it was failure caused by high work pressure and understaffing.

The private land was owned by Gunnlaug Bastesen Dale. She was the sister and the closest neighbor to Anne Bastesen. Gunnlaug Bastesen Dale's husband and thus Anne Bastesen's brother-in-law was Peder Dale. Gunnlaug Bastesen Dale's and Peder Dale's nephew was Yngve Dale who was the owner of YD Machine that carried out the drainage work (Nordhordland, 2019).

Investigation Report Maturity

As illustrated in Figure 9.2, the examination by Nordhordland (2019) represents a value-oriented investigation. The examination was a clarification. The investigation focused on value created by the examination, where the investigation is an investment by the client with an expectation of benefits exceeding costs. The

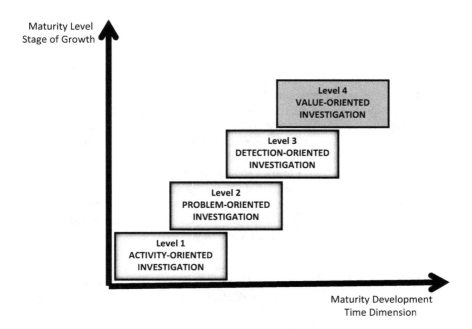

Figure 9.2 Maturity level for the Nordhordland (2019) investigation at Alver municipality

ambition of the investigation was that the result would be valuable to the client. The report provides solid evidence in terms of pictures of drainage work on private property.

The report did not suggest crime or police reporting. This is in line with recommendations and guidelines for private investigations, where examiners should constrain themselves to reconstruct events and sequences of events. A private examiner is never to take on all three roles of detective, prosecutor, and judge. Rather, the examination should provide sufficient evidence for an assumed prosecutor to decide whether or not an offense has been committed, and whether or not the offender belongs in the criminal justice system.

The Nordhordaland (2019) examination satisfies such requirements. As the major political party decided to pursue the matter despite reluctance in the municipal council, it was not difficult to turn findings in the examination report into a police report. By adding legal elements, a lawyer helped transform information into a document directing the police toward handling the case in the criminal justice system.

Police Investigation Outcome

The municipal council decided not to report the Bastesen case to the police. However, the main political party in the municipality decided to report the case on their own to the police. Despite administrative and political consideration in two control committees and one municipal council, it was still unclear to the party whether misconduct and crime had occurred that should be investigated and prosecuted. The politicians were concerned about this and wanted an independent assessment by the police.

It took some time before the police decided what to do with the report from Alver. The political party headed by Morten Klementsen reported the case to the local police station on September 14, 2020. Two months later, on November 12, there was a police response. How much time the police had actually spent on the case during this period was a reasonable issue to question. Because when the police conclusion was sent out in a press statement to newspapers, it actually raised more new questions than provided answers. Police attorney Kjetil Linge Tomren in the Bergen police district announced in the press release that the case was being dismissed on the basis of an overall assessment of the case information as it was currently available. Tomren started by writing that the police, upon receipt of the report, must assess the probability that something criminal has actually happened, and that an investigation will be able to clarify the case so that one might reach conviction. He did not go into this further.

A natural interpretation is that the police in this case was uncertain both whether something criminal had happened and whether they would be able to investigate the case. But we do not know, since the police wrote nothing to explain their consideration. However, the police attorney pointed out that the municipality itself had made undesirable findings, but the findings did not necessarily mean criminal offenses. Here again, the police attorney did not elaborate further.

The case was reported precisely because the political party wanted the police to assess whether the unwanted findings could be grounds for criminal prosecution. Basically, everything the police attorney wrote in the press statement was known from before. He further mentioned that the municipality itself had not wished to report the case, and that the parent organization for the local political party had tried to withdraw the case. At the same time, the attorney emphasized that such circumstances are not decisive for the police conclusion. Nevertheless, it is sensational that the police include irrelevant criteria when dismissing a case. The first is the statement that the municipality itself did not report the case. There can be a number of reasons for this. For example, there tends to be close ties in many directions between those involved and the administration and politicians in smaller municipalities such as Alver. The Alver councilor had also looked at the matter completely differently than Nordhordland (2019) from the start. The councilor claimed early that the technical manager was a victim of a lack of internal control. Based on this, Nydal (2020b) phrased the question:

> Should the councilor's position weigh more heavily than an independent audit company that has examined the case on behalf of the control committee?

The second irrelevant issue was that the parent organization had wanted to withdraw the case. The police should know that the only one qualified to withdraw a report is the one who submitted the report. After the local political party headed by Morten Klementsen resigned from the parent organization, Trym Aafløy from the parent organization went to the police with a request to withdraw the case because he did not want the political party to be involved in a possible lawsuit. It is unacceptable that outsiders can interfere and withdraw cases that have been reported to the police.

Hauken (2020) reported: "Professor reacts to the decision: -This is amateur work":

> Professor Petter Gottschalk is clear in his reaction to the police assessment, and says that the political party should deliver the police report again. Professor Petter Gottschalk at BI has previously stated to the newspaper that the police should take charge in the habilitation case in former Meland municipality. He reacts strongly to the decision.

- The police have not done their job here. This is amateur work, says Gottschalk to the newspaper, before he continues.
- Only the person who delivers a message to the police can withdraw it. This is simply a police service error. Secondly, the police have not notified those who submitted the report about the case not being investigated. Gottschalk further says that the police should only decide whether there is a basis for an investigation, i.e. whether there is strong suspicion that something criminal has happened.

- My commitment for the police to investigate is not that I want the person in question to be convicted. Doubts should always benefit suspects. But the elite of society escape too easily. Why should you and I follow laws and regulations, if they are not caught at the top for abusing their positions? Gottschalk thinks the political party must now submit the report again.
- It is the smartest thing to do instead of complaining about the current assessment. That the police have dropped the case is happening on the wrong basis.

Then Heimdal (2020) reported that police attorney Kjetil Linge Tomren said that the police would consider re-examining the case after a telephone conversation with political party leader Morten Klementsen:

Tomren says that after dialogue with Klementsen, he sees that there are nuances in the case related to the political party, which have not been known to the police. These will be considered in the event of a complaint. The police will reconsider the case if there is an appeal against the decision.

Nydal (2020b) wrote in another local newspaper:

We cannot document what are the facts here, but as the basic premise of dismissing the case appears to us, it seems that this case has been handled lightly, and that the police have needed some arguments to conclude as they do. BI professor Petter Gottschalk is also clear on this.

We have deliberately been careful at allowing external sources to comment on the case before the police had concluded, but now we think it is relevant to include his views. The BI professor is one of the country's foremost experts on economic crime and tells the newspaper Strilen that dismissing the case is misconduct by the police and is happening on the wrong basis. He therefore urges the political party to report the case again.

References

Adler, P.S. and Kwon, S.W. (2002). Social capital: Prospects for a new concept, *Academy of Management Review*, 27 (1), 17–40.

Agnew, R. (2014). Social concern and crime: Moving beyond the assumption of simple self-interest, *Criminology*, 52 (1), 1–32.

Craig, J.M. and Piquero, N.L. (2016). The effects of low self-control and desire-for-control on white-collar offending: A replication, *Deviant Behavior*, 37 (11), 1308–1324.

Fjeld, E.L. (2020). Bland åpen og ryddig (Mix open and tidy), local Norwegian newspaper *Strilen*, June 16, www.strilen.no.

Füss, R. and Hecker, A. (2008). Profiling white-collar crime. Evidence from German-speaking countries, *Corporate Ownership & Control*, 5 (4), 149–161.

Gottfredson, M.R. and Hirschi, T. (1990). *A General Theory of Crime*, Stanford University Press, Stanford.

Hauken, H.R. (2020). Professor reagerer på avgjerda: Dette er amatørarbeid (Professor reacts to the decision: -This is amateur work), *Local Norwegian Newspaper Strilen*, November 13, www.strilen.no (Published on paper Friday, November 20, p. 6).

Heimdal, S. (2020). Politiet vil vurdere å behandle saka på nytt (The police will consider re-examining the case), *Local Norwegian Newspaper Nordhordland*, November 13, www.nordhordland.no (Published in the paper version on November 18, p. 13).

Huisman, W. and Erp, J. (2013). Opportunities for environmental crime, *British Journal of Criminology*, 53, 1178–1200.

Jones, S., Lyman, D.R. and Piquero, A.R. (2015). Substance use, personality, and inhibitors: Testing Hirschi's predictions about the reconceptualization of self-control, *Crime & Delinquency*, 61 (4), 538–558.

Kroneberg, C. and Schultz, S. (2018). Revisiting the role of self-control in situational action theory, *European Journal of Criminology*, 15 (1), 56–76.

Lange, D. (2008). A multidimensional conceptualization of organizational corruption control, *Academy of Management Journal*, 33 (3), 710–29.

Nordhordland. (2019). *Forenkla forvaltningskontroll (Simplified management control)*, audit firm Nordhordland Revisjon, December 20, Alver, Norway, p. 32.

Nordpoll, A.L. (2020). Anne Bastesen vedgår at ho godkjente rekningar for kommunen som ho aldri burge ha godkjent (Anne Bastesen admits that she approved bills for the municipality that she should never have approved), *Local Norwegian Newspaper Strilen*, June 16, www.strilen.no.

Nydal, T.R. (2020a). Alver kommune bør være åpen (Alver municipality should be open), *Local Norwegian Newspaper Nordhordland*, May 26, www.nordhordland.no.

Nydal, T.R. (2020b). Avisa Nordhordland meiner: Politiet har klussa det unødvendig til i grunngjevinga for å legge vekk saka (The newspaper Nordhordland means: The police have messed it up unnecessarily in the reasoning for dismissing the case), *Local Norwegian Newspaper Nordhordland*, November 17, www.nordhordland.no (the paper version on November 18, p. 14).

Paternoster, R., Jaynes, C.M. and Wilson, T. (2018). Rational choice theory and interest in the "fortune of others", *Journal of Research in Crime and Delinquency*, 54 (6), 847–868.

Petrocelli, M., Piquero, A.R. and Smith, M.R. (2003). Conflict theory and racial profiling: An empirical analysis of police traffic stop data, *Journal of Criminal Justice*, 31 (1), 1–11.

Pinto, J., Leana, C.R. and Pil, F.K. (2008). Corrupt organizations or organizations of corrupt individuals? Two types of organization-level corruption, *Academy of Management Review*, 33 (3), 685–709.

Reyns, B.W. (2013). Online routines and identity theft victimization: Further expanding routine activity theory beyond direct-contact offenses, *Journal of Research in Crime and Delinquency*, 50, 216–238.

Welsh, D.T. and Ordonez, L.D. (2014). The dark side of consecutive high performance goals: Linking goal setting, depletion, and unethical behavior, *Organizational Behavior and Human Decision Processes*, 123, 79–89.

Wheelock, D., Semukhina, O. and Demidov, N.N. (2011). Perceived group threat and punitive attitudes in Russia and the United States, *British Journal of Criminology*, 51, 937–959.

10 Victimization of Social Security Clients

Social security fraud is normally concerned with recipients of social security benefits who were not entitled to such benefits. This case study is concerned with opposite roles between the social security agency and the social security recipients. Recipients were entitled to benefits that they were denied by the agency. The social security agency defrauded entitled recipients of social security benefits. If entitled recipients nevertheless had received financial payments, then the agency claimed repayment and reported the recipients to the police. In the criminal justice system, several recipients were wrongly convicted to prison sentences, and they had to serve time in jail.

This case study is concerned with public administration's abuse of power to hurt financially entitled social security recipients and to hurt them legally by investigation, prosecution, conviction, and in some cases incarceration for alleged wrongdoing. The case illustrates what the outcome can be when government institutions, which are supposed to ensure that public authorities do not cause injustice and miscarriage of justice by harming individuals, do not have the competence and willingness required to do so and do not react or communicate adequately. In the perspective of convenience theory, blame game, institutional deterioration, and neutralization techniques are some of the convenience themes that can explain the deviant practice in Norwegian social security.

When the deviant behavior by the social security agency in Norway and the following miscarriage of justice were detected, the Norwegian government appointed a committee to conduct an internal investigation by examining why legitimate benefit receivers were harmed by denial of payments and punishment for benefit receipts. The report of investigation was published in the form of an official government publication NOU (2020). This chapter evaluates the maturity of the investigation report, which seems to suffer from dominance of legal issues and lack of answers to the basic question of who is responsible for what happened to harmed benefit receivers.

Social Security Agency Scandal

A scandal is a publicized instance of transgression that runs counter to social norms, typically resulting in condemnation and discredit and other consequences such as bad press, disengagement of key constituencies, the severance of network

DOI: 10.4324/9781003363934-11

ties, and decrease in key performance indicators (Piazza and Jourdan, 2018). Depending on how accounts of a scandal evolve over time, shifts in attribution of blame and scapegoating might occur. For example, law professor Ingunn Ikdahl blamed the ministry for the social security scandal (Solberg, 2020).

The scandal in this case is concerned with wrongful prosecution and conviction of individuals who received social security benefits (Meldalen and Lofstad, 2019; NTB, 2019). The case is concerned with miscarriage of justice. Misleading interpretations of laws caused conviction and incarceration of innocent individuals for alleged social security scam (Larsen, 2019; Lofstad, 2019). The scandal is particularly interesting in the social conflict perspective, where white-collar offenders may feel entitled to violate and then modify the law, while social security recipients are at the bottom of social status and have to accept whatever happens to them (Petrocelli et al., 2003; Schwendinger and Schwendinger, 2014).

The Norwegian Labor and Welfare Administration, NAV, was embroiled in a controversy after it incorrectly interpreted rules from the European Union (EU). While not being a member of EU, Norway is part of the European Economic Area (EEA), which cooperates with the EU on legal and other matters. The controversy quickly developed into a serious scandal with demands made for the authority's chief executive, Sigrun Vågeng, to resign. Politicians were also quickly critical, with left-wing Red party leader Bjørnar Moxnes calling for the case of a scandal where the minister in charge of labor and social issues in the Norwegian government, Anniken Hauglie, should resign. Socialist party leader Audun Lysbakken described it as a catastrophe, while Prime Minister Erna Solberg said that it was incredibly unfair and should not happen in Norway (NTB, 2019). State prosecutor Tor-Aksel Busch asked all law enforcement agencies to review recent social security criminal cases (Meldalen and Lofstad, 2019).

NAV is responsible for around a third of Norway's state budget. The authority administers social security programs, including unemployment benefits, pensions, and child benefits. Compared to other countries, the welfare benefits in Norway are quite good. For example, sickness leave and unemployment only cause minimal reductions in income and thus marginal reductions in standard of living for the benefit receivers.

On Monday, October 29, 2019, the authority admitted it had made critical errors in its interpretation of sickness benefits, which is support for people who need medical treatment or other activities to help them get back to work. Sickness benefits are called work assessment allowances in Norway, which also include support for people who are unable to work due to a sick child's care needs. At least 48 individuals had been wrongly convicted of social security scam, out of which 36 individuals had served time in jail (Lofstad, 2019).

The issue specifically affected people who received benefits while living in Norway but staying temporarily in another EEA country. NAV practiced rules for being on work assessment allowances or other care benefits incorrectly. NAV thought that benefit receivers had to stay in Norway when on benefits. However, as an EEA country, not only the flow of capital but also the flow of people is encouraged within Europe. EU regulations made this explicit for social security in 2012, when it was documented that receivers of social security benefits could travel and stay wherever they like within EEA.

Thirty-six receivers of social security benefits were not just in a difficult situation in their lives; they were denied further benefits, they had to pay back received money, and they had to serve time in jail, because they had stayed temporarily abroad. They were victims of miscarriage of justice, which is considered extremely serious in Norway. When people are asked how many guilty persons should be free to avoid incarcerating an innocent person, people tend to say at least 100. In the Norwegian culture, it is extremely serious wrongdoing to punish innocent persons (Larsen, 2019).

Over the course of many years, the NAV has applied the requirement of stay in Norway under the Norwegian National Insurance Act for recipients of social security benefits, such as sickness compensation, attendance allowance, and work assessment allowance, in a manner contrary to and in conflict with European commitments. Within Europe, Norwegians are allowed to move freely independent of their status. Employees at NAV as well as ministry officials, police investigators, state prosecutors, defense lawyers, judges at criminal courts, officers at correctional institutions, academic researchers, and law professors have all ignored or misunderstood the European social security regulation. While not a member of the European Union, Norway has signed a number of treaties requiring the country to align with most EU regulations.

The requirement of stay in Norway laid down in the National Insurance Act has remained in place through several legislative amendments and has not been the subject of much debate, since corrective EEA regulations were ignored. There was and is broad political agreement that benefit recipients should be followed closely by NAV in order to get them back to work as quickly as possible. For many recipients, it has been practically feasible to stay abroad and at the same time comply with planned follow-up measures. Many have nevertheless been refused benefits, because NAV has worked based on the assumption that prior permission is required for a stay abroad, and that permission may be given only for up to four weeks per year, corresponding to statutory holiday. Yet many were not on holiday; they were exercising their right under the EU/EEA social security regulation to stay elsewhere in the EEA – such as with their own family if they are of foreign origin, such as Poles working in Norway. NAV did not recognize or acknowledge this fact of wrongfully denying benefits and punishing recipients.

The cases were not viewed as particularly complicated, and the legal issues relating to EEA law were not identified when NAV adopted decisions to report cases to the police. Similarly, prosecutors and judges viewed cases from NAV as obvious and straightforward to handle in the criminal justice system. Nobody questioned the misrepresentation in the criminal justice system, where defense lawyers spent little time and effort on each case. Low-level defendants receive far less support compared to high-level defendants. While street crime is often concerned with the lower levels, white-collar crime is often concerned with the upper levels in terms of status and success (Logan et al., 2019; Piquero, 2018). Poverty and powerlessness tend to be the cause of street crime, while excessive power and greed are often the cause of white-collar crime (Galvin, 2020).

The only ground for conviction and incarceration of social benefits receivers was that they had been abroad without NAV's permission. Where the benefits recipient had traveled outside Norway without notifying or had notified that he or she was still in Norway, NAV generally reported the person for fraud to the police. The threshold for reporting was the equivalent of only USD 10,000 in Norwegian kroner. This amount can be compared to the average amount involved in white-collar crime in Norway, which is the equivalent of USD 4 million in Norwegian kroner.

Both the Norwegian prosecuting authority and the courts have largely relied on NAV's determinations, without examining the question whether or not the person in question was actually entitled to the benefit during the stay abroad. The interpretation of the law that has formed the basis for the decisions in the administrative cases has thus scarcely been tested in connection with criminal cases in the ordinary courts of law. While white-collar crime cases in Norwegian courts tend to last for several months, where defendants have ample opportunity to present various witnesses and documents, street crime cases, including NAV cases, tend to last for a few days.

The role of the National Benefits Court in Norway is to evaluate administrative decisions in individual cases for benefits receivers. This specialist court body did not consider the EEA law issue specifically until 2017, when members of the court emphasized that NAV's circulars did not convey a correct interpretation of the regulation and that NAV was requiring a stay in Norway in situations where there was no basis for such a requirement. Subsequently, a number of cases raising the same issue came before the National Insurance Court, but not all court members understood what their colleagues had realized a few months earlier, which is that NAV was failing to consider EEA law in cases involving stays abroad for persons who were registered as residents in Norway. Thus for a while the court was failing to convey a clear and consistent – and correct – interpretation of the law and was instead reaching decisions in individual cases without reference to the relevant EEA rules.

The vast majority of court members who finally found that the EU/EEA regulation was applicable started to apply the same interpretation of it. Nevertheless, NAV case workers considered the returned cases from the court as exceptions rather than the result of a new practice aligned with EEA rules. The chair of the National Insurance Court may decide that more than two members are to take part in a case if the decision may become "determinative for practice". This was not done. It took one and a half years from the time the court delivered the first principle-setting ruling until the NAV contacted the Ministry of Labor and Social Affairs to get the practice changed. Active and competent defense lawyers were completely absent in this process, since their clients were similar to street criminals rather than rich and influential white-collar criminals (Galvin, 2020; Logan et al., 2019; Piquero, 2018).

It took NAV two years after the first ruling before publishing internal notices of amended practice, and six months later the extent of the error became known (NOU, 2020: 28):

> The Committee takes the view that NAV, the Ministry and the National Insurance Court all share responsibility for its having taken such a long time before the practice was rectified. In the Committee's view, one reason is that the National Insurance Court has viewed itself too much as a court of law that communicates only through rulings in individual cases. It seems that the body has lost sight of the fact that the National Insurance Court is intended to be a hybrid between an appeal body and a court, an institution with a particular responsibility for ensuring legal certainty for ordinary people finding themselves in demanding situations and up against a powerful opponent – the State.
>
> The absence of critical thinking, apt organization and conduct in keeping with the responsibility the bodies have, has led to a situation in which the importance of EEA law has been a blind spot for virtually everyone involved. The result has been that certain individuals have wrongfully had their payments stopped, received claims for repayment of social security benefits, been labeled as social security fraudsters and also been sentenced to prison terms on incorrect grounds.
>
> The case illustrates what the outcome can be when the institutions that are supposed to ensure that public authorities do not cause injustices to individuals do not have the resources required to do so, are not substantively up to date and do not react or communicate adequately.

Internally at NAV, a blame game started when the scandal became publicly known. The first looser in the blame game was announced on December 4, 2019, which was one month after the scandal became public. One of the senior executives reporting to Vågeng resigned from her position. The media reported (Ruud and Spence, 2019):

> Kjersti Monland will be the first to step down as a result of the social security scandal. She will quit her job Monday, December 9.

NAV published a press release about Monland's resignation:

> Over the past few weeks, Nav has received heavy criticism for its handling of the EEA regulations related to cash benefits. Confidence in Nav is greatly weakened and many Nav employees have a difficult working day.

- I have respect and understanding for Kjersti's decision, but I am also happy that she will continue to use her expertise and capacity to the best of our organization's development work. Kjersti is also available to contribute clarification and knowledge about the coming work on the EEA case, says Sigrun Vågeng.

- I have come to the conclusion that it is both necessary and appropriate to appoint a new leader who can continue this important work, as well as strengthen the power of the department in this critical phase. All tasks in the department and the line must be able to be filled satisfactorily, both in relation to government ministries, the management of Nav and the outside world says benefits director Kjersti Monland.

Kjersti Monland became an obvious scapegoat as many commented in the Norwegian media after the announcement of her resignation from the position of benefits director (Ulserød, 2020). Scapegoating is a form of denial of responsibility accompanied with placement of blame on an individual or group of individuals (Lee and Robinson, 2000; Resodihardjo et al., 2015; Xie and Keh, 2016).

Moland's resignation occurred less than a week before an internal audit report was due. Vågeng had asked the internal audit function at NAV to conduct a review as the scandal broke. Being the client for the audit review, Vågeng decided on the mandate. This is in line with many famous internal reviews, where being the client for the review can protect the client from negative attention. But it did not.

Shortly after Monland took the blame, both government minister Hauglie and chief executive Vågeng had to resign from their posts because of the scandal.

Sigrun Vågeng had to resign and was replaced by Hans Christian Holte. In an early interview as NAV chief, he was asked how it was to take on the job (Jenssen, 2020: 54).

- You took over Nav in a terrible state of emergency, right after the investigation report of the scandal that came with bitter criticism of the agency. Many people had for years been convicted and sent to prison, branded as fraudsters – because they had traveled abroad while receiving social security benefits from Norway, but it was the Norwegian interpretation of the regulations that was wrong.
- I think it is fair to say that this scandal has shaken the agency. It has clearly hit us very hard. It is not just about competence and law. For me this case is twofold. We are talking about a blind spot. Nav, the ministry, the social security court, the lawyers, academica – everyone had this blind spot. And Nav was an important part of it.

Offender Convenience Themes

The offender is the social security agency NAV in Norway. In the financial motive dimension of convenience theory, the politicians in Norway do not like what they call benefits export, where Norwegians receive social benefits and spend the money outside the country. Norwegian governments – both left-wing and right-wing governments in recent decades – have stressed that receivers of sickness compensation, attendance allowance, and work assessment allowance should stay in the country. They dislike receivers spending the money in countries where they get much more value for their money. Instead, the governments would like to avoid paying and recover what is already paid. The purpose is to make it less attractive to become benefit receivers and to make it more attractive to be workers paying tax. The financial motive is thus to make savings in social security payments.

The reluctance of an agency to follow EEA rules becomes stronger when the rules are both complicated and in conflict with political priorities (Ferraro et al., 2005; Holt and Cornelissen, 2014; Judge et al., 2009; Mawritz et al., 2017; Srivastava and Goldberg, 2017; Weick, 1995). This is anomie in the sense of low commitment to rules that do not fit. Trying to follow the law may result in inefficient business practices that depress organizational results and hurt careers of organizational members. Noncompliance might allow the agency to be more successful in the eyes of the government. Rule complexity combined with rule inappropriateness encourages deviant behavior (Kroneberg and Schultz, 2018). The situational action perspective addresses how environments shape opportunities for deviant behavior and, subsequently, how modifications in environments can increase deviant opportunities (Huisman and Erp, 2013).

In the organizational opportunity dimension of convenience theory, employees in the social security agency are never challenged by social security recipients. Recipients lack access to resources to protect their rights. In the perspective of critical criminology, social security clients have no protection. The organizational setting allows employees in the social security agency to enjoy their status relative to their clients. They also enjoy their status when reporting alleged recipient wrongdoing cases to the police. The police consider reports from the social security agency to be well documented with no need for further investigations. Next in line, the public prosecutors trust both the agency and the police. Finally in the line, the judges in district courts trust prosecutors, the police, as well as the agency. The thorough documentation from the agency travels through the criminal justice system without any questioning on its way to conviction of innocent individuals. Thirty-six individuals were wrongfully convicted of abuse of social security benefits and incarcerated.

The convenience theme of status in the organizational setting against clients can derive from the agency language that people do not understand (Ferraro et al., 2005; Holt and Cornelissen, 2014; Judge et al., 2009; Mawritz et al., 2017; Srivastava and Goldberg, 2017; Weick, 1995). The status theme in the criminal justice system can derive from the blame game, where employees at the agency assume that their reports are evaluated before any convictions occur (DeScioli and Bokemper, 2014; Eberly et al., 2011; Gangloff et al., 2016; Hurrell, 2016; Keaveney, 2008; Lee and Robinson, 2000; Resodihardjo et al., 2015; Schnatterly et al., 2018; Schoultz and Flyghed, 2016, 2019, 2020a, 2020b; Sonnier et al., 2015; Xie and Keh, 2016). If someone is wrongfully convicted, then it is the fault of the criminal justice system, rather than that of the agency.

EEA law applies to Norwegian legislation, but the incorporation of EEA social security regulation into Norwegian law was ignored by application of the Norwegian National Insurance Act instead. The ignorance was in line with the perspective of rule complexity (Boghossian and Marques, 2019; Eberlein, 2019;

Huisman, 2020; Lehman et al., 2020; Maher et al., 2019; Schoepfer and Piquero, 2006), where public agencies can claim that the complexity of having both EEA laws and local Norwegian laws that were never aligned made it difficult to be compliant. While EEA commitments are supposed to overrule local Norwegian laws, rule complexity prevented compliance, and concealment of agency wrongdoing was convenient.

As suggested by Lehman et al. (2020), rule complexity can create a situation where nobody is able to tell whether an action represents a violation of the law. It is thus impossible to understand what is right and what is wrong. Some laws, rules, and regulations are so complex that compliance becomes random, where compliance is the action of complying with laws, rules, and regulations. The regulatory legal environment is supposed to define the boundaries of appropriate agency conduct. However, legal complexity is often so extreme that even specialist compliance officers struggle to understand what to recommend to executives in organizations. The regulatory inspection does not work for compliance. Agency executives can thus find the large gray zone in legal matters a convenient space for misconduct and offenses based on political signals from ministers and other politicians. This is especially so when operating internationally and globally where states do not agree on what should be legal and illegal activities (Boghossian and Marques, 2019; Eberlein, 2019; Maher et al., 2019; Pontell et al., 2020).

NOU (2020) suggests that NAV had a culture with many clear weaknesses. For example, the tradition of not asking questions about established truths at NAV might be explained by both organizational conditions and individual attitudes. In some public agencies, executives use language that people do not understand (Ferraro et al., 2005). Some public sector agencies are involved in the blame game by misleading attribution to others (Eberly et al., 2011) without any sense of responsibility for deviance. The NOU (2020) report of investigation is yet another example of blame game, where all are to blame. By sharing blame with a number of other actors in public administration and the criminal justice system, nobody will ultimately feel especially responsible for having incarcerated innocent social security recipients. There was institutional deterioration based on legitimacy (Rodriguez et al., 2005), inability to control because of social disorganization between various parts of the public sector (Hoffmann, 2002), and interference and noise in signals of wrongdoing (Karim and Siegel, 1998). There was lack of control in principal–agent relationships (Bosse and Phillips, 2016), where police investigators trusted examiners at NAV, while defense attorneys and court judges trusted police investigators.

Weakened competence tends to cause institutional deterioration. Institutional deterioration can occur conveniently as a result of external legitimacy where deviance is the norm (Rodriguez et al., 2005). Institutional deterioration often occurs at the same time as social disorganization, which further improves the opportunity structure for deviance without notice. The disorganization perspective argues that structural conditions lead to higher levels of social disorganization – especially of weak social controls – in organizations and between organizations, which in turn results in higher rates of deviance (Pratt and Cullen, 2005). While the objective of NAV's distribution processes of authority has been described as a "lean and strategic" directorate that leads and coordinates a line organization in which the substantive competence in the agency is close to the users, the Directorate nevertheless has the same formal substantive responsibility as previously without being able to exercise that responsibility in a principal–agent perspective (Bosse and Phillips, 2016).

Problems in principal–agent relationships belong to the convenience theme of opportunity-concealment-chaos as illustrated in Figure 10.1. Lack of oversight and guardianship causes chaos. The agency perspective suggests that a principal is often unable to control an agent who does work for the principal. The agency perspective assumes narrow self-interest among both principals and agents. The interests of principal and agent tend to diverge, they may have different risk willingness or risk aversion, there is knowledge asymmetry between the two parties, and the principal has imperfect information about the agent's contribution (Bosse and Phillips, 2016; Chrisman et al., 2007; Desai, 2016; Pillay and Kluvers,

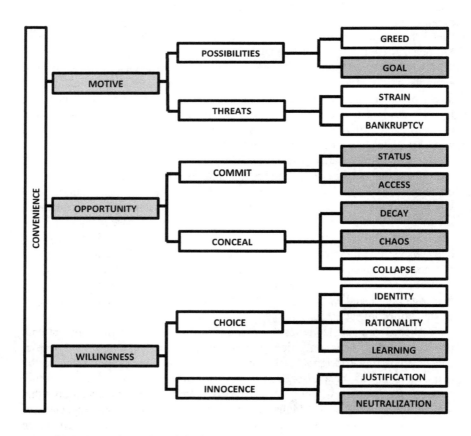

Figure 10.1 Convenience themes in the case of NAV

2014; Williams, 2008; Williams et al., 2019). The principal–agent challenge was not only a problem in the decentralization and distribution of competence within NAV, but also a problem in the relationship between the Ministry and the NAV Directorate.

Problems in sensemaking do also belong to the convenience theme of opportunity-concealment-chaos. An important part of the agency's mission is to prevent and detect benefits fraud and other misuses of social security schemes. Travel abroad has been relatively easy to spot, particularly since NAV has acquired technological tools enabling tracking of IP addresses. In a number of cases, stays in the EEA elsewhere than in Norway have formed the sole basis for decisions to stop or claim repayment of benefits, without further consideration of whether the stay abroad has impeded follow-up in the individual case. NAV employees fell into the trap of sensemaking of actions without understanding those actions in a relevant context (Bernburg et al., 2006; Hamann, 2019; Holt and Cornelissen, 2014; Weick, 1995; Weick et al., 2005). Since travel abroad was easy to spot, the perceived crime signal was a real noise signal called false alarm in the signal detection perspective (Karim and Siegel, 1998; Rooij and Fine, 2020; Szalma and Hancock, 2013).

In the willingness dimension of convenience theory, social security recipients are considered losers and potential criminals at the level of street criminals. Employees at social security agency have to be cautious when granting benefits to such individuals. In the perspective of social conflict, it is acceptable for the agency to make mistakes since employees have an identity in the privileged position (Bernat and Whyte, 2020; Petrocelli et al., 2003; Rothe, 2020; Rothe and Medley, 2020; Schwendinger and Schwendinger, 2014; Tombs and Whyte, 2003; Zysman-Quirós, 2020). According to the social conflict perspective, the justice system is biased and designed to protect the wealthy and powerful (Schoultz and Flyghed, 2019). It is not designed to protect the poor and powerless. The losers in society are to be taken care of in a way determined by the winners (Michel, 2016). If the losers deviate from arrangements determined by the winners, then they are quickly sanctioned in countries such as Norway.

The practice of reporting innocent individuals to the police might be explained by learning from others because of differential association (Sutherland, 1983), where the action is according to authority as obedience (Baird and Zelin, 2009). NAV had a collectivist value orientation (Bussmann et al., 2018) where a peer pressure (Gao and Zhang, 2019) led to individual application of neutralization techniques (Sykes and Matza, 1957).

As illustrated in Figure 10.1, the motive for NAV was to follow political signals to avoid payments to social security clients who traveled abroad. The crime against clients was possible because of the status of government agencies compared to the rights of low-level clients. The social security agency and the criminal justice system had access to resources to ignore signals of deviance. There were elements of decay and chaos as well in the Norwegian public administration regarding the country's legal commitments in Europe. Wrongdoing among employees at NAV was the result of learning and neutralization.

Fraud Investigation Outcome

NOU (2020: 26) argues that a major cause of the misapplication of the requirement of stay in Norway has been a failure to align the provisions of the National Insurance Act correctly with the rules under EEA law:

> The attention of successive governments has been directed at efficient social security administration, combating social security fraud and reduction of export of benefits. Rather less attention has been directed at considerations of safeguarding the rights of individuals.

In draft legislative amendments, the Ministry of Labor and Social Affairs has not had a tradition of explaining the limitations placed by EEA law on the application of the National Insurance Act rules imposing a requirement of stay in Norway. It is claimed that there is solid knowledge of the relevant EEA law in the ministry, but that knowledge has not resulted in legislative texts or clear preparatory documents. When the new social security regulation was implemented by the national regulation of June 1, 2012, that implementation was not accompanied by preparatory documents or other guidance as to how the rules were to be interpreted, and it was not spelled out in the act that the rules imposing a requirement of stay in Norway had to be waived in a number of practical situations. The ministry proceeded on the basis that the social security regulation from EEA law did not entail any significant changes. NAV was still to ensure correct practice through circulars. The problem was that NAV was misinterpreting EEA law in its circulars, even though NAV interpretations were questioned from time to time (NOU, 2020: 26):

> Through the years questions have arisen on a number of occasions, both within and outside NAV, about various aspects of practices relating to the requirement of stay in Norway and the relationship to EEA law. One reason why the error nevertheless was not discovered earlier is that all previous sources of discussion about the EEA rules – internally in NAV, with the Ministry and with the EFTA Surveillance Authority (ESA) – have been treated and written off as individual cases. No one, apparently, has lifted their gaze or taken the initiative to undertake any kind of systematic review in order to ensure uniform, correct practice. In the absence of critical review, officials handling cases in NAV have continued to base themselves on existing circulars, thereby continuing to misapply the rules.

NOU (2020: 26) suggests that NAV has been characterized by a management culture with clear weaknesses:

> There has been no tradition of asking questions about established truths or making pronouncements about issues not falling within one's own sphere of responsibility. The agency has had some case-handling officials with solid competence in EEA matters, but they have not worked with the specific rules

relating to the benefits in question; few have viewed the rules in their overall context. A number of case-handling officials have told the Committee of substantive uncertainty, particularly in relation to EEA law issues. In the Labor and Welfare Directorate, the quality control of new elements in circulars dealing with the EEA rules has, in some cases, such as the introduction of the new social security regulation in 2012, consisted in referring the circular to a case-handling official in the Directorate having broad but general knowledge of EEA law. The circulars contain no indication of any uncertainty about the interpretation of the provisions of the EU regulation. The Directorate assumed that the interpretation would be challenged if it was incorrect and that NAV Appeals or the National Insurance Court would, if necessary, correct the interpretation in the circular.

This did not happen, however. Instead, NAV overturned decisions in individual cases in which the interpretation was challenged, but the interpretation of the rules on which the overturning was based did not result in changes in the circulars.

NOU (2020: 27) investigators found a few examples of case-handling officials in NAV having expressed uncertainty about the interpretation in the circulars through informal internal channels:

No answers were given to those questions of interpretation and nor were they raised through formal channels. The Committee has not received any documentation indicating that employees warned that the rules were being applied incorrectly.

The practical work of implementing the social security regulations in the agency seems to have been characterized by a lack of competence, capacity, communication and critical thinking. Nor has sufficient attention been paid to general EEA law in the work on the rules, circulars and practical management of benefits. This has led to people being refused benefits they ought to have had, or losing benefits they were entitled to receive. Many have been served with wrongful claims for repayment. A number of people have also served prison terms to which they should not have been sentenced.

The NAV circulars are intended to ensure correct, uniform practice by having front-line case-handling officials familiarize themselves and be trained to apply rules that put the requirements of the law into practice, without a need to interpret and apply the law directly by front-line employees. This approach aims to simplify the case-handling procedure and ensure equal treatment for similar beneficiaries and legal certainty. The approach is, however, vulnerable to error, especially when the set of rules in question is virtually invisible to the average benefits recipient, as EEA law was in this case (NOU, 2020: 27):

It becomes particularly serious when the consequence of an incorrect interpretation of the rules by NAV may be baseless criminal proceedings brought against individuals. Viewed in the light of the importance of the circulars, the Committee takes the view that the processes employed by the Directorate for the implementation of the new EU/EEA social security regulation were inadequate and undeniably blameworthy.

It has been claimed from a number of quarters that, over time, the Directorate's substantive competence has been weakened by several rounds of reorganizations and staffing reductions.

NOU (2020) investigators found that the question whether the Directorate has the necessary capacity and competence to manage the substantive responsibility imposed on it had not been raised to the level of a formal discussion within the ministry, although it had been a topic of discussion in more informal fora. The investigators express no view on whether it has been expedient to "slim down" the Directorate, but note that the efficiency measures that had been implemented have led to a situation in which the Directorate seems to lack the competence- and resource-related prerequisites for safeguarding the substantive responsibility imposed on it in a sound manner (NOU, 2020: 27):

> The Directorate has not managed to coordinate the different result areas in NAV. This is worrying. For those Ministry employees who did know what the EU/EEA social security regulations entailed, the interpretation it is now known was relied on by NAV was shocking. The Ministry was not aware of NAV's long-standing practice in the area, however. That, and the fact that the Ministry has lacked systems to ensure better knowledge of NAV's practice is, in the Committee's view, worrisome.

The principal–agent challenge was thus not only a problem in the decentralization and distribution of competence within NAV but also a problem in the relationship between the ministry and the NAV Directorate.

NOU (2020: 28) suggests that an error that strikes in this way can easily "slip under the radar":

> The state's opponent in this area is not strong or organized and, where benefits recipients have had access to legal counsel, it has seldom been of assistance. Very few of the lawyers who have been involved in the cases, whether it be in connection with an appeal or proceedings before the National Insurance Court or the ordinary courts of law, have realized the EEA law issue involved. When a lawyer in a criminal case raised the point of EEA law, the submission was rejected on the ground that the accused was under a duty to abide by "Norwegian rules".
>
> Nor did the Supreme Court of Norway see any problem with sentencing a person to a prison term for having had stays in another EEA country without permission from NAV during periods when there was no follow-up in which to participate. The Supreme Court based itself solely on the wording of the

National Insurance Act, even though the Main Part of the EEA Agreement has been Norwegian law since 1994, and the social security regulations have been implemented in Norway through national regulations since 1994, with primacy over the requirements of the National Insurance Act. A reading of the general exceptions laid down in the National Insurance Act, to which no reference is made in the provisions on requirement of stay in Norway, together with the Norwegian regulation implementing the social security regulation and Article 21 of the regulation, shows – on a correct interpretation – that the requirement of stay in Norway cannot be applied as per the wording of the National Insurance Act. The Supreme Court undertook no such reading.

Investigation Report Maturity

After the report NOU (2020) was released, several experts were surprised that everybody and thus nobody was blamed for the scandal. Ulserød (2020: 22) phrased the question "Do someone escape too easily from responsibility for the social security scandal?":

> The Nav scandal is another public administration scandal that is allegedly about many who have failed. Does the official story mean that someone escapes responsibility too cheaply? When the investigation committee that has reviewed the so-called Nav scandal presented its report on August 4, the summary from our political authorities was that there had been a system failure. "The investigation report confirms a system failure in this area for a number of years", said Torbjørn Røe Isaksen, who was the minister of labor and social affairs. His predecessor, Anniken Hauglie, also talked about "the system failure" when she was interviewed in relation to the investigation committee's report.

The investigative committee had seven members in addition to three persons in the secretariat for the committee. Among the seven committee members, five members were trained in law, one was trained in economics, and one was a trained nurse. The dominance of law in the committee can be justified by the legal issues mentioned in the mandate. However, from a perspective of knowledge strategy to reconstruct past events and sequences of events as the main focus of the mandate, the biased knowledge structure in the committee seems a problem. The mandate focuses on the handling and roles in the case of wrongfully applying a local law to the detriment of international law. The mandate is concerned not with legal interpretations but rather with actors and actors, which is typical for an investigation: What happened? When did it happen? When did it happen? Who did what to make it happen or not happen? Why did it happen? While the basic theme is law, the investigation is concerned with finding out what went wrong, which has nothing to do with application of legal expertise. Rather, the knowledge strategy should focus on application of expertise to retrieve and interpret information.

Since the main sources to retrieve and interpret information were documents and interviews, the relevant knowledge strategy would be competence in archival analysis and investigative interviewing. While there is no single training addressing these specific competence areas, relevant knowledge derives from psychology, criminology, and management. The formalism of law as the dominating knowledge in the committee is evident in the investigation report, which reduces the extent of new insights created by the committee.

In terms of information strategy, the committee selected documents and interviews as information sources, which seems relevant for the mandate. However, the application of this information strategy was passive and reactive. The committee addressed relevant agencies for information, and they expressed areas of interest. They left it to each agency to determine the relevance of documents selected and interviewees suggested. This shortcoming is acknowledged by the committee, despite the fact that all agencies signed a cooperation agreement (NOU, 2020: 19):

> All bodies have signed the declaration. The directorate of labor and welfare proposed an amendment to the declaration, stating that the directorate has identified all information which, in the opinion of the directorate of labor and welfare, is relevant to the committees work. The committee chose not to accept such an adjustment in the declaration.
>
> Despite the committee's assumption that the agencies have submitted all relevant information, the committee has no guarantee that this has actually happened. In this respect, the committee would like to emphasize in particular that a number of minutes from the EFTA working group on social security were first sent to the committee on May 18, 2020, and then upon express request. The ministry of labor and social affairs had originally only sent minutes from the meetings of this working group in 2009. When the committee in connection with the review of the minutes from conversations with employees in the ministry learned that the ministry reported on its work with assessment of Regulation 883/2004 during meetings in EFTA working group on social security October 19, 2005 and September 28–29, 2006, we requested that these minutes also be submitted.

The shortcoming in the information strategy does not only regard the extent of relevant documents reviewed. There also was also a passive approach to the selection of relevant interviewees as persons were nominated from the relevant agencies (NOU, 2020: 20):

> The committee has conducted formal interviews with a total of 54 individuals. Many of these people are covered by the government's instructions and had a duty to explain themselves to the committee. The persons who have not had a duty to explain, including employees and managers in the prosecuting

authority and the courts, have all agreed to explain themselves to the committee. The selection of persons for interviews is partly based on the committee's own inquiries and partly on direct input from relevant agencies. The committee has emphasized talking to employees and former employees as well as managers and former managers in the various agencies that the committee's mandate includes, and people who represent different parts and levels within these agencies.

The interviews were formal in nature and lacked the advantages of investigative interviewing. Collins and Carthy (2019) studied the relationship between rapport and communication during investigative interviews. Attention, positivity, and coordination are important rapport components. Rapport is a close and harmonious relationship in which individuals understand each other and are sympathetic to each other. The purpose of investigative interviewing is to gain information, and persons providing information may not always be motivated to do so, especially if the persons perceive being subject to suspicion or blame for misconduct. The aim is for the examination interviewer and the information source to have a productive relationship that builds on cooperation and respect. An interview takes place because the interviewer assumes that the subject of an interview has information of value to the interviewer. It is important to use non-judgmental language in interviews, which can have a positive impact on interactions.

The interviews by the committee were very different. They were not only formal but also distant and procedural. Everyone attending from the committee and the secretariat had prepared questions. The interaction effect did not occur as answers seldom are followed up by the interviewer since there is the next interviewer in line to continue the questioning. While the formal committee approach is common in political settings such as national parliaments, a goal-oriented investigation with the purpose of reconstructing past events and sequences of events suffers from the number of participants and the formal roles applied by attendees. This is an obvious shortcoming in this case where people would have told more if interviewees found themselves in a more comfortable setting.

NOU (2020) does not contribute to any clarification compared to what was already known in advance. The report does not reconstruct events and sequences of events, and it does not contribute to insights into what happened, when it happened, and who did what to make it happen or not happen. Rather, the report is mainly an assessment of what was already known. Therefore, the investigation cannot achieve a higher score than level 2 in Figure 10.2.

One of the reasons for lack of new insights was the procedure for selection of interviewees and the conduct of interviews. Examiners only interviewed people recommended to them, and they conducted interviews as a communication event rather than as a goal-oriented procedure.

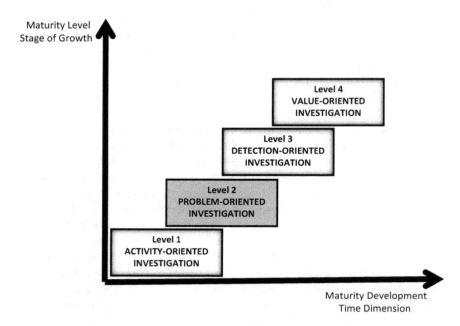

Figure 10.2 Maturity model for internal private investigation applied to the NOU

References

Baird, J.E. and Zelin, R.C. (2009). An examination of the impact of obedience pressure on perceptions of fraudulent acts and the likelihood of committing occupational fraud, *Journal of Forensic Studies in Accounting and Business*, 1 (1), 1–14.

Bernat, I. and Whyte, D. (2020). Chapter 9: State-corporate crimes, in: Rorie, M.L. (editor), *The Handbook of White-Collar Crime*, Wiley & Sons, Hoboken, pp. 191–208.

Bernburg, J.G., Krohn, M.D. and Rivera, C. (2006). Official labeling, criminal embeddedness, and subsequent delinquency, *Journal of Research in Crime and Delinquency*, 43 (1), 67–88.

Boghossian, J. and Marques, J.C. (2019). Saving the Canadian fur industry's hide: Government's strategic use of private authority to constrain radical activism, *Organization Studies*, 40 (8), 1241–1268.

Bosse, D.A. and Phillips, R.A. (2016). Agency theory and bounded self-interest, *Academy of Management Review*, 41 (2), 276–297.

Bussmann, K.D., Niemeczek, A. and Vockrodt, M. (2018). Company culture and prevention of corruption in Germany, China and Russia, *European Journal of Criminology*, 15 (3), 255–277.

Chrisman, J.J., Chua, J.H., Kellermanns, F.W. and Chang, E.P.C. (2007). Are family managers agents or stewards? An exploratory study in privately held family firms, *Journal of Business Research*, 60 (10), 1030–1038.

Collins, K. and Carthy, N. (2019). No rapport, no comment: The relationship between rapport and communication during investigative interviews with suspects, *Journal of Investigative Psychology and Offender Profiling*, 16 (1), 18–31.

Desai, V.M. (2016). Under the radar: Regulatory collaborations and their selective use to facilitate organizational compliance, *Academy of Management Journal*, 59 (2), 636–57.

DeScioli, P. and Bokemper, S. (2014). Voting as a counter-strategy in the blame game, *Psychological Inquiry*, 25, 206–214.

Eberlein, B. (2019). Who fills the global governance gap? Rethinking the roles of business and government in global governance, *Organization Studies*, 40 (8), 1125–1146.

Eberly, M.B., Holley, E.C., Johnson, M.D. and Mitchell, T.R. (2011). Beyond internal and external: A dyadic theory of relational attributions, *Academy of Management Review*, 36 (4), 731–753.

Ferraro, F., Pfeffer, J. and Sutton, R.I. (2005). Economics language and assumptions: How theories can become self-fulfilling, *Academy of Management Review*, 30 (1), 8–24.

Galvin, M.A. (2020). Gender and white-collar crime – Theoretical issues, *Criminal Justice Studies*, doi: 10.1080/1478601X.2020.1709954.

Gangloff, K.A., Connelly, B.L. and Shook, C.L. (2016). Of scapegoats and signals: Investor reactions to CEO succession in the aftermath of wrongdoing, *Journal of Management*, 42, 1614–1634.

Gao, P. and Zhang, G. (2019). Accounting manipulation, peer pressure, and internal control, *The Accounting Review*, 94 (1), 127–151.

Hamann, R. (2019). Dynamic de-responsibilization in business-government interactions, *Organization Studies*, 40 (8), 1193–1216.

Hoffmann, J.P. (2002). A contextual analysis of differential association, social control, and strain theories of delinquency, *Social Forces*, 81 (3), 753–785.

Holt, R. and Cornelissen, J. (2014). Sensemaking revisited, *Management Learning*, 45 (5), 525–539.

Huisman, W. (2020). Chapter 10: Blurred lines: Collusions between legitimate and illegitimate organizations, in: Rorie, M.L. (editor), *The Handbook of White-Collar Crime*, Wiley & Sons, Hoboken, pp. 139–158.

Huisman, W. and Erp, J. (2013). Opportunities for environmental crime, *British Journal of Criminology*, 53, 1178–1200.

Hurrell, S.A. (2016). Rethinking the soft skills deficit blame game: Employers, skills withdrawal and the reporting of soft skills gaps, *Human Relations*, 69 (3), 605–628.

Jenssen, H.L. (2020). Hans Christian Holte: Skandalen har helt klart truffet oss veldig tungt (Hans Christian Holte: The scandal has clearly hit us very hard), *Daily Norwegian Business Newspaper Dagens Næringsliv*, October 2, www.dn.no.

Judge, T.A., Piccolo, R.F. and Kosalka, T. (2009). The bright and dark sides of leader traits: A review and theoretical extension of the leader trait paradigm, *The Leadership Quarterly*, 20, 855–875.

Karim, K.E. and Siegel, P.H. (1998). A signal detection theory approach to analyzing the efficiency and effectiveness of auditing to detect management fraud, *Managerial Auditing Journal*, 13 (6), 367–375.

Keaveney, S.M. (2008). The blame game: An attribution theory approach to marketer-engineer conflict in high-technology companies, *Industrial Marketing Management*, 37, 653–663.

Kroneberg, C. and Schultz, S. (2018). Revisiting the role of self-control in situational action theory, *European Journal of Criminology*, 15 (1), 56–76.

Larsen, M.H. (2019). NAV-svindel straffes hardere enn hvitsnippforbrytelser (NAV fraud punished harder than white-collar crime), *Daily Norwegian Newspaper Aftenposten*, November 1, www.aftenposten.no.

Lee, F. and Robinson, R.J. (2000). An attributional analysis of social accounts: Implications of playing the blame game, *Journal of Applied Social Psychology*, 30 (9), 1853–1879.

Lehman, D.W., Cooil, B. and Ramanujam, R. (2020). The effects of rule complexity on organizational noncompliance and remediation: Evidence from restaurant health inspections, *Journal of Management*, 46 (8), 1436–1468.

Lofstad, R. (2019). Hentet ut av fengsel etter ni dager (Brought out of jail after nine days), *Daily Norwegian Newspaper Dagbladet*, October 30, www.dagbladet.no.

Logan, M.W., Morgan, M.A., Benson, M.L. and Cullen, F.T. (2019). Coping with imprisonment: Testing the special sensitivity hypothesis for white-collar offenders, *Justice Quarterly*, 36 (2), 225–254.

Maher, R., Valenzuela, F. and Böhm, S. (2019). The enduring state: An analysis of governance-making in three mining conflicts, *Organization Studies*, 40 (8), 1169–1192.

Mawritz, M.B., Greenbaum, R.L., Butts, M.M. and Graham, K.A. (2017). I just can't control myself: A self-regulation perspective on the abuse of deviant employees, *Academy of Management Journal*, 60 (4), 1482–1503.

Meldalen, S.G. and Lofstad, R. (2019). Måtte selje leilighet etter feilaktig NAV-dom (Had to sell apartment after incorrect NAV judgment), *Daily Norwegian Newspaper Dagbladet*, October 30, www.dagbladet.no.

Michel, C. (2016). Violent street crime versus harmful white-collar crime: A comparison of perceived seriousness and punitiveness, *Critical Criminology*, 24, 127–143.

NOU. (2020). Blindsonen: Gransking av feilpraktiseringen av folketrygdlovens oppholdskrav ved reiser i EØS-området (The blind spot: Investigation of the incorrect practice of the National Insurance Act's residence requirements when traveling in the EEA area), *Norges offentlige utredninger* (Norway's public inquiries), 2020 (9), 328.

NTB. (2019). SV og Rødt vurderer mistillit – krever klare NAV-svar fra Hauglie (SV and Red assess distrust – require clear NAV answers from Hauglie), *Daily Norwegian Business Newspaper Dagens Næringsliv*, November 4, www.dn.no.

Petrocelli, M., Piquero, A.R. and Smith, M.R. (2003). Conflict theory and racial profiling: An empirical analysis of police traffic stop data, *Journal of Criminal Justice*, 31 (1), 1–11.

Piazza, A. and Jourdan, J. (2018). When the dust settles: The consequences of scandals for organizational competition, *Academy of Management Journal*, 61 (1), 165–190.

Pillay, S. and Kluvers, R. (2014). An institutional theory perspective on corruption: The case of a developing democracy, *Financial Accountability & Management*, 30 (1), 95–119.

Piquero, N.L. (2018). White-collar crime is crime: Victims hurt just the same, *Criminology & Public Policy*, 17 (3), 595–600.

Pontell, H.N., Ghazi-Tehrani, A.K. and Burton, B. (2020). Chapter 22: White-collar and corporate crime in China, in: Rorie, M.L. (editor), *The Handbook of White-Collar Crime*, Wiley & Sons, Hoboken, pp. 347–362.

Pratt, T.C. and Cullen, F.T. (2005). Assessing macro-level predictors and theories of crime: A meta-analysis, *Crime and Justice*, 32, 373–450.

Resodihardjo, S.L., Carroll, B.J., Eijk, C.J.A. and Maris, S. (2015). Why traditional responses to blame games fail: The importance of context, rituals, and sub-blame games in the face of raves gone wrong, *Public Administration*, 94 (2), 350–363.

Rodriguez, P., Uhlenbruck, K. and Eden, L. (2005). Government corruption and the entry strategies of multinationals, *Academy of Management Review*, 30 (2), 383–396.

Rooij, B. and Fine, A. (2020). Chapter 15: Preventing corporate crime from within: Compliance management, whistleblowing, and internal Monitoring, in: Rorie, M.L. (editor), *The Handbook of White-Collar Crime*, Wiley & Sons, Hoboken, pp. 229–245.

Rothe, D.L. (2020). Moving beyond abstract typologies? Overview of state and state-corporate crime, *Journal of White-Collar and Corporate Crime*, 1 (1), 7–15.

Ruud, S. and Spence, T. (2019). Kjersti Monland går av som ytelsesdirektør i Nav (Kjerti Monland resigns as benefits director at Nav), *Daily Norwegian Newspaper Aftenposten*, December 4, www.aftenposten.no.

Schnatterly, K., Gangloff, K.A. and Tuschke, A. (2018). CEO wrongdoing: A review of pressure, opportunity, and rationalization, *Journal of Management*, 44 (6), 2405–2432.

Schoepfer, A. and Piquero, N.L. (2006). Exploring white-collar crime and the American dream: A partial test of institutional anomie theory, *Journal of Criminal Justice*, 34 (3), 227–235.

Schoultz, I. and Flyghed, J. (2016). Doing business for a 'higher loyalty' How Swedish transnational corporations neutralize allegations of crime, *Crime, Law and Social Change*, 66 (2), 183–198.

Schoultz, I. and Flyghed, J. (2019). From "we didn't do it" to "we've learned our lesson": Development of a typology of neutralizations of corporate crime, *Critical Criminology*, doi: 10.1007/s10612-019-09483-3.

Schoultz, I. and Flyghed, J. (2020a). From "we didn't do it" to "we've learned our lesson": Development of a typology of neutralizations of corporate crime, *Critical Criminology*, 28, 739–757.

Schoultz, I. and Flyghed, J. (2020b). Denials and confessions: An analysis of the temporalization of neutralizations of corporate crime, *International Journal of Law, Crime and Justice*, doi: 10.1016/j.ijlcj.2020.100389.

Schwendinger, H. and Schwendinger, J. (2014). Defenders of order or guardians of human rights? *Social Justice*, 40 (1–2), 87–117.

Solberg, S.M. (2020). Jussprofessor mener regjeringen må ta hovedansvaret for Nav-skandalen (Law professor thinks the government must carry the main responsibility for the Nav scandal), *Web-Based Norwegian Newspaper Nettavisen*, November 2, www.nettavisen.no.

Sonnier, B.M., Lassar, W.M. and Lassar, S.S. (2015). The influence of source credibility and attribution of blame on juror evaluation of liability of industry specialist auditors, *Journal of Forensic & Investigative Accounting*, 7 (1), 1–37.

Srivastava, S.B. and Goldberg, A. (2017). Language as a window into culture, *California Management Review*, 60 (1), 56–69.

Sutherland, E.H. (1983). *White Collar Crime – The Uncut Version*, Yale University Press, New Haven.

Sykes, G. and Matza, D. (1957). Techniques of neutralization: A theory of delinquency, *American Sociological Review*, 22 (6), 664–670.

Szalma, J.L. and Hancock, P.A. (2013) A signal improvement to signal detection analysis: fuzzy SDT on the ROCs, *Journal of Experimental Psychology: Human Perception and Performance*, 39 (6), 1741–1762.

Tombs, S. and Whyte, D. (2003). Scrutinizing the powerful: Crime, contemporary political economy, and critical social research, in: Tombs, S. and Whyte, D. (editors), *Unmasking the Crimes of the Powerful*, Lang, New York, pp. 3–48.

Ulserød, T. (2020). Slipper noen for billig unna ansvaret for trygdeskandalen? (Do someone escape too easily from responsibility for the social security scandal?), *Daily Norwegian Newspaper Aftenposten*, Monday, August 17, p. 22–23.

Weick, K.E. (1995). What theory is not, theorizing is, *Administrative Science Quarterly*, 40, 385–390.

Weick, K.E., Sutcliffe, K.M. and Obstfeld, D. (2005). Organizing and the process of sensemaking, *Organization Science*, 16 (4), 409–421.

Williams, J.W. (2008). The lessons of 'Enron' – Media accounts, corporate crimes, and financial markets, *Theoretical Criminology*, 12 (4), 471–499.

Williams, M.L., Levi, M., Burnap, P. and Gundur, R.V. (2019). Under the corporate radar: Examining insider business cybercrime victimization through an application of routine activities theory, *Deviant Behavior*, 40 (9), 1119–1131.

Xie, Y. and Keh, H.T. (2016). Taming the blame game: Using promotion programs to counter product-hrm crises, *Journal of Advertising*, 45 (2), 211–226.

Zysman-Quirós, D. (2020). Chapter 23: White-collar crime in South and Central America: Corporate-state crime, governance, and the high impact of the Odebrecht corruption case, in: Rorie, M.L. (editor), *The Handbook of White-Collar Crime*, Wiley & Sons, Hoboken, pp. 363–380.

11 Donald Trump Investigations

If the belief in the American dream is strong, then financial resources can help directly. The dark side of the American dream implies that if legal means seem inconvenient then white-collar crime might be a convenient option. America is often described as a land of opportunity in which anyone, regardless of race or ethnicity, can succeed. Although this maxim is typically taken to refer to opportunities for social and economic advancement, it applies as well to opportunities to commit certain forms of crime. "Trump: An American Dream" is a four-part British television documentary, exploring the journey of Donald Trump through five decades. The first episode was shown in 2017. In the opportunity dimension, Trump had for a while status combined with an ability to conceal potential wrongdoing by various corporate structures and law firm initiatives. Government agencies seem still unable to develop their allegations and accusations into evidence that might lead to conviction.

Investigative journalists at the UK newspaper *The Guardian* reported in March 2022 that the likelihood of criminal charges against the former president of the United States was rising. Some ex-prosecutors called on the US department of justice to accelerate investigations (Stone, 2022). Not only was Donald Trump facing charges for attempts to overturn a presidential election. He also faced charges for fraud (Eisen et al., 2021; James, 2020).

According to the petition by the attorney general, there were accusations against Trump related to misleading statements of financial conditions, misleading asset valuations, and misleading reports for other assets (James, 2020). Similarly, Eisen et al. (2021) list allegations of falsifying business records, alleged tax fraud, alleged insurance fraud and scheme to defraud banks, and enterprise fraud allegations.

Offender Convenience Themes

If assuming that the allegations and accusations are correct, then convenience theory can be applied to identify potential convenience themes for motive, opportunity, and willingness, as illustrated in Figure 11.1. Donald Trump has been a strong advocate for the American dream of prosperity. The American dream suggests that the greatest and most satisfying experience in life is to become economically

DOI: 10.4324/9781003363934-12

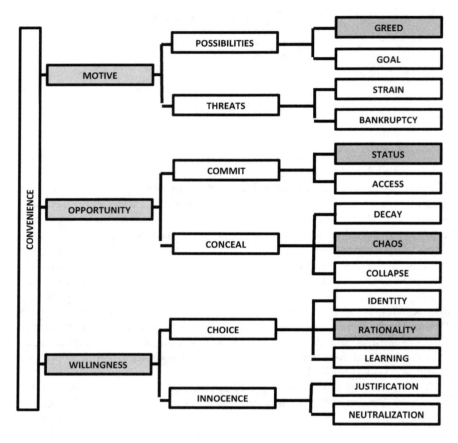

Figure 11.1 Convenience themes for Donald Trump

rich and that everyone can indeed become rich if he or she works hard enough and smart enough (Schoepfer and Piquero, 2006). It is a one-dimensional emphasis on the desirability of material success and individual achievement in life. The American dream is a set of cultural beliefs saying that in the United States, everyone can be economically successful. It instructs all Americans to strive for material success, suggesting that hard work will bring high rewards (Cullen et al., 2010: 170):

> The American dream has positive effects, because it creates strong desires for upward mobility and allows some people who might otherwise have been mired in the bottom of society to achieve enormous wealth. But this dream also has a dark side. The difficulty is that the American dream preaches universal success – that is, that it tells everyone that economic mobility not only is to be cherished but also is within reach. But this dream confronts harsh

reality: the unequal American class structure. Opportunities for success are not universal but differentially available.

If the belief in the American dream is strong, then financial resources can help directly. The dark side of the American dream implies that if legal means seem inconvenient then white-collar crime might be a convenient option (Pratt and Cullen, 2005; Trahan et al., 2005). As argued by Benson et al. (2021: 10), the American dream might be pursued by crime:

> America is often described as a land of opportunity in which anyone, regardless of race or ethnicity, can succeed. Although this maxim is typically taken to refer to opportunities for social and economic advancement, it applies as well to opportunities to commit certain forms of crime.

"Trump: An American Dream" is a four-part British television documentary, exploring the journey of Donald Trump through five decades. The first episode was shown in 2017.

In the opportunity dimension, Trump had for a while status combined with an ability to conceal potential wrongdoing by various corporate structures and law firm initiatives. Government agencies seem still unable to develop their allegations and accusations into evidence that might lead to conviction. In the personal willingness dimension, it was apparently a rational choice by Trump to avoid public scrutiny. The rational choice assumption about offending is based on a normative foundation where advantages and disadvantages are subjectively compared (Müller, 2018). When there is no perceived likelihood of detection, then there is no deterrence effect to prevent offenses (Comey, 2009). Rational choice is concerned with benefits of crime exceeding costs (Pratt and Cullen, 2005), where the perceived likelihood of incarceration is a cost element.

Fraud Investigation Outcome

There are two reports here. One is written by the attorney general of the State of New York (James, 2020), and the other is written by governance studies at Brookings (Eisen et al., 2021). While James (2020) relied mainly on financial statements as information sources for the investigation, Eisen et al. (2021) relied mainly on newspaper reports as information sources.

Among other allegations, the attorney general investigated potential misrepresentation to banks. James (2020) argued that misleading financial statements from Trump granted him and his organization access to credit. Deutsche Bank accepted Trump's personal guaranty as the goodwill attached to the Trump name might have significant financial value. Trump also provided a personal guaranty for a $170 million loan in connection with the Trump International Hotel in Washington, DC. The office of the attorney general (OAG) obtained evidence, but not necessarily of misconduct or crime (James, 2020: 50):

Evidence obtained by the OAG establishes that Donald Trump, Jr. personally certified on an annual basis the truth and accuracy of the Statements of
Financial Condition of Donald J. Trump for 2016, 2017, 2018, and 2019. On
some such certifications, Donald Trump, Jr. specified that he was doing so as
"attorney in fact" for Donald J. Trump.

Among other allegations, Brookings investigators suggested tax fraud (Eisen
et al., 2021: 28):

Based on the public reporting as to the fringe benefits investigation, prosecutors may seek to charge the Trump Organization (or those who received the
benefits) with multiple tax fraud acts here under Section 1801. Elements of
that section may be met, for example, if fringe benefits were misdescribed
or entirely omitted from relevant filings and/or if appropriate taxes were not
paid in connection with those benefits. The class of felony or misdemeanor is
harder to ascertain because the exact value of the benefits and their impact on
tax liabilities is unclear from the public records.

Brooking investigators also discussed why Trump and his organization might be
able to avoid criminal liability. One reason could be expired statutes of limitations. Fringe benefits in tax filings, for example, have a five-year or possibly only
two-year limitations period. Brooking investigators made recommendations on
how to avoid the short time limits. They suggested that prosecutors could use
three independent methods. First, prosecutors could charge a broader conspiracy.
Second, prosecutors could suggest prior bad acts. Third, prosecutors could argue
that the "the statute of limitations should be extended as to Trump because he has
been outside of New York "continuously" over at least the last four years, during
the term of his presidency" (Eisen et al., 2021: 40).

Investigation Report Maturity

Both reports have obvious shortcomings. None of them carried out interviews
to gain insights into the allegations. Both relied on secondary data from either
accounting or media. Eisen et al. (2021: 53) admitted to investigation limitations:

As we have noted from the start, this report is based on publicly available
information, which we have assembled and analyzed in light of the potentially governing statutes and relevant legal principles. We do not have any
inside prosecutorial information, and are not privy either to unreported evidence uncovered by the prosecuting authorities, or to the particular insights
that they have gleaned from their intense efforts in connection with the
investigation. We thus cannot offer a definitive judgment or prediction of
either what will occur, or what action should be taken in light of the complete record.

James (2020) was more certain about what action should be taken. The final heading in the 114-page document was "claim for relief," where the petitioner requested that the court entered a judgment regarding Donald J. Trump, Donald Trump Jr., and Ivanka Trump. While the petition document was in the name of Letitia James as the attorney general of the State of New York, the investigation report was signed by Austin Thompson, an attorney admitted to the bar of the state. He affirmed in the document that he was authorized to make the verification, and that he was acquainted with the facts in the matter of the report. In addition to Thompson, nine named individuals at the office of the New York State attorney general had worked on the investigation report. They were all labeled "Attorneys for the People of the State of New York".

The attorney general investigation by James (2020) is assigned level 2 in the maturity model, while the analysis by Eisen et al. (2021) is assigned level 1 in the maturity model in Figure 11.2.

Donald Trump continued to be an important person in the center of attention not only in the United States but also globally. Barak (2022: 53) labeled him an outlaw:

> In terms of being an *outlaw*, Trump is the real deal. Meaning that Donald is habitually breaking laws of all kinds, while he remains free at large to take care of his businesses as usual. Donald is also an outlaw within a community

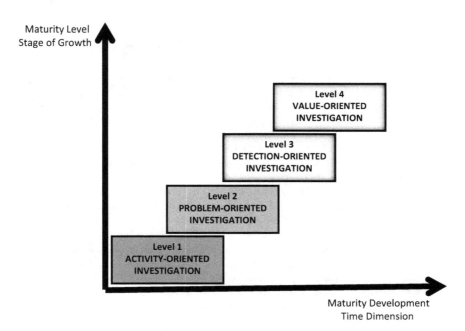

Figure 11.2 Maturity of investigations by the Attorney General and by Brookings

of outlaws because he has no moral compass, and he has no loyalty to anyone besides himself. In a few words, Trump has no honor among thieves, and he has no honor among the law-abiding. The Donald is not an outlaw out of negligence or unfamiliarity with the illegalities of the marketplace, the Constitution, or civil laws. On the contrary, Trump knows the subtle differences between lawfully right and unlawfully wrong.

Moreover, Donald appreciates that the legal system and the laws distinguishing between right and wrong, justifiable and not justifiable, legal and illegal are fluid in theory and practice, and they are subject to valuation and interpretation. Trump also understands that the administration of justice can often be malleable. Based on Trump's unmatched number of lawsuits as both plaintiff and defendant, Donald generally knows the rules of the legal games as well as anyone with the exceptions of those who litigate the law for a living. Should Donald not know where the lines are drawn between lawlessness and lawfulness, it then becomes the business of his arsenal of attorneys to find out where those lines are supposed to be as they seek to evade or move them. Unlike most powerful people who may go up to the lines of wrongdoing and have some reluctance of stepping over, Donald has no such inhibitions especially when it comes to bending, if not breaking, those legalities standing in the way of his pursuing the objects of his needs or desires.

This quote is from a book by criminologist Gregg Barak entitled *Criminology on Trump* in the book series entitled "Crimes of the Powerful".

References

Barak, G. (2022). *Criminology on Trump*, Routledge, London.

Benson, M.L., Feldmeyer, B., Gabbidon, S.L. and Chio, H.L. (2021). Race, ethnicity, and social change: The democratization of middle-class crime, *Criminology*, 59 (1), 10–41.

Comey, J.B. (2009). Go directly to prison: White collar sentencing after the Sarbanes-Oxley act, *Harvard Law Review*, 122, 1728–1749.

Cullen, F.T., Cloward, R.A. and Lloyd E.O. (2010). Delinquency and opportunity, in: Cullen, F.T. and Wilcox, P. (editors), *Encyclopedia of Criminological Theory* (Volume 1), Sage Publications, Los Angeles, pp. 170–174.

Eisen, N., Perry, E.D., Ayer, D. and Cuti, J.R. (2021). *New York State's Trump Investigation: An Analysis of the Reported Facts and Applicable Law*, Brookings Governance Studies, Washington D.C., www.brookings.edu.

James, L. (2020). *The Trump Organization, Inc.; DJT Holdings LLC; DJT Holdings Managing Member LLC; Seven Springs LLC; Eric Trump; Charles Martabano; Morgan, Lewis & Bockius, LLP; Sheri Dillon; Mazars USA LLC; Donald J. Trump; Donald Trump, Jr.; and Ivanka Trump*, Petition by the Attorney General of the State of New York to the Supreme Court of the State of New York, January 18.

Müller, S.M. (2018). Corporate behavior and ecological disaster: Dow Chemical and the Great Lakes mercury crisis, 1970–1972, *Business History*, 60 (3), 399–422.

Pratt, T.C. and Cullen, F.T. (2005). Assessing macro-level predictors and theories of crime: A meta-analysis, *Crime and Justice*, 32, 373–450.

Schoepfer, A. and Piquero, N.L. (2006). Exploring white-collar crime and the American dream: A partial test of institutional anomie theory, *Journal of Criminal Justice*, 34 (3), 227–235.

Stone, P. (2022). Likelihood of criminal charges against Trump rising, experts say, *The Guardian*, March 11, www.theguardian.com.

Trahan, A., Marquart, J.W. and Mullings, J. (2005). Fraud and the American dream: Toward an understanding of fraud victimization, *Deviant Behavior*, 26 (6), 601–620.

12 South Sudan Financial Flows

The Commission interviewed over 40 witnesses and examined 110 confidential records pertaining to corruption, embezzlement, and misappropriation as well as environmental harms in South Sudan. This seems to be a good information strategy. The Commission "was satisfied that there are reasonable grounds to believe that an incident or pattern of conduct had occurred only when it had obtained a reliable body of information, consistent with other material, upon which a reasonable and ordinarily prudent person would believe that the incident or pattern of conduct had occurred". This was no value-oriented investigation for the United Nations. Probably, no extensive investigation represents a profitable investment for the UN. However, an investigation might add value to stakeholders in the country if the report was to be taken serious by application of the strategies of carrot or stick. Unfortunately, the report seems to be one of many that end up on the shelf in an office at the United Nations in New York. The privileged elite in South Sudan can disregard the report by claiming that the investigators did not understand the situation in their country. They can express a strong dislike against all foreigners who criticize their internal affairs.

Lundin Energy in Sweden was accused of wrongdoing in South Sudan (Schoultz and Flyghed, 2020). The civil war caused the deaths of thousands of people, the forced displacement of almost 200,000 people, and numerous cases of rape, torture, and abduction. Villages were put on fire. According to the outside-in sources, executives at Lundin Energy knew that such crime was committed and that Lundin Energy enabled some of it, took no effective action to stop their occurrence, and worked alongside their perpetrators to secure oil and gas activities. Communities were allegedly violently displaced from areas where Lundin Energy planned to operate (BHR Resource Center, 2018).

In their analysis of the Lundin Energy case, Schoultz and Flyghed (2020: 7) found that the initial account of the scandal was characterized by appeal to higher loyalties, denial of knowledge, and condemnation of the condemner:

> The vice president of exploration, Alexander Schneiter, who had lived in Sudan during the ten-year period that the company had been present in the country, had not seen any of the phenomena witnessed by the various aid and human rights organizations. "I have instead seen the opposite. How villages have

DOI: 10.4324/9781003363934-13

grown up along the road and how people's conditions have improved as a result of having better communications. Our presence means a form of security for the population". Nor had the company's CEO, Ian Lundin, "seen any burning villages, only tribes that are fighting one another". Representatives of Lundin Petroleum used denial of knowledge, in the form of an interpretative denial, which involves assertions of not having known what was happening at the time.

This chapter reviews an investigation report focusing on the "staggering amounts of money and other wealth" that "have been illicitly siphoned from South Sudan's public coffers and resources" (Commission, 2021: 1).

Offender Convenience Themes

Figure 12.1 illustrates convenience themes for accused offenders at Lundin. There were possibilities for individual and corporate gain. There was lack of oversight and guardianship as well as criminal market forces in terms of chaos and collapse. The findings by Schoultz and Flyghed (2020) indicate rationality.

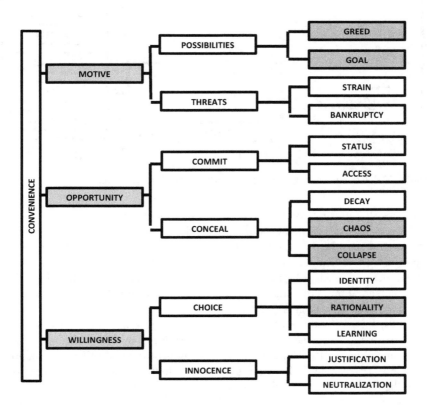

Figure 12.1 Convenience themes for Lundin

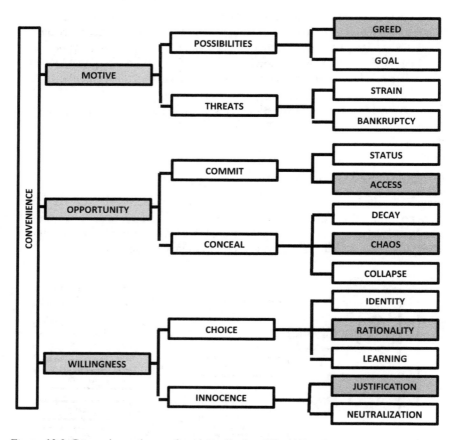

Figure 12.2 Convenience themes for Al Cardinal and Kur Ajing Ater

Figure 12.2 illustrates convenience themes for the main suspects of Al Cardinal and Kur Ajing Ater in South Sudan involved in misconduct such as bribing the British company De La Rue PLC. Investigators at the Commission (2021) also reported harm to health and environmental crime. The total fraud scam involving government officials, politicians, generals, and other members of the elite might be explained at the individual level of possibilities for climbing in the hierarchy of human needs and desires.

Status, success, and wealth – often based on greed – were probably important to all of them. Power and influence can be achieved by membership in criminal financial networks. There were obvious signs of rational self-interest among offenders. This is one of the witness statements in the report: "Get any company from the registrar, and you will see the names of Government officials".

Access to resources to commit fraud is common among elite members in the country. Revenues from both oil and other sources are available to people in powerful positions. There is no control of elite members or guardianship against their wrongdoing.

Offenders can justify their wrongdoing by arguing that fraud is common in a corrupt country. Furthermore, since the criminal justice system is not concerned with white-collar crime, there is a signal that such crime is not considered serious. For example, everyone knows that Al Cardinal spent state income to buy housing estates in the United Kingdom for himself without any interest from the criminal justice system in South Sudan. It was a rational choice to offend since benefits exceeded costs.

Fraud Investigation Outcome

The Commission (2022: 40) concluded that there were "reasonable grounds to believe that a significant proportion of oil revenue continues to be diverted and stolen". Regarding non-oil revenue, the investigators found that payments identified in three case studies alone amounted to a total value of more than USD 73 million. One of the case studies concerned allegations of corruption related to a Sudanese businessman. He was linked to acts of corruption involving the government procurement of vehicles (Commission, 2021: 21):

> One of the major challenges underpinning the misappropriation of non-oil revenues relates to poor procurement procedures. For example, as far back as 2007 and 2008, the Auditor General's Reports on Financial Statements for these years are published on the National Audit Chamber website. Both of these reports detailed poor procurement procedures in southern Sudan prior to its independence in 2011, including for goods procured without signed contracts, payments made without supporting documents, single source procurements, and a lack of records to ensure that goods which were paid for had actually been delivered.

Investigation Report Maturity

The Commission (2021) interviewed over 40 witnesses and examined 110 confidential records pertaining to corruption, embezzlement, and misappropriation as well as environmental harms. This seems to be a good information strategy. The Commission (2021: 9) "was satisfied that there are reasonable grounds to believe that an incident or pattern of conduct had occurred only when it had obtained a reliable body of information, consistent with other material, upon which a reasonable and ordinarily prudent person would believe that the incident or pattern of conduct had occurred". This criterion is different from the traditional and stronger requirement of incident occurrence beyond any reasonable doubt.

While the procedure applied by the examiners seems convincing, the lack of substantial findings makes the result seem like a problem-oriented investigation as indicated in Figure 12.3.

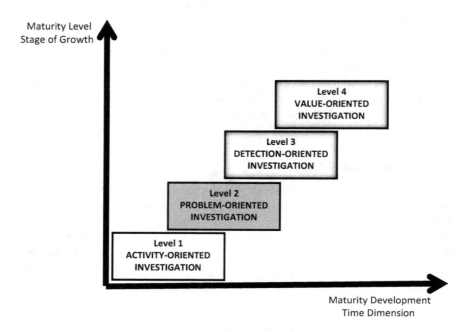

Figure 12.3 Maturity of investigations by the commission in South Sudan

This was no value-oriented investigation for the United Nations. Probably, no extensive investigation represents a profitable investment for the UN. However, an investigation might add value to stakeholders in the country if the report was to be taken serious by application of the strategies of carrot or stick. Unfortunately, the report seems to be one of many that end up on the shelf in an office at the United Nations in New York. The privileged elite in South Sudan can disregard the report by claiming that the investigators did not understand the situation in their country. They can express a strong dislike against all foreigners who criticize their internal affairs.

References

BHR Resource Center. (2018). Lundin Energy lawsuit (re complicity in war crimes, Sudan), *Business & Human Rights Resource Centre*, October 18, www.business-human-rights.org.

Commission. (2021). *Human Rights Violations and Related Economic Crimes in the Republic of South Sudan* (Human Rights Council, Forty-eighth session: Agenda item 4 Human rights situations that require the Council's attention), 13 September–08 October 2021. Conference room paper of the Commission on Human Rights in South Sudan.

Schoultz, I. and Flyghed, J. (2020). Denials and confessions: An analysis of the temporalization of neutralizations of corporate crime, *International Journal of Law, Crime and Justice*, doi: 10.1016/j.ijlcj.2020.100389.

13 Danish Bestseller in Myanmar

This case study applies the perspective of social license to operate. The perspective of social license suggests that legal and social obligations and expectations provide separate but interacting issues for assessing the extent to which business conduct is aligned with norms in the community. While each business enterprise serves a number of purposes in the community such as employment and goods and services, the business conduct has to meet both legal and social requirements to operate. The community does not exist to serve the business enterprise. Rather, each corporate entity exists to serve the community with benefits without violating the legal and social license. The social license can be part of a bottom-up as well as an outside-in effort to enhance the social control of business activity. Business enterprises attempt to respond to indicate that their activities are not only legally legitimate but also socially legitimate. The expression is often used when a company's activities may face disapproval – especially when such disapproval could result in resistance that could harm their business interests.

The Danish law firm Offersen Christoffersen was commissioned to assess whether the company Bestseller had economic relations with the military junta in Myanmar in violation of the Danish Ministry of Foreign Affairs' or the EU's guidelines and rules for sanctions. The law firm had to also assess whether Bestseller's due diligence in Myanmar lived up to international standards for corporate social responsibility (Christoffersen and Mikkelsen, 2021).

Bestseller had 2,700 branded chain stores across 38 markets worldwide, and their products were sold in 15,000 multi-brand and department stores. Bestseller seemed to violate its social license to operate when it placed orders in Myanmar after the military coup in the country (Reed, 2022):

> In garments, multinational companies such as H&M, Bestseller and Primark brought in supply-chain investors and created jobs, mostly women, during Myanmar's decade of democratic transition, which ended with a coup. While some have suspended their Myanmar operations, others are quietly still buying.

Bestseller faced serious criticism (Einarsdottir, 2021; Thomsen, 2021), including negative comments from the Danish foreign minister (Ritzau, 2021) and the

DOI: 10.4324/9781003363934-14

fashion industry (Einarsdottir, 2021). A report by the United Nations showed that companies producing clothes in Myanmar had financial relations to the military.

The military in Myanmar carried out a coup on February 1, 2021, and established a junta of generals to rule the country. In 2022, the junta executed four democracy activists (Nystuen, 2022). The European Union introduced sanctions against the junta on March 22 and April 19, 2021. Sanctions were implemented to harm military financial interests in the country, and the sanctions were targeted at companies with financial relations to the junta. Bestseller had since 2014 produced clothes at several factories in Myanmar.

Challenging the Social License

The foreign minister in Denmark, Jeppe Kofod, was upset over Bestseller's use of factories in Myanmar (Ritzau, 2021):

> The military is in power in Myanmar. According to the UN report, factories that Bestseller uses are effectively owned by the military. Two of the factories used by Danish clothing giant Bestseller in Myanmar in recent years are cooperating with the military in the country, according to a UN report. And this could have consequences, Denmark's foreign minister Jeppe Kofod told the newspaper. He is greatly exasperated by the cooperation.
>
> I would like to make it quite clear that I think it is highly problematic if Bestseller chooses to have clothes produced in factories controlled by the military dictatorship in Myanmar, according to the UN, he told the newspaper.

Bestseller faced serious criticism from the clothing and fashion industry that could harm the company's outlets and their brands (Einarsdottir, 2021):

> Bestseller receives criticism for alleged military connections in crisis-stricken Myanmar. The Danish fashion giant Bestseller is once again in bad weather. This time it is due to their connections in crisis-hit Myanmar. Bestseller, which owns about twenty fashion brands such as Vero Moda, Only and Jack & Jones, produces at three factories in the industrial zone Ngwe Pinlae outside the city of Yangon. A report from 2019 to the UN Human Rights Council points out that the zone is controlled by the industrial conglomerate Myanmar Economic Holdings Limited (MEHL). Their owners consist of the military and individuals in the military leadership, among them chief of staff Min Aung Hlaing who is mainly responsible for the recent bloody attacks on civilians in the country where over 700 people have been killed, writes Fashion Forum.

Because of the criticism, Bestseller was "among the companies that froze orders from the south-east Asian country because of human rights concerns and civil unrest" (Reed and Nilsson, 2021). The European Union targeted Myanmar's lucrative energy sector in sanctions and put companies under pressure to divest from the country and cut off indirect funding for the junta. The EU imposed "sanctions against almost two dozen Myanmar government and military officials as well as a state-backed oil and gas group" (Meixler and Creery, 2022). Nevertheless, the Danish company wanted to resume its business in Myanmar again (Reed and Nilsson, 2021):

> Bestseller, which describes itself as a champion of sustainable development and whose Myanmar suppliers have about 48,000 workers, concluded that the three factories were not on military-owned land, and it had not violated EU sanctions. The Danish group also said it had "started to resume business in Myanmar again".

To legitimate a resumption of its business in Myanmar again, Bestseller argued that their business did not benefit the military junta (Reed and Nilsson, 2021):

> Proceeds from the garment industry for the most part do not directly benefit the country's military, unlike industries such as gemstones, timber, and oil and gas. However, Bestseller commissioned an independent investigation into its business in the country to investigate the status of three of its factories in an industrial zone linked to Myanmar Economic Holdings, a military-controlled conglomerate that has been placed under sanctions by the US, EU and UK since the coup.

Surprisingly, Bestseller's response to the threat of losing the company's social license to operate was to commission an investigation primarily into the legal license to operate by lawyers as examiners.

Bestseller's Convenience Themes

Assuming that the allegations against the company were correct, it is possible to identify convenience themes for the offender as illustrated in Figure 13.1. There was a corporate threat against supply of quality goods at low prices from Myanmar. At the same time, the possibility of continued supply would ensure more profits. The company had access to resources to continue their business in Myanmar, and the lack of oversight and guardianship by the international community created a chaotic situation. It was a rational choice for the company to continue its business in Myanmar that they justified by the employment they provided to thousands of poor people in the country.

The founder of Bestseller was Troels Holch Povlsen, and his son Anders Holch Povlsen developed the business into 2,700 retail stores and 15,000 retail customers. The number of employees was 17,000 at Bestseller headquartered in Brande, Denmark. The son became a billionaire and remained the CEO and sole owner of the international retail clothing chain as a privately held and family-owned clothing company. In a statement, Anders Holch Povlsen said:

> we cannot imagine anything worse than if our company, in any way possible, should contribute to the situation Myanmar now finds itself in. Our work in the country to date has been about the exact opposite – contributing positively to the country's development, both economically and politically.
>
> (Larsen, 2021)

He argued that continuing operations in Myanmar would help poor people, where almost half of the population lives below the poverty line. He claimed that it would cause serious harm to the population if international businesses had to withdraw from Myanmar. He argued that corporate social responsibility implies staying in Myanmar, while critics argued that the only responsible thing to do would be to close down business in Myanmar as long as a military clique was in power in the country.

This CEO reasoning is in line with the motive of social concern for others. Agnew (2014) introduced the motive of social concern for wrongdoing, where there is a desire to help others, and thus moving beyond the assumption of simple self-interest. However, as argued by Paternoster et al. (2018), helping others can be a self-interested, rational action that claims social concern.

The CEO reasoning for the motive of corporate possibilities might also be founded in the historical tradition of reputation benefits from being an employer in Myanmar. When the previous military dictatorship collapsed, and Aung San Suu Kyi was elected president in the country, being an employer of workers caused a corporate reputation improvement by the Myanmar "fairytale" (Mortensen et al., 2019). With the Nobel Peace Prize winner Kyi in front as president of Myanmar, Bestseller and other companies contributed to raising the standard of living in the country. By establishing factories in Myanmar with very low wages for employees, Bestseller and others could claim that they contributed to the adventurous improvements for local people. At the same time, the companies were making substantial profits from sale of the garments on markets in Europe. If withdrawing from production in Myanmar, Bestseller faced the threat of significant reduction in profits and possible economic losses in the clothing business as indicated in Figure 13.1.

In the opportunity structure, Bestseller management had access to resources to continue operations in Myanmar, as indicated in Figure 13.1. The company had also an opportunity to conceal potential links to the junta by avoiding direct trade with garment factories. Instead, Bestseller did business with local vendors that had links to the factories. In the principal–agent perspective of detachment (Bosse and Phillips, 2016), Bestseller as a principal appeared detached from factories as agents that were producing clothes for the company.

The innocent justification might rely on an argument that many other foreign companies operated the same business structure as Bestseller in Myanmar.

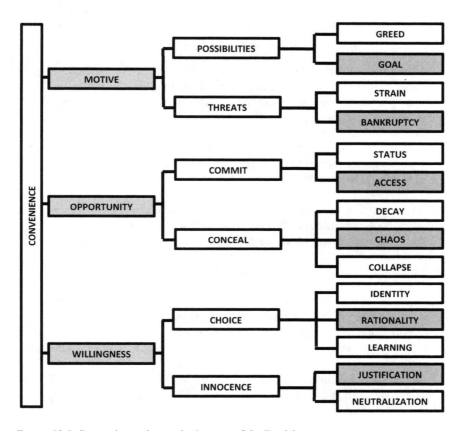

Figure 13.1 Convenience themes in the case of the Danish company

Furthermore, the employment argument of securing a minimum standard of living among workers could also be used to justify continued operations in Myanmar despite junta dictatorship in the country.

The Fraud Investigation Report

The mandate for the examiners asked them to conduct a review of whether Bestseller had lived up to the highest international standards for corporate social responsibility, inclusive the United Nation's guidelines for human rights and business and OECD's guidelines for multinational enterprises. The other part of the mandate asked examiners to review whether Bestseller had economic relationships with the military and thus had acted in violation of the rules from the Danish foreign ministry and the European Union.

Examiners argued that discontinuing activities in Myanmar would be a breach of Bestseller's corporate social responsibility (Christoffersen and Mikkelsen, 2021: 120):

> Myanmar's situation is bleak, not just politically but also economically. In case many international companies decide to halt their activities in Myanmar, it would cause an economic meltdown and lead to widespread and serious poverty and famine. It is therefore, in our view, in clear breach of Bestseller's corporate social responsibility, should they decide not to continue with their economic and social activities in Myanmar. It is therefore our recommendation, that Bestseller as quickly as possible resume their activities in Myanmar.

One main question that examiners were commissioned to answer was whether Bestseller had economic relations with the military in Myanmar as a result of 3 of the 30 factories, from which Bestseller sourced products, were placed in the Ngwe Pinlae industrial zone. Based on the review, examiners did not believe that there were reasonable grounds to assume that the three factories were located on plots of land that were owned, directly or indirectly, by the military. Neither did examiners believe that there were reasonable grounds to assume that the three factories had paid administration fees, directly or indirectly, to the military. Based on the volatile situation in Myanmar, examiners recommended that Bestseller should continue to exercise considerable due diligence in order to avoid breaching the EU sanctions.

Another main question addressed by the examiners was whether Bestseller had acceptable standard in its corporate social responsibility (Christoffersen and Mikkelsen, 2021: 121):

> We are clearly of the opinion that there is no doubt that Bestseller lived up to their corporate social responsibility in accordance with the highest international standards in relation to their activities in Myanmar.

A third main question was whether Bestseller, in case of economic relations with the military, was in breach of Danish or EU guidelines and rules. Examiners found that there were no reasonable grounds to assume that Bestseller had any economic relations with the military in Myanmar as a result of their activities in the Nwge Pinlae industrial zone. They found no evidence of breaches of the sanctions from the EU.

The conclusions drawn by examiners were based on various documents from Bestseller including emails, minutes of meetings, and contracts. They interviewed a number of people where some interviewees had to remain anonymous because of safety issues. Some relevant information sources never responded to requests from the examiners. The investigation is assigned maturity level 2 in Figure 13.2.

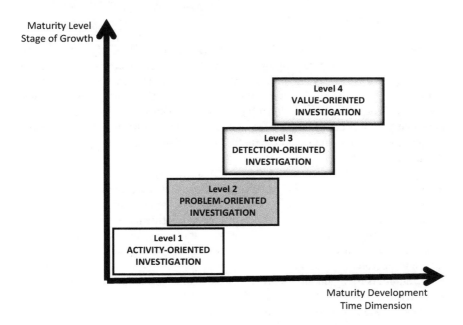

Figure 13.2 Maturity of investigations by Christoffersen and Mikkelsen

Regaining the Social License

The investigation by Christoffersen and Mikkelsen (2021) was an attempt to regain not only the legal license to operate but also the social license to operate in Myanmar. The main argument for continuing Bestseller business in the country that had been occupied by a military dictatorship was concerned with avoidance of poverty. The firm claimed that 48,000 persons in Myanmar were dependent on new orders of clothing from Bestseller. The story was told that not only employees would suffer, but also their families. Furthermore, the firm claimed that their continued business activities in Myanmar in no way would benefit the military junta. Investigators strongly recommended Bestseller to place new orders when their report was released on May 10, 2021.

However, on August 27, 2021, Bestseller announced that they had stopped their business in Myanmar already and that they would place no new orders (Bestseller, 2021):

> Following the announcement from IndustryALL Global Union and their Myanmar affiliate, the Industrial Workers Federation of Myanmar (IWEM), Bestseller will not place new orders in the country until an impact assessment and dialogue with experts, NGOs, trade unions and other relevant

stakeholders with a clear focus on the wellbeing of garment workers in Myanmar has been conducted.

The report by Christoffersen and Mikkelsen (2021) was obviously not sufficient to regain the social license since global and local unions were still skeptical to business activities in Myanmar. The only relevant attempt to regain the license seemed to be by not placing new orders in Myanmar. The argument that poor workers and their families would suffer income loss was contradicted by the argument that the well-being of garment workers in the country was not guaranteed and that the military junta would benefit from Bestseller business in the country (Thomsen, 2021).

Furthermore, while stakeholders felt sorry for citizens in Myanmar who suffered under the boycott, stakeholders also knew that there are always innocent victims of various sanctions. For example, when hospital employees go on strike to gain higher wages, patients waiting in line for treatment become innocent victims. Therefore, it may not come as a surprise that the innocent-victim approach suggested by the investigators did not work for Bestseller to regain the social license to operate in Myanmar.

The attempts to regain the social license by Bestseller management can be studied in terms of factors that are needed to earn the license as suggested by Saenz (2019) and Sale (2021) as illustrated in Table 13.1.

Table 13.1 Attempts to regain the social license by Bestseller executives

Social legitimacy	Violation	Correction
Pragmatic legitimacy	Supporting business benefiting military junta	Withdraw from further business that could benefit the military junta in Myanmar
Moral legitimacy	Military junta hurting innocent civilians	Keep readiness to return to business in Myanmar if social license from local unions
Cognitive legitimacy	Profiting from poor people in the country	Keep readiness to return to business in Myanmar if acceptable to garment industry
Trust vulnerability	**Violation**	**Correction**
Risk tolerance	Ignorance of transition from democracy to dictatorship	Alignment with other corporations and national guidelines
Adjustment level	Military junta's power regulation of business conduct	Home country's guidelines for business abroad
Relative power	Retail customers in chain stores reacted to misconduct	Avoidance of garments marked "Made in Myanmar"

Social License to Operate

This case study has applied the perspective of social license to operate. The perspective of social license suggests that legal and social obligations and expectations provide separate but interacting issues for assessing the extent to which business conduct is aligned with norms in the community. While each business enterprise serves a number of purposes in the community such as employment and goods and services, the business conduct has to meet both legal and social requirements to operate. The community does not exist to serve the business enterprise. Rather, each corporate entity exists to serve the community with benefits without violating the legal and social license. The social license can be part of a bottom-up as well as an outside-in effort to enhance the social control of business activity (Haines et al., 2022). Business enterprises attempt to respond to indicate that their activities are not only legally legitimate but also socially legitimate (Saenz, 2019: 296):

> The expression is often used when a company's activities may face disapproval – especially when such disapproval could result in resistance that could harm their business interests. Failure to engage all segments of the community, to inform them, and to solicit their opinions is often seen as evidence of illegitimacy by those who are excluded. It is typically preferable for companies to communicate directly with the masses and not rely solely on those occupying leadership positions.

Sources of license authority are a combination of people and knowledge. The main people sources of license authority are bottom-up activists and outside-in activists. The bottom-up approach to executive compliance focuses on organizational measures by employees to make wrongdoing less convenient for potential offenders (Haines et al., 2022). Compliance refers to obeying the formal and informal rules, regulations, and norms in force at a given time and place (Durand et al., 2019).

The main knowledge sources of license authority are insights, reflections, and assessments of benefits and harm (Rooney et al., 2014: 210):

> Other critical components include the reputation of the organization, previous relationships with communities, the level of transparency the organization operates with, and whether the organization is trusted to do the things they say they will. Social license relies critically on social aspects of knowledge diffusion, and contested "truth" claims often based on radically different ontologies, epistemologies, and axiologies.

Control by stakeholders is concerned with a negative discrepancy between the desired and current state of affairs. Control mechanisms attempt to reduce the discrepancy through adaptive action in the form of behavioral reactions (Direnzo and Greenhaus, 2011). Control mechanisms attempt to influence and manage the process, content, and outcome of work (Kownatzki et al., 2013). Control involves processes of negotiation in which various strategies are developed to produce particular outcomes. Control is therefore a dynamic process that regulates behavior through a set of modes, rules, or strategies (Gill, 2019).

There are various types of control mechanisms with various targets (Chown, 2020: 752):

> For example, prominent frameworks delineate controls based on whether they are formal or informal, coercive, normative, peer-based, or concertive. Controls are also divided based on whether they target employees' behaviors by implementing processes or rules that ensure individuals perform tasks in a particular manner, target their outputs by assessing employees based on measurable items such as profits or production, or target the inputs to the production process by controlling the human capital and material inputs utilized by the organization.

At its core, top-down control refers to the manner in which "an organization's managers can use different types of control mechanisms – such as financial incentives, performance management, or culture – to monitor, measure, and evaluate workers' behaviors and influence them toward achieving the organization's goals in efficient and effective ways" (Chown, 2020: 713). Similarly, at its core, bottom-up control refers to the manner in which organizational members can use different types of control mechanisms – such as whistleblowing, transparency, resource access, or culture – to monitor, measure, and evaluate executives' avoidance of deviant behaviors and influence them toward achieving the organization's goals in efficient and effective ways. While the hierarchical structure remains with executives at the top of the organization in charge of the business, bottom-up control is a matter of stakeholder involvement in compliance. While top-down control is often a formal and rigid system, bottom-up control can be an informal and flexible system based on social influence (Haines et al., 2022: 185):

> Criminalization, foundational analytical territory for criminology, forms part of a "bottom up" strategy where it becomes "social property", untethered from law and formal criminal justice. Criminalization as social property comprises a central element of "social control influence" over corporate harm. This is justice in the vernacular with media, social movements and citizen watchdogs exerting pressure, demanding change and bringing business to account.

When noticing wrongdoing at the top of the organization, improvisation might be a key capability for organizational members and citizen watchdogs. Capability refers to the ability to perform (Paruchuri et al., 2021), while improvisation refers to the spontaneous process by which planning and execution happen at the same time (Mannucci et al., 2021). Rather than following formal reporting lines to people who are not trustworthy, improvisation is a matter of spontaneous action in response to unanticipated occurrences, in which individuals find a way to manage unexpected problems.

Bottom-up approaches are a matter of people in the organization who prevent potential offenders from wrongdoing and who detect offenses and offenders having committed misconduct and crime. A different approach in the same line of reasoning is the outside-in approach, where outsiders rather than insiders prevent and detect wrongdoing in the organization. The outside-in approach involves various stakeholders in the community such as citizens, media, unions, politicians, and action groups.

The term "stakeholder" refers to someone with an interest or concern in something, especially in business (Gomulya and Mishina, 2017). A stakeholder is someone who can affect or be affected by the business, and a stakeholder is someone who associates with the business and does or does not derive utility from the association (Lange et al., 2022: 9):

> Utility here describes the satisfaction, gratification, or need fulfillment that a stakeholder receives by virtue of interacting with or being associated with the business.

A stakeholder typically injects some kind of resource into the business with the expectation of receiving some form of return. Nason et al. (2018) argued that a stakeholder is someone who derives own identity to some extent from attributes of the business. Lange et al. (2022) argued that a stakeholder should not necessarily be viewed as someone having a single-minded focus on own utility but rather as someone having an outcome in mind that often will be of utility for groups of people based on a kind of solidarity. Nason et al. (2018: 259) suggested that a stakeholder provides "intense feedback when there are major discrepancies between their expectations and the firm's actual social performance".

The rise of social media, non-government organizations, as well as the knowledge level among citizens has led to the strengthening of stakeholder demands (Panda and Sangle, 2019: 1085):

> As a result, firms often find themselves in conflicts. The cost of these conflicts for the firm is the opportunity cost of future projects due to loss of reputation, and for the stakeholders, it is the loss of opportunities, both social and economical, that could have been brought by the projects. The tension between firms and stakeholders creates a dynamic environment where following compliance is not enough, and social acceptance is equally important as government licenses. Such an acceptance is termed as "social license to operate" (SLO). SLO exists when a project is seen as having the broad, ongoing approval and acceptance of society to conduct its activities.

Panda and Sangle (2019: 1086) further argued that there is a growing awareness among stakeholders of their power to make their voices heard:

> The rise of social media has resulted in organized movements against corporations as well as in the demand for greater transparency from firms. The

number and type of stakeholders for a firm are no longer confined in their immediate surroundings. Most multinational corporations have "global stakeholders" who may not directly have a stake in the firm but are interested in its social, economic, and environmental impacts. Firms practicing opaqueness are at a greater risk than those open to stakeholder inspection.

Panda and Sangle (2019) found that SLO is deeply rooted in stakeholder theory. It is a theory of business ethics to promote managerial matters during different environmental situations. According to Waheed and Zhang (2022), the theory supports social issues by assisting the strategic decisions of organizations. It takes into account the evolving role of stakeholders, from being bystanders in a company to being a part in the decision-making processes (Panda and Sangle, 2019).

However, the monitored enterprise might find it easier to challenge the authority of outsiders compared to insiders who belong to the enterprise. Outsiders can be challenged whether they count in authorizing or denying the company their social license. Outsiders can be challenged whether they are entitled to speak based on their claimed membership and representation of the community.

One potential source of license authority is activist groups and non-government organizations that take cases to the courts. While a case is pending, the accused company tends to become passive by awaiting the outcome of the trial. However, bringing a case in front of a judge is only a matter of legal license to operate. The judge is to apply the law to the issues and cannot apply other criteria that citizens are concerned about.

Another potential source of license authority is name-and-shame lists where academics consider firms that are ethical and compliant versus firms that are not ethical and compliant. When Russia invaded Ukraine in February and March 2022 (Grønningsæter, 2022), the Yale School of Management in the United States updated on a daily basis a list of companies that had terminated their business in Russia as well as those that remained. The two lists were for a while updated every hour by Professor Jeffrey Sonnenfeld and his research team at the Yale Chief Executive Leadership Institute to reflect new announcements from companies in real time (Sonnenfeld, 2022a, 2022b).

References

Agnew, R. (2014). Social concern and crime: Moving beyond the assumption of simple self-interest, *Criminology*, 52 (1), 1–32.

Bestseller. (2021). *Not Placing New Orders in Myanmar*, Bestseller, August 27, www.bestseller.com.

Bosse, D.A. and Phillips, R.A. (2016). Agency theory and bounded self-interest, *Academy of Management Review*, 41 (2), 276–297.

Chown, J. (2020). The unfolding of control mechanisms inside organizations: Pathways of customization and transmutation, *Administrative Science Quarterly*, 66 (3), 711–752.

Christoffersen, J. and Mikkelsen, M.S. (2021). *Redegjørelse: Bestseller A/S' samfundsansvar i Myanmar (Statement: Bestseller Ltd.'s Social Responsibility in Myanmar)*, law firm Offersen Christoffersen, Copenhagen, Denmark, May 10, 122 pages.

Direnzo, M.S. and Greenhaus, J.H. (2011). Job search and voluntary turnover in a boundaryless world: A control theory perspective, *Academy of Management Review*, 36 (3), 567–589.

Durand, R., Hawn, O. and Ioannou, I. (2019). Willing and able: A general model of organizational responses to normative pressures, *Academy of Management Review*, 44 (2), 299–320.

Einarsdottir, I.E. (2021). Bestseller får kritikk for påståtte militærforbindelser i kriserammede Myanmar (Bestseller receives criticism for alleged military connections in crisis-stricken Myanmar), *Fashion Industry Magazine Melk & Honning*, April 20, www.melkoghonning.no.

Gill, M.J. (2019). The significance of suffering in organizations: Understanding variation in workers' responses to multiple modes of control, *Academy of Management Review*, 44 (2), 377–404.

Gomulya, D. and Mishina, Y. (2017). Signaler credibility, signal susceptibility, and relative reliance on signals: How stakeholders change their evaluative processes after violation of expectations and rehabilitative efforts, *Academy of Management Journal*, 60 (2), 554–583.

Grønningsæter, F. (2022). Russlands svarte økonomi (Russia's black economy), *Norwegian Business Magazine Kapital*, 5, 16–23.

Haines, F., Bice, S., Einfeld, C. and Sullivan, H. (2022). Countering corporate power through social control: What does a social licence offer? *The British Journal of Criminology*, 62, 184–199.

Kownatzki, M., Walter, J., Floyd, S.W. and Lechner, C. (2013). Corporate control and the speed of strategic business unit decision making, *Academy of Management Journal*, 56 (5), 1295–1324.

Lange, D., Bundy, J. and Park, E. (2022). The social nature of stakeholder utility, *Academy of Management Review*, 47 (19), 9–30.

Larsen, M. (2021). Danish company Bestseller urges EU to take action on Myanmar, *ScandAsia* (Nordic News and Business Promotion in Asia), April 21, www.scandasia.com.

Mannucci, P.V., Orazi, D.C. and Valck, K. (2021). Developing improvisation skills: The influence of individual orientations, *Administrative Science Quarterly*, 66 (3), 612–658.

Meixler, E. and Creery, J. (2022). EU targets Myanmar's lucrative energy sector in latest sanctions, *Financial Times*, published February 22, www.ft.com.

Mortensen, N.H., Danwatch, K.L.H., Myanmar Now, Cha, P.T. and Frontier. (2019). Baksiden av eventyret om "Made in Myanmar" (The flip side of the fairytale about "Made in Myanmar"), *Norwegian Foreign Aid Magazine Bistandsaktuelt*, April 29, www.bistandsaktuelt.no.

Nason, R.S., Bacq, S. and Gras, D. (2018). A behavioral theory of social performance: Social identity and stakeholder expectations, *Academy of Management Review*, 43 (2), 259–283.

Nystuen, M.M. (2022). Demokratiforkjempere henrettet av Myanmars militærjunta (Pro-democracy activists executed by Myanmar's military junta), *Daily Norwegian Newspaper Aftenposten*, July 26, p. 10.

Panda, S.S. and Sangle, S. (2019). An exploratory study to investigate the relationship between social license to operate and sustainable development strategies, *Sustainable Development*, 27, 1085–1095.

Paruchuri, S., Han, J.H. and Prakash, P. (2021). Salient expectations? Incongruence across capability and integrity signals and investor reactions to organizational misconduct, *Academy of Management Journal*, 64 (2), 562–586.

Paternoster, R., Jaynes, C.M. and Wilson, T. (2018). Rational choice theory and interest in the "fortune of others", *Journal of Research in Crime and Delinquency*, 54 (6), 847–868.

Reed, J. (2022). Stay or go: The dilemma for multinationals in Myanmar, *Financial Times*, January 25, www.ft.com.

Reed, J. and Nilsson, P. (2021). H&M and Primark resume Myanmar orders for first time since coup, *Financial Times*, May 21, www.ft.com.

Ritzau. (2021). Kofod fortørnet over Bestsellers brug af fabrikker i Myanmar (Kofod upset over Bestseller's use of factories in Myanmar), *Danish Broadcasting TV2*, April 18, www.nyheder.tv2.dk.

Rooney, D., Leach, J. and Ashworth, P. (2014). Doing the social in social license, *Social Epistemology*, 28 (3–4), 209–218.

Saenz, C. (2019). Building legitimacy and trust between a mining company and a community to earn social license to operate: A Peruvian case study, *Corporate Social Responsibility and Environmental Management*, 26 (2), 296–306.

Sale, H.A. (2021). The corporate purpose of social license, *Sothern California Law Review*, 94 (4), 785–842.

Sonnenfeld, J. (2022a). The great business retreat matters in Russia today – Just as it mattered in 1986 South Africa, *Fortune*, March 7, www.fortune.com.

Sonnenfeld, J. (2022b). Over 300 companies have withdrawn from Russia – But some remain, *Yale School of Management*, March 10, www.som.yale.edu.

Thomsen, C.B. (2021). Dansk tøjgigant vil ikke støtte brutalt militær og trækker sig ud af Myanmar – I hvert fald for en periode, *Danish Daily Newspaper Politiken*, September 16, www.politiken.dk.

Waheed, A. and Zhang, Q. (2022). Effect of CSR and ethical practices on sustainable competitive performance: A case of emerging markets from stakeholder theory perspective, *Journal of Business Ethics*, 175, 837–855.

14 Embezzlement of Client Funds

This chapter does not present another case study of fraud examiners in corporate investigations. Instead, this chapter reviews the case of attorney fraud in a law firm. The chapter starts with a brief review of law firm business. Next, crime convenience theory is applied to the case by identifying relevant convenience themes for financial motive, organizational opportunity, and personal willingness. Then, a brief application of crime signal detection theory is presented. In the discussion, governance in the form of restrictions based on convenience theory is discussed. Prevention and detection of wrongdoing is at the core of governance to secure compliance with laws, regulations, rules, and guidelines. The lack of transparency among stakeholders in the case of the law firm is detrimental to governance. The discourse and rituals of transparency, account-giving, and verification are central to governance. This chapter starts with a brief review of law firm business. Next, crime convenience theory is applied to the case by identifying relevant convenience themes for financial motive, organizational opportunity, and personal willingness. Then, a brief application of crime signal detection theory is presented. In the discussion, governance in the form of restrictions based on convenience theory is discussed.

In 2019, attorney Halstein Sjølie at law firm Liljedahl in Norway admitted to fraud of 30 million Norwegian kroner (about three million US dollars). Victims of his fraud were law firm clients as well as law firm partners (Bøyum, 2019; Tveit, 2019). Sjølie was prosecuted by the National Authority for Investigation and Prosecution of Economic and Environmental Crime, which is the serious fraud office in Norway (NTB, 2019).

The case of Sjølie is interesting both in the perspective of crime convenience theory and crime signal detection theory. Sjølie was able to practice his fraud for quite some time, which is interesting to analyze in terms of convenience in his financial motive, professional opportunity, as well as willingness for deviant behavior. He was finally detected, which is interesting to analyze in terms of crime signal alertness, signal reflection, pattern recognition, as well as personal knowledge of crime signal assessment.

One of the partners in the law firm, attorney Bjørn Haugen, commented in the media that he knew nothing until the Financial Supervisory Authority of Norway

DOI: 10.4324/9781003363934-15

had removed attorney Sjølie's authorization to be in the real estate business (Fange, 2019):

- I have worked with him for 23 years, and one has both a friendship and a trusted relationship. For an attorney, client funds are untouchable, so it was a shock when this became known, says Haugen.

We approached attorney Bjørn Haugen for an interview, and he agreed to provide empirical insights into our research questions: What convenience themes can be relevant for a fraudulent partner in a law firm? Why are fraud signals not detected internally in a law firm?

In addition to our interview with the victimized colleague Haugen in the law firm, Spurkland (2021) interviewed offender Sjølie and presented the interview in her book. One of the statements by the offender in the book is that "I suffered from a world champion syndrome" (Spurkland, 2021: 215), which apparently meant that he could achieve whatever he set out to accomplish.

This chapter starts with a brief review of law firm business. Next, crime convenience theory is applied to the case by identifying relevant convenience themes for financial motive, organizational opportunity, and personal willingness. Then, a brief application of crime signal detection theory is presented. In the discussion, governance in the form of restrictions based on convenience theory is discussed.

Law Firm Business Characteristics

Liljedahl was a small law firm with four attorneys and one assistant. The law firm was located in the town of Moss outside of the capital Oslo in Norway. Attorney Halstein Sjølie was both in the legal business and in the real estate business (Bøyum, 2019; Fange, 2019; NTB, 2019; Tveit, 2019).

Attorneys are knowledge workers who provide legal services to clients (Litchfield et al., 2021). Knowledge represents the fuel that feeds the engine of creative idea generation (Mannucci and Yong, 2018). Knowledge is a matter of understanding, where complexity, dynamism, and stochasticity make it difficult – but not impossible – to understand. Ignorance and reluctance represent barriers to understanding, while curiosity and imagination can help the knowledge worker understand (Arikan et al., 2020). Attorney Sjølie was a successful knowledge worker as a high earner in the law firm Liljedahl (Spurkland, 2021).

A law firm is a business enterprise often with high expectations regarding partner income (Litchfield et al., 2021). The partners own the firm, and they share revenues according to some distribution key. A law firm is a professional service firm characterized by knowledge intensity, low capital intensity, and a professional workforce. Knowledge intensity refers to the reliance and dependence on a substantial body of knowledge for the production of the firm's output. Relative to other firms, knowledge-intensive firms may display more autonomy for knowledge workers and more informality in organizational processes as a way to better satisfy lawyers' preferences for autonomy. While the business logic in legal practice might dominate in terms of revenues and profit sharing among law firm partners, everyday working life in the firm may seem informal and autonomous. Specific manifestations of autonomy may include greater decentralization of decision-making and greater participation in firm-level decisions (Nordenflycht, 2010). Just like nobody else was involved in attorney Sjølie's affairs, Sjølie was not involved in the affairs of any of the other partners in the law firm. There was autonomy and independence (Spurkland, 2021).

Law firms belong to the legal services industry. "For more than a century", Paquin (2021: 1) argued, "concerns have been expressed over what has been seen as the decline of law from a profession to a business". The commercialization of law practice is visible in the large, multinational law firms that have replaced traditional law firms with a father and a son or a few colleagues educated at the same law school. Nevertheless, the doctrine of professionalism is upheld within most legislation where lawyers are professionals based on moral, institutional, and scholarly elements, where professionalization is a process of control of the market (Chan and Li, 2021).

Crime Convenience Themes

Attorney Halstein Sjølie was convicted to five years and six months in prison for fraud of approximately 100 million Norwegian kroner (about ten million US dollars). He was sentenced to pay compensation to 15 victims of about NOK 50 million (Sfrintzeris and Ording, 2021). His fraud was detected when a victim reported it to the Norwegian authority for financial control. The victim had bought a hotel from Sjølie. After the transaction, the victim discovered that she had inherited Sjølie's old debt that was still associated with the hotel that she had acquired.

In the beginning, the fraud consisted of what the offender labeled rolling embezzlement, where one embezzlement act was replaced by the next as explained by Sjølie (Spurkland, 2021: 215):

> Let's say that a million kroner came in that was going to a client. Then you can borrow that million for a while, and before it is paid out, a new million comes in elsewhere. To begin with, there was a harmless character in the embezzlements. Harmless is in imitation, because no one discovered it and no one was harmed by them. But then something like this is never harmless. It's no less wrong that it actually worked.

One of his sources was testamentary gifts to the Salvation Army. A donor can deposit his or her will with a lawyer who executes the gift when the donor is dead. Nobody controls whether the lawyer actually does what the donor has written in the will.

The attorney fraud can be analyzed by application of convenience theory, which suggests that the offender has a financial motive, an organizational opportunity, and a willingness for deviant behavior (Asting and Gottschalk, 2022; Braaten and Vaughn, 2019). The structural model of convenience theory is illustrated in Figure 14.1, where there are a total of 14 potential convenience themes. When

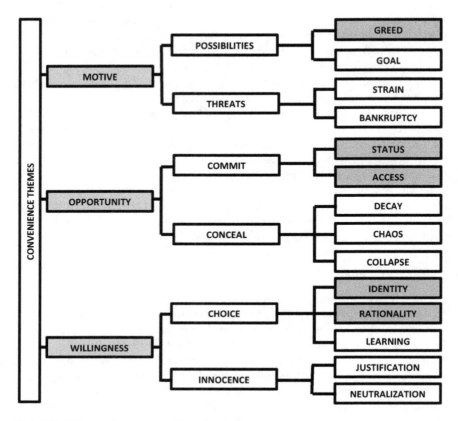

Figure 14.1 Convenience propositions for deviant attorney

applying the model to a case, the research task is to link information from both offender interview and victim interview to identify the most obvious convenience themes in the case.

Financial Motive

The motive for Sjølie was individual possibilities as indicated in the figure. His ambition was to expand his professional activities from a successful legal service provider to a real estate agent and then becoming a real estate entrepreneur. He bought various properties including some hotels (Spurkland, 2021: 216):

> After a few years, we had a real estate company and a real estate complex in Moss, and a total of six hotels around Norway.

Through rolling embezzlement and later plain embezzlement and fraud, he expanded his empire of various properties. He thought of himself as a world champion for whom nothing was impossible (Spurkland, 2021: 199):

> had a kind of world champion syndrome, you might say. And for many years it went well, very well – Until it didn't work out anymore.

Initially, his fraud scheme was not caused by threats of any kind. Therefore, the convenience theme of motive-threats-individuals is not emphasized in the figure (Spurkland, 2021: 215):

> He had high income and no personal financial problems. He did not want a Rolex, a new car or a new wine cellar. He was not exposed to any kind of threat.

His motive was to explore possibilities, he was ambitious, and he wanted to accomplish too much (Spurkland, 2021: 215).

> I have pondered a lot about the why question. Why did I start with that, and why did I not quit before the problems grew? To put it bluntly, I think the reason is this: I wanted too much, more than I could handle. And then I cut some corners to make it happen.

Possibilities include reaching business objectives by ignoring whether or not means are legitimate or illegitimate (Campbell and Göritz, 2014; Jonnergård et al., 2010; Kang and Thosuwanchot, 2017). Ends simply justify means that might represent crime. Welsh and Ordonez (2014) found that high performance goals cause unethical behavior. Dodge (2009: 15) suggested that tough rivalry among executives make them commit crime to attain goals: "The competitive environment generates pressures on the organization to violate the law in order to attain goals". Sjølie reasoned in the same way (Spurkland, 2021: 216):

> I knew what I was doing was not legal, and it did not feel good to do it. But there is something called the goal sanctifies the means. I got it in a way that as long as I got it so that no one gets hurt by it, I had to live with the fact that I stretch the elastic a bit.

He explained why he was hit by the so-called world champion syndrome (Spurkland, 2021: 215):

> You can get that after many years of success. I was used to being able to handle everything. If I got a problem, I just worked on it for 24 hours straight, and then it was solved. I was overconfident.

His motive was not to make his law firm rich or to avoid bankruptcy of the law firm. Therefore, the convenience themes of motive-possibilities-corporate and motive-threats-corporate are not emphasized in the figure.

Attorney Haugen told in our interview with him that attorney Sjølie was divorced from his first wife and married his second wife. Haugen suggested then a financial motive of negative life events. The perspective of negative life events implies that events such as divorce, accident, lack of promotion, and sudden cash problems can cause offenders to consider financial crime as a convenient solution. They may perceive being victims of unfortunate circumstances that they have to compensate in some ways (Engdahl, 2015).

Organizational Opportunity

Status is a convenience theme that seems to apply to Sjølie as an offender. Status is an individual's social rank within a formal or informal hierarchy or the person's relative standing along a valued social dimension. Status is the extent to which an individual is respected and admired by others, and status is the outcome of a subjective assessment process (McClean et al., 2018). High-status individuals enjoy greater respect and deference from, as well as power and influence over, those who are positioned lower in the social hierarchy (Kakkar et al., 2020: 532):

> Status is a property that rests in the eyes of others and is conferred to individuals who are deemed to have a higher rank or social standing in a pecking order based on a mutually valued set of social attributes. Higher social status or rank grants its holder a host of tangible benefits in both professional and personal domains. For instance, high-status actors are sought by groups for advice, are paid higher, receive unsolicited help, and are credited disproportionately in joint tasks. In innumerable ways, our social ecosystem consistently rewards those with high status.

Especially individuals with high status based on prestige rather than dominance tend to be excused for whatever wrongdoing they commit. Individuals who attain and maintain high rank by behaving in ways that are assertive, controlling, and intimidating are characterized as dominant. Individuals who attain and maintain high ranks by their set of skills, knowledge, expertise and their willingness to share these with others are characterized as prestigious (Kakkar et al., 2020).

Sjølie described his former status this way (Spurkland, 2021: 209):

> I had been a person that people listened to. I enjoyed a lot of trust. Now I can count on them looking at me like a fool. And the trust I had is gone. The transition there, it's sad and awkward.

Law firm partner Haugen confirmed that Sjølie had a very high status in the local community. He was a member of the city council. After each election, all political parties gathered at the law firm office to discuss how to share various positions among the politicians. Haugen said Sjølie was a strategist able to position his thoughts politically.

Sjølie had access to resources to commit financial crime by rolling embezzlement as well as theft of testamentary gifts. He explained his form of rolling embezzlement in the previous quote, where he characterized his fraud scheme as harmless (Spurkland, 2021). He could ignore a dead person's last will by not notifying the rightful recipient. When he entered the real estate market as a broker, his organizational opportunity structure improved since a buyer of property always deposited the purchase price with the broker before the amount was transferred to the seller at a later point in time.

Haugen told that Sjølie as an attorney actively helped people in his network to set up their last will and asked them to deposit the will in the law firm. The alternative would typically be to deposit their testaments in the district court or with someone trusted in the family.

For five years he kept the rolling of client funds going. He replaced an embezzlement with a new embezzlement, prepared fictitious invoices, and forged client bank statements. Everything happened unnoticed. At most, he handled values of around NOK 200 million (about USD 20 million) every day. At that time, his business had expanded to include far more than the legal profession. In 2014, he went into real estate, he sold a plot of land and made some money, and sold a couple of other properties and earned a little more.

A white-collar offender has typically legitimate access to resources to commit financial crime (Kempa, 2010; Huisman and Erp, 2013; Williams et al., 2019). Money laundering is a typical example in the legal profession (Benson, 2018). A resource is an enabler applied and used to satisfy human and organizational needs. According to Petrocelli et al. (2003), access to resources equates access to power. Others are losers in the competition for resources (Wheelock et al., 2011). In the conflict perspective suggested by Petrocelli et al. (2003), the upper class in society exercises its power and controls the resources. White-collar offenders have legitimate access to premises (Benson and Simpson, 2018; Williams et al., 2019), and they have specialized access in routine activities (Cohen and Felson, 1979).

Haugen told that Sjølie was able to mislead the external auditor. Sjølie's wife did the accounting separately for her husband. When the auditor showed up, the wife was absent, making the office manager in the law firm unable to present Sjølie's part to the auditor. In addition, there were often two versions of Sjølie's accounting, one real and the other for the audit.

Personal Willingness

The willingness of Sjølie for deviant behavior seems to derive from his world champion syndrome, which apparently meant that he could achieve whatever he set out to accomplish. He thought of himself as a world champion for whom nothing was impossible. For many years it went very well. He was used to being able to handle everything. If he had a problem, he just worked around the clock, and then it was solved. He did not feel sorry for his victims as he told himself that he harmed nobody.

After detection, however, his views changed regarding his deviant behavior (Spurkland, 2021: 207):

> There is no excuse. It is important for me to bring it out. I am not a victim in any way. It is myself and my actions that have put me in this situation. It is my fault and no one else.
>
> It is the worst thing, that my actions have created problems and losses for other people. And now I cannot even make up for it. This bothers me. But it should do that.

There is no attempt to justification of his wrongdoing. There is no innocence suggested by the offender. Rather, crime was committed as a choice based on identity and rationality as indicated in Figure 14.1. Identity is the first convenience theme in the willingness category. Crime as a choice can be based on an identity that makes it acceptable for elite members to break the law (Petrocelli et al., 2003), a professional deviant identity (Obodaru, 2017), an identity of a narcissist expecting preferential treatment (Zvi and Elaad, 2018), deviant identity labeling (Mingus and Burchfield, 2012), reputation adaptation to individual labels (Bernburg et al., 2006), and narcissistic identification with the organization (Galvin et al., 2015; Toubiana, 2020). Professional identity is how an individual sees himself or herself in relation to work. The self-concept is a complex cognitive structure containing all of a person's self-representations. According to the identity perspective, roles and identities are interdependent concepts. Identity enactment refers to acting out an identity or claiming the identity by engaging in behaviors that conform to role expectations and that allow the identity to become manifest.

The rational choice assumption about offending is based on a normative foundation where advantages and disadvantages are subjectively compared (Müller, 2018). When there is no perceived likelihood of detection, then there is no deterrence effect to prevent offenses (Comey, 2009). If there is a certain perceived likelihood, then willingness might depend on the perceived consequences. For potential white-collar offenders it can be frightening to think of time in jail or prison. Research has shown that some white-collar offenders suffer from special sensitivity in prison, while others have special resilience ability in prison (Button et al., 2018, 2020; Logan, 2015; Logan et al., 2019; Long et al., 2021), which means that they cope better with incarceration than other inmates. Deterrence comes from whether or not an offender has to go to prison, rather than the severity of sanction in terms of imprisonment length. Generally, the severity of punishment has shown to have no effect on recidivism (Mears and Cochran, 2018).

Rational choice is concerned with benefits of crime exceeding costs (Pratt and Cullen, 2005), where the perceived likelihood of incarceration is a cost element. Another cost element is media exposure, where investigative journalists often are the first to disclose suspected white-collar crime and the offender. Press reporters' detection of misconduct and crime "represented an important ingredient of the nineteenth-century newspaper" (Taylor, 2018: 346), and this is certainly also the case so far in the twenty-first-century media.

The economic model of rational self-interest is all about weighing up the pros and cons of alternative courses of action. When the desire increases, then the benefits in the rational benefit-cost comparison increase, which in turn influences willingness. The rational choice perspective simply states that when benefits exceed costs, we would all do it. The perspective is explicitly a result of the self-regarding preference assumption, where rationality is restricted to self-interested materialism (Paternoster et al., 2018). Individuals and organizations are less likely to comply if they conclude that following laws, rules, and regulations is less profitable than violating those laws, rules, and regulations (Peeters et al., 2020).

Crime Signal Detection Theory

Crime signal detection theory suggests that there are four possible outcomes in the decision matrix of an observer (Karim and Siegel, 1998). First, the observer notices a noise signal when it is a crime signal (called a miss). Second, the observer notices a crime signal when it is a crime signal (called a hit). Third, the observer notices a noise signal when it is a noise signal (called a correct identification). Finally, the observer notices a crime signal when it is a noise signal (called a false alarm). The more frequent false alarms and misses occur, the greater the opportunity is successfully to conceal white-collar crime. Szalma and Hancock (2013) found that potential observers typically have low signal alertness and that most people lack the ability to recognize and interpret patterns in signals.

Attorney Haugen told in our interview with him that attorney Sjølie offered him to participate and invest in one of the first real estate projects. Haugen was reluctant to do so, not because he suspected misconduct and crime but because he feared that he would have to invest more to make the project a reality. Haugen perceived Sjølie as a big spender, who bought and developed properties in expensive ways and then tried to get all expenses covered by high prices at the sale of the properties. Therefore, Haugen was concerned with lack of profitability and not concerned with potential wrongdoing.

Attorney Haugen said that he neither trusted what Sjølie was doing nor what Sjølie was telling. The latter he exemplified with Sjølie's divorce, where Sjølie had bragged about his first wife, but then changed the story completely after the divorce. Nevertheless, Haugen never suspected Sjølie of any wrongdoing.

Despite his skepticism toward Sjølie, Haugen continued working in the same firm with Sjølie. His reason was that Sjølie was a nice guy, and everyday life at the law firm was quite pleasant. Also, Haugen was the chairperson in the law firm, although he realized that he never really functioned in that position. Very often, Sjølie said he would take care of this and that, which Haugen accepted, since Haugen was busy with his clients. We were supposed to have regular meetings to review administrative issues and financial issues, but we never had time for that. Haugen noticed that some of the accounting was strange, but he never raised the issue with Sjølie. In other matters, when Haugen questioned Sjølie, then Sjølie responded by saying that he would take care of it. Haugen was then reluctant to check whether or not Sjølie had done anything about it.

As mentioned earlier, Sjølie's fraud was detected when a victim reported it to the Norwegian authority for financial control. However, the authority did not tell the Norwegian police. It was Haugen who reported his colleague to the police when he learned about the involvement of the financial supervisory authority of Norway.

Transparency for Governance

Prevention and detection of wrongdoing is at the core of governance to secure compliance with laws, regulations, rules, and guidelines (Durand et al., 2019). The lack of transparency among stakeholders in the case of the law firm is detrimental to governance. The discourse and rituals of transparency, account-giving, and verification are central to governance (Mehrpouya and Salles-Djelic, 2019: 13):

> Transparency has been a normative shell through which financial accounting and audit standards have been pushed around the world. Under the contemporary governance paradigm, financial disclosure regimes are an important dimension of what it means to make organizations, states and individuals transparent and accountable. Champions of transparency, such as the former head of the IMF, Michel Candessus, describe transparency as the "golden rule" of the new international financial system, "absolutely central to the task of civilizing globalization". . . . Transparency implies unhindered access to information for the public. However, the definition of the public, targets and beneficiaries of transparency, along with associated programs and technologies, has been contested and has evolved through time.

Transparency enables normative institutional pressure concerned with conformity, where deviance and nonconformity are disliked, disapproved, or even dismissed (Witt et al., 2021).

Prevention and detection of wrongdoing is a matter of reduction in convenience for potential offenders. It is a matter of less convenience to commit and conceal crime. Traditionally, control in organizations is concerned with top-down approaches, where executives attempt to direct their employees' attention, behaviors, and performance to align with the organizations' goals and objectives.

However, we suggest turning the challenge of control upside down by a bottom-up approach as well as an outside-in approach. The bottom-up approach to executive compliance focuses on organizational measures to make white-collar crime less convenient for potential offenders. At its core, bottom-up control refers to the manner in which organizational members can use different types of control mechanisms – such as whistleblowing, transparency, resource access, or culture – to monitor, measure, and evaluate executives' avoidance of deviant behaviors and influence them toward achieving the organization's goals in efficient and effective ways.

In addition to bottom-up approaches, outside-in approaches should be recognized as supplements to control of white-collar crime. Outside organizations, there are various professionals who can either help white-collar offenders commit and conceal crime or help prevent and detect white-collar individuals in organizations. Lawyers can report suspicious transactions on client accounts, certified accountants as well as auditors can blow the whistle on suspected value assessments, bank officials can react to attempts to use tax havens for corruption payments, and employees in health care can detect wrongdoing in pharmaceutical firms.

In conclusion, based on the theory of convenience, this chapter has identified themes that made white-collar crime convenient for the offender in the case study. In the perspective of governance, the themes can serve as indicators of bottom-up as well as outside-in approaches that might reduce the convenience of crime for white-collar offenders. Traditionally, control in organizations is concerned with top-down approaches, where executives attempt to direct their employees to align their work with organizational objectives. This chapter has introduced the challenge of directing privileged individuals such as deviant attorneys to align their work with laws, rules, and ethics.

References

Arikan, A.M., Arikan, I. and Koparan, I. (2020). Creation opportunities: Entrepreneurial curiosity, generative cognition, and Knightian uncertainty, *Academy of Management Review*, 45 (4), 808–824.

Asting, C. and Gottschalk, P. (2022). Attorney fraud in the law firm: A case study of crime convenience theory and crime signal detection theory, *Deviant Behavior*, doi: 10.1080/01639625.2022.2071657.

Benson, K. (2018). Money laundering, anti-money laundering and the legal profession, in: King, C., Walker, C. and Gurule, J. (editors), *The Palgrave Handbook of Criminal and Terrorism Financing Law*, Pagrave Macmillan, Cham, pp. 109–133.

Benson, M.L. and Simpson, S.S. (2018). *White-Collar Crime: An Opportunity Perspective*, (3rd Edition), Routledge, New York.

Bernburg, J.G., Krohn, M.D. and Rivera, C. (2006). Official labeling, criminal embeddedness, and subsequent delinquency, *Journal of Research in Crime and Delinquency*, 43 (1), 67–88.

Bøyum, J.M. (2019). Advokat kjøpte tre hotell i Sogn – no har han tilstått underslag av 30 millionar (Attorney bought three hotels in Sogn – now he has admitted embezzlement of 30 millions), *Norwegian Local Newspaper Porten*, November 7, www.porten.no.

Braaten, C.N. and Vaughn, M.S. (2019). Convenience theory of cryptocurrency crime: A content analysis of U.S. federal court decisions, *Deviant Behavior*, doi: 10.1080/01639625.2019.1706706.

Button, M., Gough, D., Shepherd, D. and Blackbourn, D. (2020). White collar criminals' experience of imprisonment in England and Wales: Revisiting the "special sensitivity" debate, *Deviant Behavior*, 41 (12), 1585–1600.

Button, M., Shepherd, D. and Blackbourn, D. (2018). "The higher you fly, the further you fall": White-collar criminals, "special sensitivity" and the impact of conviction in the United Kingdom, *Victims & Offenders*, 13 (5), 628–650.

Campbell, J.L. and Göritz, A.S. (2014). Culture corrupts! A qualitative study of organizational culture in corrupt organizations, *Journal of Business Ethics*, 120 (3), 291–311.

Chan, K.W. and Li, T. (2021). Empowering judicial scriveners as litigators in Japan: Is it justifiable and of value? *International Journal of the Legal Profession*, doi: 10.1080/09695958.2020.1742720.

Cohen, L.E. and Felson, M. (1979). Social change and crime rate trends: A routine activity approach. *American Sociological Review*, 44, 588–608.

Comey, J.B. (2009). Go directly to prison: White collar sentencing after the Sarbanes-Oxley act, *Harvard Law Review*, 122, 1728–1749.

Dodge, M. (2009). *Women and White-collar Crime*, Prentice Hall, Saddle River.

Durand, R., Hawn, O. and Ioannou, I. (2019). Willing and able: A general model of organizational responses to normative pressures, *Academy of Management Review*, 44 (2), 299–320.

Engdahl, O. (2015). White-collar crime and first-time adult-onset offending: Explorations in the concept of negative life events as turning points, *International Journal of Law, Crime and Justice*, 43 (1), 1–16.

Fange, P.Ø. (2019). Advokat innrømmer å ha underslått millioner av klientenes penger (Attorney admits to have embezzled millions of clients' money), Norwegian public broadcasting *NRK*, November 1, www.nrk.no.

Galvin, B.M., Lange, D. and Ashforth, B.E. (2015). Narcissistic organizational identification: Seeing oneself as central to the organization's identity, *Academy of Management Review*, 40 (2), 163–181.

Huisman, W. and Erp, J. (2013). Opportunities for environmental crime, *British Journal of Criminology*, 53, 1178–1200.

Jonnergård, K., Stafsudd, A. and Elg, U. (2010). Performance evaluations as gender barriers in professional organizations: A study of auditing firms, *Gender, Work and Organization*, 17 (6), 721–747.

Kakkar, H., Sivanathan, N. and Globel, M.S. (2020). Fall from grace: The role of dominance and prestige in punishment of high-status actors, *Academy of Management Journal*, 63 (2), 530–553.

Kang, E. and Thosuwanchot, N. (2017). An application of Durkheim's four categories of suicide to organizational crimes, *Deviant Behavior*, 38 (5), 493–513.

Karim, K.E. and Siegel, P.H. (1998). A signal detection theory approach to analyzing the efficiency and effectiveness of auditing to detect management fraud, *Managerial Auditing Journal*, 13 (6), 367–375.

Kempa, M. (2010). Combating white-collar crime in Canada: Serving victim needs and market integrity, *Journal of Financial Crime*, 17 (2), 251–264.

Litchfield, R.C., Hirst, G. and Knippenberg, D. (2021). Professional network identification: Searching for stability in transient knowledge work, *Academy of Management Review*, 46 (2), 320–340.

Logan, M.W. (2015). *Coping with Imprisonment: Testing the Special Sensitivity Hypothesis for White-Collar Offenders*. A dissertation to the Graduate School of the University of Cincinnati in partial fulfillment of the requirements for the degree of Doctor of Philosophy in the Department of Criminal Justice, Cincinnati, OH.

Logan, M.W., Morgan, M.A., Benson, M.L. and Cullen, F.T. (2019). Coping with imprisonment: Testing the special sensitivity hypothesis for white-collar offenders, *Justice Quarterly*, 36 (2), 225–254.

Long, J., Logan, M.W. and Morgan, M.A. (2021). Are white-collar prisoners special? Prison adaptation and the special sensitivity hypothesis, *Journal of Criminal Justice*, 77, doi: 10.1016/j.crimjus.2021.101863.

Mannucci, P.V. and Yong, K. (2018). The differential impact of knowledge depth and knowledge breadth on creativity over individual careers, *Academy of Management Journal*, 61 (5), 1741–1763.

McClean, E.J., Martin, S.R., Emich, K.J. and Woodruff, T. (2018). The social consequences of voice: An examination of voice type and gender on status and subsequent leader emergence, *Academy of Management Journal*, 61 (5), 1869–1891.

Mears, D.P. and Cochran, J.C. (2018). Progressively tougher sanctioning and recidivism: Assessing the effects of different types of sanctions, *Journal of Research in Crime and Delinquency*, 55 (2), 194–241.

Mehrpouya, A. and Salles-Djelic, M.L. (2019). Seeing like the market; Exploring the mutual rise of transparency and accounting in transnational economic and market governance, *Accounting, Organizations and Society*, 76, 12–31.

Mingus, W. and Burchfield, K.B. (2012). From prison to integration: Applying modified labeling theory to sex offenders, *Criminal Justice Studies*, 25 (1), 97–109.

Müller, S.M. (2018). Corporate behavior and ecological disaster: Dow chemical and the great lakes mercury crisis, 1970–1972, *Business History*, 60 (3), 399–422.

Nordenflycht, A. (2010). What is a professional service firm? Toward a theory and taxonomy of knowledge-intensive firms, *Academy of Management Review*, 35 (1), 155–174.

NTB. (2019). Advokat siktet for å ha underslått titalls millioner kroner av klienters penger (Attorney charged for having embezzled tens of millions of kroner from clients' money), *Norwegian Daily Financial Newspaper Finansavisen*, November 1, www.finansavisen.no.

Obodaru, O. (2017). Forgone, but not forgotten: Toward a theory of forgone professional identities, *Academy of Management Journal*, 60 (2), 523–553.

Paquin, J. (2021). From partners to team leaders: Tracking changes in the Canadian legal profession, *International Journal of the Legal Profession*, doi: 10.1080/09695958.2020.1830098.

Paternoster, R., Jaynes, C.M. and Wilson, T. (2018). Rational choice theory and interest in the "fortune of others", *Journal of Research in Crime and Delinquency*, 54 (6), 847–868.

Peeters, M., Denkers, A. and Huisman, W. (2020). Rule violations by SMEs: The influence of conduct within the industry, company culture and personal motives, *European Journal of Criminology*, 17 (1), 50–69.

Petrocelli, M., Piquero, A.R. and Smith, M.R. (2003). Conflict theory and racial profiling: An empirical analysis of police traffic stop data, *Journal of Criminal Justice*, 31 (1), 1–11.

Pratt, T.C. and Cullen, F.T. (2005). Assessing macro-level predictors and theories of crime: A meta-analysis, *Crime and Justice*, 32, 373–450.

Sfrintzeris, Y. and Ording, O. (2021). Eksadvokat dømt for underslag av 100 millioner (Former lawyer convicted of embezzlement of 100 million), *Daily Norwegian Newspaper VG*, October 1, www.vg.no.

Spurkland, M. (2021). *Ut av krisen: Beretninger om sammenbrudd og tilsynelatende håpløshet, men også om mot og den ukjente styrken som bor i oss alle (Out of the Crisis: Reports of Collapse and Apparent Hopelessness, but also about the Courage and the Unknown Strength that Lives in All of Us)*, Cappelen Damm, Oslo.

Szalma, J.L. and Hancock, P.A. (2013) A signal improvement to signal detection analysis: fuzzy SDT on the ROCs, *Journal of Experimental Psychology: Human Perception and Performance*, 39 (6), 1741–1762.

Taylor, J. (2018). White-collar crime and the law in nineteenth-century Britain, *Business History*, 60 (3), 343–360.

Toubiana, M. (2020). Once in orange always in orange? Identity paralysis and the enduring influence of institutional logics on identity, *Academy of Management Journal*, 63 (6), 1739–1774.

Tveit, T. (2019). Advokaten som eig Morgedal hotel er sikta for grovt underslang (The attorney who owns Morgedal hotel is charged with serious embezzlement), *Norwegian Local Newspaper Vest-Telemark blad*, November 1, www.vtb.no.

Welsh, D.T. and Ordonez, L.D. (2014). The dark side of consecutive high performance goals: Linking goal setting, depletion, and unethical behavior, *Organizational Behavior and Human Decision Processes*, 123, 79–89.

Wheelock, D., Semukhina, O. and Demidov, N.N. (2011). Perceived group threat and punitive attitudes in Russia and the United States, *British Journal of Criminology*, 51, 937–959.

Williams, M.L., Levi, M., Burnap, P. and Gundur, R.V. (2019). Under the corporate radar: Examining insider business cybercrime victimization through an application of routine activities theory, *Deviant Behavior*, 40 (9), 1119–1131.

Witt, M.A., Fainshmidt, S. and Aguilera, R.V. (2021). Our board, our rules: Nonconformity to global corporate governance norms, *Administrative Science Quarterly*, 1–36, doi: 10.1177/00018392211022726.

Zvi, L. and Elaad, E. (2018). Correlates of narcissism, self-reported lies, and self-assessed abilities to tell and detect lies, tell truths, and believe others, *Journal of Investigative Psychology and Offender Profiling*, 15, 271–286.

15 Fraud Examination Comparison

The theory of convenience suggests that financial threats and possibilities, organizational opportunities to commit and conceal wrongdoing, as well as personal willingness for deviant behavior determine the likelihood of white-collar crime. When there is suspicion of white-collar crime, public and private organizations tend to hire fraud examiners from audit firms and law firms to reconstruct past events and sequences of events. This chapter links findings in fraud examination reports regarding crime convenience to the extent of corruption in the respective countries. Research results suggest that white-collar crime convenience increases as the extent of crime in a nation increases. The empirical research presented in this chapter is exploratory, with a number of shortcomings that need to be addressed in future studies.

The research presented in this chapter attempts to link a global corruption index to the extent of white-collar convenience based on a limited number of available fraud examination reports from various countries. The chapter aims to apply convenience theory by developing an exploratory study of the cases of examined crime across 18 jurisdictions. Methodologically, the research engages in a quantitative analysis in the form of regression of findings in examination reports linked to ranks in the corruption index. This chapter represents the first attempt to measure convenience in white-collar crime.

Transparency International is a global movement working in over 100 countries to end the injustice of corruption. They define corruption as the abuse of entrusted power for private gain. This definition is broad and covers various forms of financial crime. The definition is applied in the corruption index that Transparency International publishes every year. An interesting research question is whether fraud examination reports from various countries might indicate varying crime convenience depending on the countries' rank in the index.

Fraud examination reports are written by private investigators at audit firms and law firms that are hired by client organizations in private and public sectors to reconstruct past events and sequences of events (Gottschalk, 2020; King, 2021; Meerts, 2020). Reports are the property of client organizations that pay for the work, and reports are normally kept secret and confidential, often in relation to law enforcement, the media, as well as the public (Gottschalk and Tcherni-Buzzeo, 2017). Very seldom, reports are accessible for the purpose of research.

DOI: 10.4324/9781003363934-16

However, this research was successful in retrieving reports from 18 countries that vary on the index from number one (Denmark and New Zealand) to number 149 (Nigeria) and number 170 (Congo).

A theoretical perspective to study the extent of crime convenience is the theory of convenience for white-collar crime (Asting and Gottschalk, 2022; Braaten and Vaughn, 2019; Dearden and Gottschalk, 2020; Stadler and Gottschalk, 2021).

This chapter presents exploratory research attempting to link crime convenience by suspected white-collar offenders to the extent of corruption in the country. The research hypothesis suggests that crime convenience increases as corruption increases. While crime convenience is concerned with a phenomenon at the organizational level, the extent of corruption is a phenomenon at the national level.

The chapter starts by presenting the theory of convenience with its convenience themes. Next, fraud investigation reports from several countries are introduced. Then a convenience scale is applied before research results are presented. Finally, the shortcoming of the current research is discussed.

Crime Convenience Themes

The convenience triangle suggests that a financial motive, an organizational opportunity, and a willingness for deviant behavior make financial crime convenient for white-collar offenders. Convenience is a relative concept concerned with efficiency in time and effort as well as reduction in pain and solution to problems in legitimate versus illegitimate ways (Engdahl, 2015). A convenient individual is not necessarily neither bad nor lazy. On the contrary, the person can be seen as smart and rational (Sundström and Radon, 2015). Furthermore, Agnew (2014: 2) suggested that "crime is often the most expedient way to get what you want", and "fraud is often easier, simpler, faster, more exciting, and more certain than other means of securing one's ends".

Convenience orientation refers to a person's or persons' general preference for convenient maneuvers. A convenience-oriented person is one who seeks to accomplish a task in the shortest time with the least expenditure of human energy (Berry et al., 2002; Farquhar and Rowley, 2009). Chen and Nadkarni (2017: 34) found that many chief executive officers can be characterized by time urgency where they have the feeling of being chronically hurried:

> Time urgency is a relatively stable trait. Time-urgent people are acutely aware of the passage of time and feel chronically hurried. They often create aggressive internal deadlines and use them as markers of the timely completion of team tasks. They regularly check work progress, increase others' awareness of the remaining time, and motivate others to accomplish commitments within the allotted time.

The convenience triangle is based on the fraud triangle (Cressey, 1972; Wells, 1997), which suggests three conditions for fraud: (1) incentives and pressures, (2) opportunities, and (3) attitudes and rationalization. However, there are three distinct differences. First, convenience is a relative concept, indicating that offenders have the option of alternative actions to reach their goals that do not represent illegitimate behavior. While the fraud triangle suggests that opportunities will stimulate crime, the convenience triangle suggests that relative opportunities will stimulate crime. There is no reason to commit crime, even if there are many opportunities, as long as alternative convenient decisions may lead to the same result. It is the extent of relative convenience, and not the extent of opportunity, that determines whether an offense is attractive. A very conveniently oriented decision-maker may resort to illegal activities when legal activities are slightly more stressful. A less conveniently oriented decision-maker may try intensely to solve problems and explore opportunities without violating the law.

Second, it is in the organizational setting where offenders have access to resources so that opportunity arises to commit and conceal crime. While the fraud triangle emphasizes opportunity in general, the convenience triangle concentrates on the privileged position that offenders can abuse to commit and conceal crime. There is trust and lack of control, obedience, and fear, which create convenient opportunities. The convenient opportunity derives from legitimate access to resources in a trusted position without guardians, where resources are enablers to carry out activities that are not available to others. Opportunity convenience emerges because of an organizational structure and an organizational culture where members of the elite may feel above the law.

Third, a white-collar offender can influence the organizational opportunity over time. Therefore, opportunity in convenience theory is a dynamic rather than a static condition. By collecting decision rights, by controlling information flows, and by authoritarian leadership styles, a potential offender develops an opportunity space that grows over time. Whether intentional or not, the opportunity space changes over time as a reaction to the potential offender's behavior.

This chapter presents a structural model of convenience theory with 14 convenience themes. Offender profiling occurs when some of the 14 themes are identified as relevant for a suspected white-collar offender. This is exemplified later in the chapter.

A combination of motive, opportunity, and willingness determines the extent of white-collar crime convenience as illustrated in the structural model in Figure 15.1.

In the financial motive dimension, profit might be a goal in itself or an enabler to exploit possibilities and to avoid threats. Possibilities and threats exist both for individual members of the organization and for the organization as a whole. It is convenient to exploit possibilities and to avoid threats by financial means.

In the organizational opportunity dimension, convenience can exist both to commit white-collar crime and to conceal white-collar crime. Offenders have high social status in privileged positions, and they have legitimate access to crime resources. Disorganized institutional deterioration causes decay, lack of oversight and guardianship causes chaos, while criminal market structures cause collapse.

The personal willingness for deviant behavior focuses on offender choice and perceived innocence. The choice of crime can be caused by deviant identity, rational consideration, or learning from others. Justification and neutralization

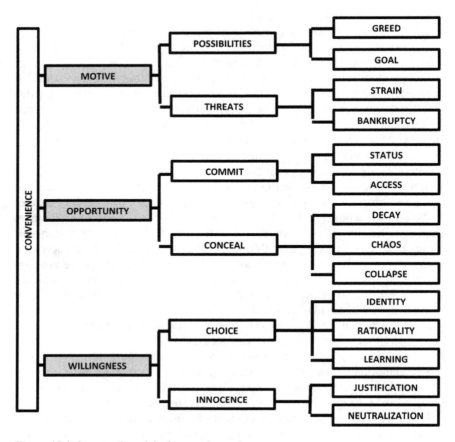

Figure 15.1 Structural model of convenience theory

cause the perceived innocence at crime. Identity, rationality, learning, justification, and neutralization all contribute to making white-collar crime action a convenient behavior for offenders.

As illustrated in the figure, there are 14 potential themes that might contribute
to a profile of the white-collar offender.

Global companies tend to adapt to local market conditions when they consider
crime-as-a-choice strategy. Grabosky and Shover (2010) discuss how crime as a
choice can receive higher attention because of higher relative attractiveness compared to alternative legitimate paths. Crime as a choice implies that "a decrease in the
availability or attractiveness of legitimate opportunities will normally increase the
attractiveness of illegal opportunities" (Coleman, 1987: 424). German technology
company Siemens used legitimate means in their domestic marketing, but resorted
to corruption in countries like India and Thailand. Norwegian fertilizer producer
Hydro used legitimate means in their domestic market but resorted to corruption in

countries like Libya. Swedish bank Swedbank as well as Danish bank Danske Bank prevented money laundering incidents in their domestic market but did let it happen in their Eastern European markets. Such examples suggest that crime convenience is higher in countries with higher levels of corruption as studied in the following.

Fraud Investigation Reports

The first investigation report in Table 15.1 is from Austria, which ranks number 15 on the corruption index. The International Biathlon Union is headquartered in Salzburg in Austria. Biathlon is a winter sport that combines cross-country skiing and rifle shooting. It is treated as a race, with contestants skiing through a cross-country trail whose distance is divided into shooting rounds. Major biathlon nations include France, Russia, Sweden, and Norway. Biathlon is a very popular sport among spectators, both present at shooting stadiums and in front of television screens all over the world. The business of biathlon events has grown significantly in recent decades, and rumors of both corruption and doping have flourished for several years in the media.

Russian doping whistleblower Grigory Rodchenkov told the media about organized doping of Russian athletes at the Sochi Winter Olympics (Ruiz and Schwirtz, 2016). He had been the head of Russia's national anti-doping laboratory (Pelley, 2018). Rodchenkov's allegations were confirmed by the independent McLaren report, leading to Russia's partial bans from the 2016 Summer Olympics and 2018 Winter Olympics. Rodchenkov's allegations and the McLaren findings led to an investigation particularly targeted at the management at the International Biathlon Union. When the IBU report was released (ERC, 2021), the *New York Times* wrote about it under the heading "Hunting trips, sex, and cash: How grooming biathlon's leader paid off for Russia: An investigation accuses biathlon's longtime president of accepting gifts from Russians and then doing the country's bidding as a doping scandal swirled" (Panja, 2021):

> The president of the International Biathlon Union told the police that the young woman who had come to his hotel in Moscow was a prostitute, but he was hazy on the details. He did not remember the date or even who had paid for her services, he said, but it had assuredly not been him. The president, Anders Besseberg, had led biathlon's governing body for more than two decades by then, and he was accustomed to receiving gifts from his Russian hosts. Like a chocolate on his pillow or a gift bag placed on a chair in his hotel room, the company of a young woman during a trip to a World Cup biathlon event was not uncommon.
>
> And for decades, according to a report commissioned by biathlon's new leadership, Besseberg repaid the Russian favors by doing the country's bidding – defending its athletes, assailing its critics and even blocking efforts to root out doping by its teams. The yearlong effort to groom Besseberg, and later his top deputy, was so effective that at the height of Russia's state-run doping scandal one Russian official boasted to a colleague that the country

had little to fear in biathlon – a grueling endurance sport that combines precision shooting with cross-country ski racing – because he had Besseberg "under his control".

Fraud examiners found Besseberg greedy and status-oriented, as illustrated by an incident related to a possible hunting trip in Canada (ERC, 2021: 64):

> Mr. Besseberg was unable to produce for the criminal authorities any evidence that he paid any of the expenses of these hunting trips himself. Jim Carrabre said that before the Vancouver Olympics in 2010, Anders Besseberg was in Canada and "since we knew that he is a passionate hunter, we offered to organize a hunt in Canada for him. Besseberg was extremely interested and asked us if we would pay for it. We said no, we (the Canadian Biathlon Union) would only organize the hunt. He would have to pay for the hunt himself. Besseberg then lost interest in the hunt".

The foregoing description of the first investigation serves to illustrate what fraud examinations are all about. Table 15.1 lists the other investigations that focused on various issues such as embezzlement, kickbacks, money laundering, accounting fraud, customer fraud, and business email compromise. For example, fraud examiners from Kroll (2017: 11) start their executive summary concerning bank fraud in Moldova with the following sentences:

> Our investigation to date has identified contemporaneous and independent documentary evidence that indicates that the Three Moldovan Banks were

Table 15.1 Corruption index ranks, reports, and investigators in select countries

Country	Rank	Investigation	Investigator
Austria	15	Biathlon President corruption	ERC (2021)
Bangladesh	246	Save the Children embezzlement	Inspector General (2012)
Canada	11	Pelham public project fraud	KPMG (2017)
Congo	170	Mercy Corp local kickbacks	Henze et al. (2020)
Denmark	1	Danske Bank money laundering	Bruun Hjejle (2018)
Germany	9	Wirecard accounting fraud	KPMG (2020)
Ghana	75	BioFuel license corruption	Kluge (2009)
Iceland	17	Samherji corruption in Namibia	Kleinfeld (2019)
Japan	19	Toshiba accounting fraud	Deloitte (2015)
Moldova	115	Moldova bank fraud	Kroll (2017)
Netherlands	8	VimpelCom corruption in Uzbekistan	Sands (2019)
New Zealand	1	Fuji Xerox customer fraud	Deloitte (2017)
Nigeria	149	National petroleum fraud	PwC (2015)
Norway	7	Business email compromise	PwC (2020)
Sweden	3	Swedbank money laundering	Clifford Chance (2020)
Switzerland	3	FIFA World Cup corruption	Garcia (2014)
USA	25	Lehman Brothers bankruptcy	Jenner Block (2010)
Vietnam	104	Embassy housing rental fraud	Duane Morris (2016)

subjected to a large, coordinated fraud, which took place over at least three years, and intensified in 2014, ultimately resulting in their collapse.

The fraud examiners investigated suspected fraud that involved the issuing of hundreds of loans to seemingly cooperating companies. They found some evidence that the loan funds ended up at a laundering mechanism in Latvia. Afterward, most of the money returned to Moldova to repay existing loans and to allow the continuation of lending, while at least USD 600 million disappeared to other destinations.

It is important to emphasize that the cases and countries are merely based on the availability of the fraud examination reports. The selected countries do not constitute a random and representative sample of all countries in terms of geographic location or economic development. Using the national corruption level to predict an arbitrarily-picked case's convenience structure has obvious analytical limitations. As emphasized in this chapter, a random investigation report from each country combined with a national corruption score is thus no obvious proof of the relationship. Nevertheless, in the perspective of exploratory research, it is interesting to establish whether white-collar crime convenience increases as the extent of crime illustrated by corruption in a nation increases.

Crime Convenience Scale

To determine the extent of crime convenience in each of the 18 cases in Table 15.1, a two-step procedure was applied. First, dominant convenience themes were identified for motive, opportunity, and willingness respectively. Next, the extent of convenience for the dominant themes was assessed on a scale from 1 (not convenient) to 10 (very convenient). Scale development was inspired by multidimensional service convenience scales in the marketing literature (Seiders et al., 2007).

Again, we use the first case from Austria as example. President Besseberg had individual possibility to benefit from Russian generosity. His motive to exploit Russian generosity does not seem very strong and is thus assessed with a score of 6 in Table 15.2. His opportunity structure to receive Russian favors was based on his high status and thus strong importance to the Russians that leads to an assessment with a score of 9 in the table. His ability to claim innocence and deny wrongdoing was based on justification, where the strength of justification is assessed with a score of 6.

The method of assessment is a qualitative review of the content of each fraud investigation report. Content analysis is any methodology or procedure that works to identify characteristics within texts attempting to make valid inferences (Bell et al., 2018; Braaten and Vaughn, 2019; Patrucco et al., 2017). Content analysis assumes that language reflects both how people understand their surroundings and their cognitive processes. Therefore, content analysis makes it possible to identify and determine relevant text in a context (McClelland et al., 2010).

It is important to emphasize the exploratory nature of the convenience scale applied here. There is certainly a need in future research to clarify the standards

Table 15.2 Extent of convenience for motive, opportunity, and willingness

Country	Motive	Opportunity	Willingness
Austria	Individual possibility 6	Commit: Status 9	Innocence: Justification 6
Bangladesh	Individual possibility 8	Conceal: Chaos 9	Choice: Learning 9
Canada	Corporate possibility 4	Commit: Access 4	Innocence: Neutralization 4
Congo	Corporate possibility 9	Conceal: Collapse 8	Choice: Learning 8
Denmark	Corporate possibility 4	Conceal: Decay 5	Innocence: Neutralization 2
Germany	Corporate threat 9	Conceal: Collapse 5	Choice: Identity 9
Ghana	Corporate threat 9	Conceal: Collapse 8	Choice: Rationality 8
Iceland	Corporate possibility 5	Conceal: Collapse 3	Innocence: Neutralization 3
Japan	Corporate threat 4	Conceal: Decay 4	Choice: Rationality 7
Moldova	Corporate possibility 8	Commit: Status 9	Choice: Identity 8
Netherlands	Corporate possibility 5	Conceal: Decay 3	Choice: Rationality 4
New Zealand	Corporate possibility 6	Commit: Access 6	Choice: Rationality 5
Nigeria	Corporate threat 8	Conceal: Collapse 8	Choice: Learning 7
Norway	Corporate threat 3	Conceal: Chaos 3	Choice: Rationality 8
Sweden	Corporate possibility 4	Conceal: Decay 5	Innocence: Neutralization 2
Switzerland	Individual possibility 7	Commit: Status 8	Innocence: Justification 6
USA	Individual threat 8	Conceal: Status 8	Innocence: Justification 6
Vietnam	Individual possibility 9	Commit: Access 5	Choice: Rationality 7

with which values will be assigned to each theme. For example, why the IBU president's motive in exploiting Russian generosity gets a score of 6 instead of 7 has a random basis of qualitatively thinking that the motive might be much stronger by an alternative offender. A concrete coding scheme would be necessary in future research to show that the value assignments are not a result of subjective judgments as is the case in the current research. There was only one single rater that applied subjective judgment, as more serious evaluation would need a multiple-rater approach.

Predicting Crime Convenience

Examining the relationship between corruption in various countries and crime convenience in organizations in those countries is a matter of correlation analysis as well as regression analysis. The data for such analyses are listed in Table 15.3. The first column lists the various countries. The second column sums up the extent of convenience from the previous table. The final column repeats the suspected white-collar crime in each case.

Correlation analysis between the second and the third column in Table 15.3 results in a correlation coefficient of .568*, which indicates a strong correlation with a significance at the 0.05 level (*2-tailed). This result implies that there is a strong positive relationship between the convenience of crime and the extent of crime internationally.

In regression analysis, corruption index ranking is applied as the independent variable that might predict convenience extent as the dependent variable.

Table 15.3 Crime convenience as dependent and corruption rank as independent variables

Country	Rank	Convenience	Investigation
Austria	15	6 + 9 + 6 = 21	Biathlon President corruption
Bangladesh	246	8 + 9 + 9 = 26	Save the Children embezzlement
Canada	11	4 + 4 + 4 = 12	Pelham public project fraud
Congo	170	9 + 8 + 8 = 25	Mercy Corp local kickbacks
Denmark	1	4 + 5 + 2 = 11	Danske Bank money laundering
Germany	9	9 + 5 + 9 = 23	Wirecard accounting fraud
Ghana	75	9 + 8 + 8 = 25	BioFuel license corruption
Iceland	17	5 + 3 + 3 = 11	Samherji corruption in Namibia
Japan	19	4 + 4 + 7 = 15	Toshiba accounting fraud
Moldova	115	8 + 9 + 8 = 25	Moldova bank fraud
Netherlands	8	5 + 3 + 4 = 12	VimpelCom corruption in Uzbekistan
New Zealand	1	6 + 6 + 5 = 17	Fuji Xerox customer fraud
Nigeria	149	8 + 8 + 7 = 23	National petroleum fraud
Norway	7	3 + 3 + 8 = 14	Business Email Compromise
Sweden	3	4 + 5 + 2 = 11	Swedbank money laundering
Switzerland	3	7 + 8 + 6 = 21	FIFA World Cup corruption
USA	25	8 + 8 + 6 = 22	Lehman Brothers bankruptcy
Vietnam	104	9 + 5 + 7 = 21	Embassy housing rental fraud

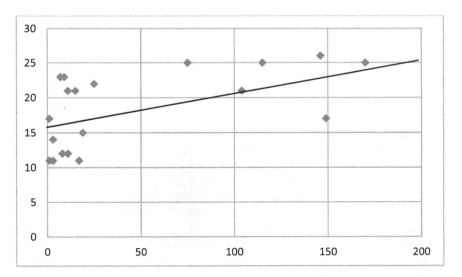

Figure 15.2 Corruption rank as predictor of convenience extent

Regression analysis results in an adjusted R square of 0.282, where the regression equation is significant at 0.01. The constant starts at 16,046 as illustrated in Figure 15.2. The slope is 0.019 as indicated by the standardized coefficient. Thus, the significance of corruption rank as predictor of convenience extent results in a slack climb rather than a steep climb in convenience.

The obvious shortcoming of this exploratory research has to be emphasized. While it is intuitively straightforward that crime convenience might increase as crime is more common in the country, that is, a causal link from corruption rank on convenience extent might exist, a random investigation report from each country combined with a national corruption score is no obvious proof of the relationship. Nevertheless, fraud investigation reports create anecdotal insights into white-collar crime convenience depending on the jurisdiction and thus on the crime convenience in relation to how common crime is in that country.

As illustrated in a similar study by Weiss et al. (2021) regarding international differences in the perception of the "American Dream", various approaches taken to the measurement of national culture can result in entirely different conclusions regarding the relationships between culture and crime. They emphasize the need for further theoretical and methodological development when conducting studies of cross-national crime rates. Similarly, this exploratory research regarding the relationship between white-collar crime convenience and the general tendency of financial crime in terms of corruption on a cross-national basis needs further theoretical as well as methodological development. This is in line with the argument of Gottfredson (2021: 28):

> Contemporary research from around the world provides a body of consistent findings, making it an indispensable tool for the evaluation of crime theory. To be valid, general theories of crime must now be able to accommodate the results of this cross-national research.

An important perspective so far neglected in this chapter is crime seriousness. It might be argued that corruption and other forms of financial crime are not only more common but implicitly less serious in countries with a lower rank on the corruption index.

Even within countries, the perceived seriousness of white-collar crime might vary. At the lower end of seriousness, Alcadipani and Medeiros (2020) found that white-collar crime tends to be perceived as and treated as corporate irresponsibility and not as misconduct, wrongdoing, offending, or law violation. Generally, when detection of crime occurs, an issue of public opinion about seriousness emerges (Cullen et al., 2009; Rosenmerkel, 2001; Unnever et al., 2009). Cullen et al. (2020) studied public opinion about white-collar crime, and they found public willingness to punish white-collar offenders. However, they found that public opinion about inflicting punishment on white-collar criminals varies depending on clarity of culpability, typical harm, violation of trust, and need to show equity. If a detected offender is successful in disclaiming responsibility for crime by not being culpable, then the preference for punitive action declines. The offender can claim one or more of the conditions of the responsible agency did not occur.

In addition to the neglected crime seriousness, variation in convenience orientation between cultures might also explain crime differences between nations. Convenience orientation is conceptualized as the value that individuals and organizations place on actions with inherent characteristics of saving time and effort as well as avoiding strain and pain. Convenience orientation can be considered a value-like construct that influences behavior and decision-making. Mai and Olsen (2016) measured convenience orientation in terms of a desire to spend as little time as possible on the task, in terms of an attitude that the less effort needed the better, as well as in terms of a consideration that it is a waste of time to spend long hours on the task. Convenience orientation toward illegal actions increases as negative attitudes toward legal actions increase. The basic elements in convenience orientation are the individual attitudes toward the saving of time, effort, and discomfort in the planning, action, and achievement of goals. Generally, convenience orientation is the degree to which an individual or a group of individuals are inclined to save time and effort to reach goals.

In conclusion, the convenience of white-collar crime depends on motive, opportunity, and willingness. As indicated in the exploratory research presented in this chapter, the convenience of white-collar crime might also depend on the extent of financial crime, such as corruption, in the country.

In a nation where corruption is more common, white-collar crime is slightly more convenient. Since convenience is a relative concept, where crime-as-a-choice is the dominating perspective, the relative attractiveness of illegitimate versus legitimate actions determines future actions. Potential offenders have the option to choose legitimate rather than illegitimate paths to solve problems and gain from possibilities. As emphasized in the discussion section, shortcoming in this study needs to be addressed in future research.

References

Agnew, R. (2014). Social concern and crime: Moving beyond the assumption of simple self-interest, *Criminology*, 52 (1), 1–32.

Alcadipani, R. and Medeiros, C.R.O. (2020). When corporations cause harm: A critical view of corporate social irresponsibility and corporate crimes, *Journal of Business Ethics*, 167, 285–297.

Asting, C. and Gottschalk, P. (2022). Attorney fraud in the law firm: A case study of crime convenience theory and crime signal detection theory, *Deviant Behavior*, doi: 10.1080/01639625.2022.2071657.

Bell, E., Bryman, A. and Harley, B. (2018). *Business Research Methods*, (2nd Edition), Oxford University Press, New York.

Berry, L.L., Seiders, K. and Grewal, D. (2002). Understanding service convenience, *Journal of Marketing*, 66, 1–17.

Braaten, C.N. and Vaughn, M.S. (2019). Convenience theory of cryptocurrency crime: A content analysis of U.S. federal court decisions, *Deviant Behavior*, doi: 10.1080/01639625.2019.1706706.

Bruun Hjejle. (2018). *Report on the Non-Resident Portfolio at Danske Bank's Estonian branch*, law firm Bruun Hjejle, Copenhagen, p. 87.

Chen, J. and Nadkarni, S. (2017). It's about time! CEOs' temporal dispositions, temporal leadership, and corporate entrepreneurship, *Administrative Science Quarterly*, 62 (1), 31–66.

Clifford Chance. (2020). *Report of Investigation on Swedbank*, law firm Clifford Chance, Washington, DC, p. 218.

Coleman, J. (1987). Toward an integrated theory of white-collar crime, *American Journal of Sociology*, 93 (2), 406–439.

Cressey, D. (1972). *Criminal Organization: Its Elementary Forms*, Harper and Row, New York.

Cullen, F.T., Chouhy, C. and Jonson, C.L. (2020). Chapter 14: Public opinion about white-collar crime, in: Rorie, M.L. (editor), *The Handbook of White-Collar Crime*, Wiley & Sons, Hoboken, pp. 211–228.

Cullen, F.T., Hartman, J.L. and Jonson, C.L. (2009). Bad guys: Why the public supports punishing white-collar offenders, *Crime, Law and Social Change*, 51, 31–44.

Dearden, T.E. and Gottschalk, P. (2020). Gender and white-collar crime: Convenience in target selection, *Deviant Behavior*, 1–9, doi: 10.1080/01639625.2020.1756428.

Deloitte. (2015). *Investigation Report, Summary Version, Independent Investigation Committee for Toshiba Corporation*, audit firm Deloitte, Tokyo, p. 90.

Deloitte. (2017). *Investigation Report*, Independent Investigation Committee, by global auditing firm Deloitte, June 10 (Ito, T., Sato, K. and Nishimura, K.), p. 89, www.fuji-filmholdings.com/en/pdf/investors/finance/materials/ff_irdata_investigation_001e.pdf.

Duane Morris. (2016). *Project House – Report, Conclusions and Notes from Interviews with Selected Landlords, Real Estate Agents and Locally Engaged Employees of the Royal Norwegian Embassy in Hanoi*, report of investigation, Hanoi, p. 172.

Engdahl, O. (2015). White-collar crime and first-time adult-onset offending: Explorations in the concept of negative life events as turning points, *International Journal of Law, Crime and Justice*, 43 (1), 1–16.

ERC. (2021). *Final Report of the IBU External Review Commission, ERC (External Review Commission)*, International Biathlon Union, Austria, 28 January, p. 220.

Farquhar, J.D. and Rowley, J. (2009). Convenience: a services perspective, *Marketing Theory*, 9 (4), 425–438.

Garcia. (2014). *Report on the Inquiry into the 2018/2019 FIFA World Cup Bidding Process, Investigatory Chamber*, FIFA Ethics Committee, Zürich, p. 359.

Gottfredson, M.R. (2021). The essential role of cross-national research in assessing theories of crime: Illustrations from modern control theory, *International Criminology*, 1, 28–37.

Gottschalk, P. (2020). Private policing of white-collar crime: Case studies of internal investigations by fraud examiners, *Police Practice and Research*, 21 (6), 717–738.

Gottschalk, P. and Tcherni-Buzzeo, M. (2017). Reasons for gaps in crime reporting: The case of white-collar criminals investigated by private fraud examiners in Norway, *Deviant Behavior*, 38 (3), 267–281.

Grabosky, P. and Shover, N. (2010). Forestalling the next epidemic of white-collar crime, *Criminology & Public Policy*, 9 (3), 641–654.

Henze, N., Grünewald, F. and Parmar, S. (2020). *Operational Review of Exposure to Corrupt Practices in Humanitarian Aid Implementation Mechanisms in the DRC*, Adam Smith International, London, p. 88.

Inspector General. (2012). Final investigation report of sub-recipient Padakhep Manabik Unnayan Kendra (PMUK) – Bangladesh, *The Office of the Inspector General*, Report No: GF-IG-11-025.

Jenner Block. (2010). *In regard Lehman Brothers Holdings Inc. to United States Bankruptcy Court in Southern District of New York*, law firm Jenner & Block, A.R. Valukas, https://jenner.com/lehman/VOLUME%203.pdf, downloaded September 23, 2018.

King, M. (2021). Profiting from a tainted trade: Private investigators' views on the popular culture glamorization of their trade, *Journal of Criminological Research Policy and Practice*, 7 (2), 112–125.

Kleinfeld, J. (2019). Anatomy of a bribe: A deep dive into an underworld of corruption, *News Organization Al Jazeera*, December 1, www.aljazeera.com.

Kluge. (2009). *Joint Investigation Report by BioFuel, Perennial and Kluge law firm regarding corruption accusations in Ghana*, law firm Kluge, Oslo.

KPMG. (2017). *The Corporation of the Town of Pelham: Forensic Review of Certain Concerns Regarding the East Fonthill Development Project*, report of investigation, audit firm KPMG, Pelham, p. 100.

KPMG. (2020). *Report Concerning the Independent Special Investigation at Wirecard AG*, audit firm KPMG, Munich, April 27, p. 74.

Kroll. (2017). *Project Tenor II, Summary Report, Report Prepared for The National Bank of Moldova, report of investigation*, audit firm Kroll, London, p. 58 (2016: Project Tenor – Scoping Phase, p. 84. 2018: Project Tenor II, Confidential Working Papers Part I to the Detailed Report, Detailed tracing analysis, 60 pages. 2018: Project Tenor II – Confidential working papers – Part II, Evidence Packs – Funds traced to: Ilan Shor, Alexandr Macloivici and Olga Bondarciuc. 2018: Project Tenor II – Detailed Report, Report Prepared for The National Bank of Moldova, 154 pages).

Mai, H.T.X. and Olsen, S.O. (2016). Consumer participation in self-production: The role of control mechanisms, convenience orientation, and moral obligation, *Journal of Marketing Theory and Practice*, 24 (2), 209–223.

McClelland, P.L., Liang, X. and Barker, V.L. (2010). CEO commitment to the status quo: Replication and extension using content analysis, *Journal of Management*, 36 (5), 1251–1277.

Meerts, C. (2020). Corporate investigations: Beyond notions of public-private relations, *Journal of Contemporary Criminal Justice*, 36 (1), 86–100.

Panja, T. (2021). Hunting trips, sex and cash: How grooming biathlon's leader paid off for Russia – An investigation accuses biathlon's longtime president of accepting gifts from Russians and then doing the country's bidding as a doping scandal swirled, *The New York Times*, January 28, www.nytimes.com.

Patrucco, A.S., Luzzini, D. and Ronchi, S. (2017). Research perspectives on public procurement: Content analysis of 14 years of publications in the Journal of Public Procurement, *Journal of Public Procurement*, 16 (2), 229–269.

Pelley, S. (2018). The Russian doping mastermind on the run, *CBS News*, February 11, www.cbsnews.com.

PwC. (2015). *Auditor-General for the Federation: Investigative Forensic Audit into the Allegations of Unremitted Funds into the Federation Accounts by the NNPC*, Nigerian National Petroleum Corporation, report of investigation, audit firm Pricewaterhouse-Coopers, Lagos, Nigeria, p. 199.

PwC. (2020) *Independent Assessment of the Cyber Fraud Incident: Report developed for Norfund, Report of Investigation*, June 30, PricewaterhouseCoopers, Oslo, Norway, p. 34.

Rosenmerkel, S.P. (2001). Wrongfulness and harmfulness as components of seriousness of white-collar offenses, *Journal of Contemporary Criminal Justice*, 17, 308–327.

Ruiz, R.R. and Schwirtz, M. (2016). Russian insider says state-run doping fueled Olympic gold, *The New York Times*, May 12, www.nytimes.com.

Sands. (2019). *Factual report Oceanteam: Investigation of related party transactions*, report of investigation, law firm Sands, Oslo, p. 256.

Seiders, K., Voss, G.B. and Godfrey, A.L. (2007). SERVCON: Development and validation of a multidimensional service convenience scale, *Journal of the Academy of Marketing Science*, 35, 144–156.

Stadler, W.A. and Gottschalk, P. (2021). Testing convenience theory for white-collar crime: Perceptions of potential offenders and non-offenders, *Deviant Behavior*, doi: 10.1080/01639625.2021.1919037.

Sundström, M. and Radon, A. (2015). Utilizing the concept of convenience as a business opportunity in emerging markets, *Organizations and Markets in Emerging Economies*, 6 (2), 7–21.

Unnever, J.D., Benson, M.L. and Cullen, F.T. (2009). Public support for getting tough on corporate crime: Racial and political divides, *Journal of Research in Crime and Delinquency*, 45 (2), 163–190.

Weiss, D.B., Santos, M.R. and Testa, A. (2021). Operationalizing the "American Dream": A comparison of approaches, *International Criminology*, 1, 281–298.

Wells, J.T. (1997). *Occupational Fraud and Abuse*, Obsidian Publishing Company, TExA.

16 Stigma or Competition Effects

It is an interesting research issue whether competitors loose or gain when an industry peer is hit by a scandal such as white-collar and corporate crime. Traditionally, it is assumed that the negative stigma effect is more common among others in the same industry rather than the positive competition effect where non-accused firms gain from the accused firm's loss. Recent research has suggested a U-shaped relationship where increasing product market overlap first causes a stigma effect and then causes a competition effect. Based on seven cases from seven different countries, this chapter suggests that the U-shape might be influenced by the local extent of white-collar and corporate crime. Specifically, this chapter suggests the following hypothesis for future research: The product market overlap between a non-accused firm and an accused industry peer will exhibit a U-shaped effect on the non-accused firm's market depending on the extent of product market overlap, where the negative stigma effect will be stronger in countries characterized by more corruption and other forms of white-collar and corporate crime, while the positive competition effect will be stronger in countries characterized by less corruption and other forms of white-collar and corporate crime.

When Telia in Sweden was hit by a corporate scandal (Schoultz and Flyghed, 2021), did the local telecommunication industry suffer? When Danske Bank in Denmark was hit by several scandals (Bruun Hjejle, 2018; Plesner, 2020), did the local banking sector suffer? When Volkswagen in Germany was hit by a scandal (Jung and Sharon, 2019), did the local automobile industry suffer? When Wirecard in Germany was hit by a scandal (Storbeck, 2021), did the local finance sector suffer? This list might be much longer, but the point should be obvious: Does an industry and thus competitors suffer of negative consequences when an industry peer is hit by a scandal? Or does suspected wrongdoing by an industry peer represent a competitive advantage for others in the local industry?

Traditionally, as argued by Naumovska and Lavie (2021: 1130), "research on misconduct suggests that accusations against industry peers generate negative consequences for non-accused firms". Researchers have thus suggested as stigma effect that generates a negative spillover, whereby other companies in the accused company's industry suffer market loss following the accusation.

Naumovska and Lavie (2021: 1131) introduced a counterargument, "predicting a positive spillover to non-accused firms following an accusation against their

DOI: 10.4324/9781003363934-17

industry peer". Alleged wrongdoing ascribed to a competitor can improve the competitive position of competing corporations in the same industry. Non-accused corporations can benefit from the revelation of financial misconduct by an industry peer. Major customers might not only consider but actually carry out a switch of their business to other companies. Then one firm's loss is its competitor's gain.

Naumovska and Lavie (2021: 1134) theorized the stigma effect versus the competition effect by suggesting that "a non-accused firm that exhibits greater product market overlap with an accused peer will be perceived as more similar to it and thus more likely than other firms to be assigned to the same industry category as the accused peer". Their research first suggested a growing negative spillover to non-accused firms at increasing product market overlap. Then they change their suggestion to a U-shaped relationship (Naumovska and Lavie (2021: 1137):

> The product market overlap between a noon-accused firm and an accused industry peer will exhibit a U-shaped effect on the non-accused firm's stock market valuation, with the expected stock market valuation first becoming more negative as the product market overlap increases and then becoming more positive with further increases in product market overlap.

This chapter is concerned with the empirical side of the stigma effect versus the competition effect. Corporate scandals are frequently investigated by fraud examiners, and this chapter reviews a convenience sample of investigation reports to identify relevant effects. In our perspective of corporate crime consequences, the presented research is exploratory to review whether one firm's loss is its competitor's loss or gain.

Corporate Crises and Scandals

Scandals are disruptive publicity of misconduct (Dewan and Jensen, 2020) and publicized instances of transgression that run counter to social norms (Hearit, 2006; Whyte, 2016). Scandals typically result in condemnation and discredit and other consequences such as bad press, disengagement of key constituencies, the severance of network ties, and decrease in performance (Piazza and Jourdan, 2018). A scandal can be an act of elite deviance that might include financial, physical, and morally harmful behavior committed by privileged members in society.

A crisis from scandals can be a fundamental threat to the organization, characterized by particular ambiguity of cause, effect, and means of resolution (Bundy and Pfarrer, 2015; König et al., 2020). A crisis is an unexpected, publicly known, and harmful event that is associated with uncertainty. Most corporate crises originate from failures within the organization. Scholars denote that organizational crises require timely responses (König et al., 2020). When the Siemens corruption scandal emerged in the public, top management attempted to blame lower-level managers (Berghoff, 2018: 423):

> At first the company defended itself with set phrases like "mishaps of individuals" and isolated offenses committed by a "gang" of criminals, or "This is not Siemens".

U-shaped prediction in the US software industry based on investors' shareholdings and stock market returns of non-accused firms.

We applied the same kind of theorizing to our convenience sample of seven accused organizations in seven different countries. Six out of seven cases are characterized by strong product market overlap. Five out of those six agree with the competition effect. One case seems to have a better fit with the stigma effect as banks in Moldova generally lost trust because of the fraud at Unibank. A potential explanation might be the greater extent of white-collar and corporate crime generally in Moldova as evidenced by that country's rank on the corruption index by Transparency International. While Moldova ranks 115, Denmark ranks 1, Norway ranks 7, Congo ranks 165 (and the Democratic Republic of Congo ranks 180), Sweden ranks 3, United States of America ranks 25, and Germany ranks 9. We return later to the low rank of Congo. The interesting deviation by Moldova might be caused by the fact that more than one bank in the country was involved in the scandal and that Moldova is considered a corrupt country based on the corruption perceptions index. While investors in Denmark, Sweden, and Germany switched financial institution away from Danske Bank, Swedbank and Wirecard to non-accused banks locally, local investors left all banks in Moldova.

The only case characterized by relatively weak product market overlap is cruise lines. We argue that Hurtigruten Cruises is different from other cruise lines in terms of the adventure offered. While other cruise lines may operate in holiday waters of warm weather, cosmopolitan cities, and paradise islands, Hurtigruten Cruises operates in exploratory waters in the north to see ice bears, reindeer, and whales in cold waters. Even among other cruise lines there might be weak product market overlap as indicated by their pricing strategies, where some trips are inexpensive with low standards, while others are exotic with extreme luxury and prices accordingly. Thus, the low product market overlap in the cruise industry might explain the stigma effect being stronger than the competition effect.

The final case of Congo is concerned with strong product market overlap among non-government organizations in the business of foreign aid. We suggest a strong product market overlap as both private donors and governments do not necessarily distinguish between various aid organizations. For example, in Norway, it is almost quite random whether you financially support Norwegian Red Cross, Norwegian People's Aid, Norwegian Refugee Council, Strømme Foundation, Care Norway, or any other of the numerous aid organizations. Strong product market overlap should, according to Naumovska and Lavie (2021), result in a competition effect stronger than the stigma effect. However, donors tend to lose faith in the efficiency and effectiveness of aid organizations when one aid organization, such as Mercy Corps, is hit by a scandal. A potential reason is the extent of white-collar crime and corporate crime already present in countries that receive foreign aid. Development aid funds might seem to disappear within bureaucratic and inefficient NGOs as well as corrupt local destinations.

Based on the small and convenient sample of countries in this study, we suggest an extension of the theoretical perspective by Naumovska and Lavie (2021), where the local situation is taken into account. Specifically, based on our conclusion regarding Moldova and Congo, we suggest that non-accused firms will suffer from a stigma effect rather than a competition effect to a greater extent in countries characterized by high levels of white-collar and corporate crime. Formulated as a research hypothesis for future research, we suggest the following angle: *The product market overlap between a non-accused firm and an accused industry peer will exhibit a U-shaped effect on the non-accused firm's market depending on the extent of product market overlap, where the negative stigma effect will be stronger in countries characterized by more corruption and other forms of white-collar and corporate crime, while the positive competition effect will be stronger in countries characterized by less corruption and other forms of white-collar and corporate crime.*

In conclusion, based on recent research regarding whether competitors lose or gain when an industry peer is hit by a scandal, this chapter has contributed to an extension of previous theorizing. While the relationship between the extent of product market overlap and stigma versus competition effects is supported, anecdotal evidence suggests that the stigma effect will be stronger and more persistent in nations with more corruption and other forms of white-collar and corporate crime. Based on exploratory research in this chapter, the following hypothesis is formulated for future research: The product market overlap between a non-accused firm and an accused industry peer will exhibit a U-shaped effect on the non-accused firm's market depending on the extent of product market overlap, where the negative stigma effect will be stronger in countries characterized by more corruption and other forms of white-collar and corporate crime, while the positive competition effect will be stronger in countries characterized by less corruption and other forms of white-collar and corporate crime.

References

Asplid, Å. (2019). Swedbank-kund: "Väldigt obehagligt" (Swedbank customer: Very unpleasant), *Swedish Business Journal Dina Penger*, December 13, www.expressen.se.

Benson, M.L. (2019). The neutralization of corporate crime: Organizational and state-facilitated denials of corporate harm and wrongdoing, *Journal of White Collar and Corporate Crime*, April 2, https://ascdwcc.org/journal-of-white-collar-and-corporate-crime/.

Berghoff, H. (2018). "Organised irresponsibility?" The Siemens corruption scandal of the 1990s and 2000s, *Business History*, 60 (3), 423–445.

Bruun Hjejle. (2018). *Report on the Non-Resident Portfolio at Danske Bank's Estonian branch*, report of investigation, law firm Bruun Hjejle, Copenhagen, Denmark, p. 87.

Buckley, N. (2018). Latvia: A banking scandal on the Baltic, *Financial Times*, February 23, www.ft.com.

Bundy, J. and Pfarrer, M.D. (2015). A burden of responsibility: The role of social approval at the onset of a crisis, *Academy of Management Review*, 40 (3), 345–369.

CDC. (2021). Cruise ship travel during Covid-19, *Centers for Disease Control and Prevention*, November 1, www.cdc.gov.

Clifford Chance. (2020). *Report of Investigation on Swedbank*, report of investigation, law firm Clifford Chance, Washington, DC, p. 218.

Dewan, Y. and Jensen, M. (2020). Catching the big fish: The role of scandals in making status a liability, *Academy of Management Journal*, 63 (5), 1652–1678.

Gottschalk, P. and Benson, M.L. (2020). The evolution of corporate accounts of scandals from exposure to investigation, *British Journal of Criminology*, 60, 949–969.

Gottschalk, P. and Tcherni-Buzzeo, M. (2017). Reasons for gaps in crime reporting: The case of white-collar criminals investigated by private fraud examiners in Norway, *Deviant Behavior*, 38 (3), 267–281.

Gray, A. (2016). Wells Fargo loses status as world's most valuable bank, *Financial Times*, September 14, www.ft.com.

Greer, C. and McLaughlin, E. (2017). Theorizing institutional scandal and the regulatory state, *Theoretical Criminology*, 21 (2), 112–132.

Hearit, K. M. (2006). *Crisis Management by Apology: Corporate Responses to Allegations of Wrongdoing*, Lawrence Erlbaum Associates, Mahwah.

Henze, N., Grünewald, F. and Parmar, S. (2020). *Operational Review of Exposure to Corrupt Practices in Humanitarian Aid Implementation Mechanisms in the DRC*, Adam Smith International, London, p. 88.

Johannessen, S.Ø. and Christensen, J. (2020). Swedbank vil ikke betale sluttpakke til toppsjef som måtte gå av etter hvitvaskingsskandale (Swedbank will not pay final package to top executive who had to leave after money laundering scandal), *Daily Norwegian Business Newspaper Dagens Næringsliv*, March 23, www.dn.no.

Jung, J.C. and Sharon, E. (2019). The Volkswagen emissions scandal and its aftermath, *Global Business & Organizational Excellence*, 38 (4), 6–15.

Kagge, G. (2021). Merkel må forklare seg om hjelp til selskap anklaget for milliardsvindel (Merkel must explain herself about help to companies accused of billion fraud), *Daily Norwegian Newspaper Aftenposten*, Thursday, April 22, p. 24.

Kim, P.H., Dirks, K.T. and Cooper, C.D. (2009). The repair of trust: A dynamic bilateral perspective and multilevel conceptualization, *Academy of Management Review*, 34 (3), 401–422.

King, M. (2020). Private investigation into economic crime: Regulation of a multidisciplinary field, *Journal of Applied Security Research*, doi: 10.1080/19361610.2020.1832018.

King, M. (2021). Profiting from a tainted trade: Private investigators' views on the popular culture glamorization of their trade, *Journal of Criminological Research Policy and Practice*, 7 (2), 112–125.

Kleinfeld, P. (2020a). Exclusive: Congo aid scam triggers sector-wide alarm, *The New Humanitarian*, June 11, www.thenewhumanitarian.org.

Kleinfeld, P. (2020b). UN wows to "maintain trust" in Congo aid effort after damning review leaked, *The New Humanitarian*, June 12, www.thenewhumanitarian.org.

König, A., Graf-Vlachy, L., Bundy, J. and Little, L.M. (2020). A blessing and a curse: How CEOs' trait empathy affects their management of organizational crisis, *Academy of Management Review*, 45 (1), 130–153.

KPMG. (2020). *Report Concerning the Independent Special Investigation at Wirecard AG*, audit firm KPMG, Munich, Germany, April 27, p. 74.

Kroll. (2017). *Project Tenor II, Summary Report, Report Prepared for The National Bank of Moldova, report of investigation*, audit firm Kroll, London, p. 58 (2016: Project Tenor – Scoping Phase, 84 pages. 2018: Project Tenor II, Confidential Working Papers Part I to the Detailed Report, Detailed tracing analysis, 60 pages. 2018: Project Tenor II – Confidential working papers – Part II, Evidence Packs – Funds traced to: Ilan Shor, Alexandr Macloivici and Olga Bondarciuc. 2018: Project Tenor II – Detailed Report, Report Prepared for The National Bank of Moldova, 154 pages).

Larsen, O.J. (2021). Tidligere bistandstopp - Bistand virker ikke (Former aid executive - Aid does not work), Norwegian broadcasting corporation *NRK*, December 13, www.nrk.no.

Makortoff, K. (2019). Swedbank chief sacked amid money laundering scandal, *The Guardian*, March 28, www.theguardian.com.

Meerts, C. (2020). Corporate investigations: Beyond notions of public-private relations, *Journal of Contemporary Criminal Justice*, 36 (1), 86–100.

Milne, R. (2020). Swedbank failings on E37bn of transactions revealed in report, *Financial Times*, March 23, www.ft.com.

Mulinari, S., Davis, C. and Ozieranski, P. (2021). Failure of responsive regulation? Pharmaceutical marketing, corporate impression management and off-label promotion of enzalutamide in Europe, *Journal of White Collar and Corporate Crime*, 2 (2), 69–80.

Naumovska, I. and Lavie, D. (2021). When an industry peer is accused of financial misconduct: Stigma versus competition effects on non-accused firms, *Administrative Science Quarterly*, 66 (4), 1130–1172.

Nechepurenko, I. (2015). Moldova parliament dismisses government amid bank scandal, *The New York Times*, October 29, www.nytimes.com.

Nestler, F. (2020). Kunden auf der Flucht (Customers on the run), *Daily German Newspaper Frankfurter Allgemeine Zeitung*, June 24, www.faz.net.

Olsen, S.M. (2019). Danske Bank mister tusindvis af kunder – men topchef venter prop i flugten (Danske Bank loses thousands of customers – but the top manager is expecting a plug in the outlet), *Daily Danish Newspaper Berlingske*, April 30, www.berlingske.dk.

Piazza, A. and Jourdan, J. (2018). When the dust settles: The consequences of scandals for organizational competition, *Academy of Management Journal*, 61 (1), 165–190.

Plesner. (2020). *Response to DFSA-letter: Anmodning om redegørelse om Danske Bank A/S'gældsinddrivelsessystem (Response to DFSA letter: Request for account concerning Danske Bank Inc.'s debt collection system)*, investigation report by Danske Bank, law firm Plesner, Copenhagen, Denmark, p. 120.

Schoultz, I. and Flyghed, J. (2021). "We have been thrown under the bus": Corporate versus individual defense mechanisms against transnational corporate bribery charges, *Journal of White Collar, and Corporate Crime*, 2 (1), 24–35.

Scott, M.B. and Lyman, S.M. (1968). Accounts, *American Sociological Review*, 33 (1), 46–62.

Seddon, M. (2016). Outrage over Moldova bank scandal threatens reforms, *Financial Times*, published January 26, www.ft.com.

Shearman Sterling. (2017). Independent Directors of the Board of Wells Fargo & Company: Sales Practices Investigation Report, Community Bank, Report of investigation, law firm *Shearman Sterling*, San Francisco, California, USA, p. 113.

Shichor, D. and Heeren, J.W. (2021). Reflecting on corporate crime and control: The Wells Fargo banking saga, *Journal of White Collar and Corporate Crime*, 2 (2), 97–108.

Storbeck, O. (2021). Prosecutors delayed arrest warrant for Wirecard's Jan Marsalek, *Financial Times*, January 29, www.ft.com.

Storbeck, O. and Morris, S. (2021). BaFin files insider trading complaint against Deutsche Bank board member, *Financial Times*, April 19, www.ft.com.

Whyte, D. (2016). It's common sense, stupid! Corporate crime and techniques of neutralization in the automobile industry, *Crime, Law and Social Change*, 66 (2), 165–181.

Wiersholm. (2020). *Granskingsrapport: Utbrudd av covid-19 på Hurtigruten-skipet MS Roald Amundsen 17–31 juli 2020 (Investigation report: Outbreak of covid-19 on Hurtigruten ship MS Roald Amundsen July 17–31, 2020)*, law firm Wiersholm, Oslo, p. 51.

Conclusion

Thirteen corporate investigation reports by fraud examiners were reviewed in this book. The fraud examinations are summarized in Table C1 in terms of convenience themes and investigation maturity. Along the dimension of motive, most cases were concerned with possibilities for individuals and/or corporations: Dechert (2021), PwC (2021), State Auditor (2020), ERC (2021), Aust-Agder (2019), Simonsen (2020), Nordhordland (2019), NOU (2020), James (2020) and Eisen et al. (2021), BHR Resource Center (2018), and Christoffersen and Mikkelsen (2021). Only two cases were concerned with threats: Hurtigruten Cruises in Norway (Wiersholm, 2020) and Mercy foreign aid in Congo (Henze et al., 2020).

The opportunity structure for committing alleged wrongdoing was frequently status of the offender and less frequently access to resources. The opportunity for concealing alleged wrongdoing was frequently chaos in terms of lacking oversight and guardianship. The willingness for alleged deviant behavior was mainly based on justification. In a justification, the actor admits responsibility for the act in question but denies its pejorative and negative content. Justifications are different from denials, excuses, or admissions. In a denial, the actor either disavows that anything untoward happened or denies responsibility for whatever it is that happened. In an excuse, the actor admits the act in question is wrong but denies having full responsibility for it. In an admission, reference is made to the wrongdoer by name as having engaged in the wrongdoing.

Based on the stage model for maturity assessment of fraud examinations in corporate investigations, PwC (2021) at Bergen University and State Auditor (2020) at the University of California at Berkley, as well as Nordhordland (2019) at Alver municipality in Norway achieved the highest score of value-oriented investigations at level 4. Dechert (2021) conducted a detection-oriented investigation of Apollo Global at level 3.

ERC (2021) at the International Biathlon Union, Simonsen (2020) at Ørland municipality, NOU (2020) at the Social security agency, BHR Resource Center (2018) in South Sudan, and Christoffersen and Mikkelsen (2021) conducted problem-oriented investigations at level 2. Investigations by Wiersholm (2020) at Hurtigruten Cruises, by Henze et al. (2020) at Mercy foreign aid in Congo, by Aust-Agder (2019) at Hove peninsula in Norway, and by James (2020) and Eisen

DOI: 10.4324/9781003363934-18

Table C1 Summary of corporate investigation reports by fraud examiners

#	Organization	Motive	Opportunity	Willingness	Investigator	Maturity
1	Apollo Global in the United States	Individual Possibility	Status, Access	Identity, Learning, Neutralization	Dechert (2021)	3
2	Bergen University in Norway	Individual Corporate Possibility	Status	Justification	PwC (2021)	4
3	Berkley University in the USA	Individual Possibility	Status	Justification, Neutralization	State Auditor (2020)	4
4	Hurtigruten Cruises in Norway	Corporate Threat	Status, Chaos, Collapse	Justification, Neutralization	Wiersholm (2020)	1
5	International Biathlon in Austria	Individual Possibility	Status, Decay	Justification, Neutralization	ERC (2021)	2
6	Mercy Foreign Aid in Congo	Individual, Corporate Threat	Access, Decay, Chaos	Rationality, Learning	Henze et al. (2020)	1
7	Hove Peninsula in Norway	Corporate Possibility	Access	Rationality	Aust-Agder (2019)	1
8	Ørland Municipality in Norway	Individual Possibility	Status	Justification Neutralization	Simonsen (2020)	2
9	Alver Municipality in Norway	Individual Possibility	Access	Neutralization	Nordhordland (2019)	4
10	Social Security Agency in Norway	Corporate Possibility	Status, Access, Decay, Chaos	Learning Neutralization	NOU (2020)	2
11	Investigations of Donald Trump	Individual, Corporate Possibility	Status, Access, Decay	Identity, Rationality, Neutralization	James (2020) Eisen et al. (2021)	1
12	South Sudan Financial Flows	Corporate Possibility	Access, Chaos	Justification, Neutralization	BHR Resource Center (2018)	2
13	Danish Bestseller in Myanmar	Corporate Possibility	Status, Access, Decay	Rationality, Learning, Justification	Christoffersen and Mikkelsen (2021)	2

et al. (2021) regarding Donald Trump achieved the lowest score of 1 in terms of examination maturity.

The structural model as applied to all case studies in this book can help future researchers and practitioners identify convenience themes in cases that they are studying. Defense lawyers as well as prosecutors may find it helpful to classify an emerging crime case by means of the structural model. Fraud examiners in corporate investigations may want to communicate their findings by means of the structural model.

The stage model as applied to all case studies in this book can help fraud examination clients assess the maturity of reports from internal investigators. Client organizations pay for the work, and they might learn from the maturity levels how to judge the performance of people working for them. Fraud examiners themselves can learn from the stage model what ambition might be appropriate in a particular assignment. The ambition should not necessarily be level 4 as the contingent approach to an investigation depends on the situation.

References

Aust-Agder. (2019). *Avtaler og beslutningsprosesser knyttet til Hove-saken (Agreements and decision-making processes related to the Hove case)*, audit firm Aust-Agder Revisjon, Arendal, September, p. 61.

BHR Resource Center. (2018). Lundin Energy lawsuit (re complicity in war crimes, Sudan), *Business & Human Rights Resource Centre*, October 18, www.business-human-rights.org.

Christoffersen, J. and Mikkelsen, M.S. (2021). *Redegjørelse: Bestseller A/S' samfundsansvar i Myanmar (Statement: Bestseller Ltd.'s Social Responsibility in Myanmar)*, law firm Offersen Christoffersen, Copenhagen, Denmark, May 10, p. 122.

Dechert. (2021). *Investigation of Epstein/Black Relationship and Any Relationship between Epstein and Apollo Global Management*, law firm Dechert, report of investigation, New York, p. 21.

Eisen, N., Perry, E.D., Ayer, D. and Cuti, J.R. (2021). *New York State's Trump Investigation: An Analysis of the Reported Facts and Applicable Law*, Brookings Governance Studies, Washington, DC, www.brookings.edu.

ERC. (2021). Final Report of the IBU External Review Commission, ERC (External Review Commission), International Biathlon Union, Austria, 28 January, p. 220.

Henze, N., Grünewald, F. and Parmar, S. (2020). *Operational Review of Exposure to Corrupt Practices in Humanitarian Aid Implementation Mechanisms in the DRC*, Adam Smith International, London, p. 88.

James, L. (2020). *The Trump Organization, Inc.; DJT Holdings LLC; DJT Holdings Managing Member LLC; Seven Springs LLC; Eric Trump; Charles Martabano; Morgan, Lewis & Bockius, LLP; Sheri Dillon; Mazars USA LLC; Donald J. Trump; Donald Trump, Jr.; and Ivanka Trump*, Petition by the Attorney General of the State of New York to the Supreme Court of the State of New York, January 18.

Nordhordland. (2019). *Forenkla forvaltningskontroll (Simplified management control)*, audit firm Nordhordland Revisjon, December 20, Alver, p. 32.

NOU. (2020). Blindsonen: Gransking av feilpraktiseringen av folketrygdlovens oppholdskrav ved reiser i EØS-området (The blind spot: Investigation of the incorrect practice of the National Insurance Act's residence requirements when traveling in the EEA area), *Norges offentlige utredninger* (Norway's public inquiries), 2020 (9), 328.

PwC. (2021). *Universitet i Bergen: Gjennomgang av "konseptet" (The University of Bergen: Review of "the concept")*, investigation report, PricewaterhouseCoopers, Oslo, March 11, p. 68.

Simonsen. (2020). *Rapport om mottatt varsel vedrørende forhold ved jordmortjenesten i Ørland kommune (Report on notification received regarding conditions at the midwifery service in Ørland municipality)*, report of investigation, May 20, law firm Simonsen Vogt Wiig, Oslo, p. 36.

State Auditor. (2020). *University of California, California State Auditor, 621 Capitol Mall*, report of investigation, Sacramento, CA, p. 82.

Wiersholm. (2020). *Granskingsrapport: Utbrudd av covid-19 på Hurtigruten-skipet MS Roald Amundsen 17–31 juli 2020 (Investigation report: Outbreak of covid-19 on Hurtigruten ship MS Roald Amundsen July 17–31, 2020)*, law firm Wiersholm, Oslo, 51 pages.

Index Gottschalk Fraud Examinations